D1569220

Turning Points of the Irish Revolution

Previously Published Works

*The Irish Experience during the
Second World War: An Oral History*

Turning Points of the Irish Revolution

The British Government, Intelligence, and the Cost of Indifference, 1912–1921

Benjamin Grob-Fitzgibbon

TURNING POINTS OF THE IRISH REVOLUTION
© Benjamin Grob-Fitzgibbon, 2007.

Portions of Part 1 of this work were previously published as "Neglected Intelligence: How the British Government Failed to Quell the Ulster Volunteer Force, 1912–1914," *Journal of Intelligence History*, Volume 6, Issue 1, Summer 2006, pp. 1–23. Used with permission by the *Journal of Intelligence History*.

First published in 2007 by
PALGRAVE MACMILLAN™
175 Fifth Avenue, New York, N.Y. 10010 and
Houndmills, Basingstoke, Hampshire, England RG21 6XS
Companies and representatives throughout the world.

PALGRAVE MACMILLAN is the global academic imprint of the Palgrave Macmillan division of St. Martin's Press, LLC and of Palgrave Macmillan Ltd. Macmillan® is a registered trademark in the United States, United Kingdom and other countries. Palgrave is a registered trademark in the European Union and other countries.

ISBN-13: 978–1–4039–8003–8
ISBN-10: 1–4039–8003–9

Library of Congress Cataloging-in-Publication Data

Grob-Fitzgibbon, Benjamin John.
    Turning points of the Irish Revolution : the British government, intelligence, and the cost of indifference, 1912–1921 / Benjamin Grob-Fitzgibbon.
        p. cm.
    Includes bibliographical references and index.
        ISBN 1–4039–8003–9 (alk. paper)
        1. Ireland—History—1910–1921. 2. Ireland—History—Easter Rising, 1916. 3. Ireland—History—War of Independence, 1919–1921. I. Title.
DA962.G76 2007
941.5082′1—dc22   2006052012

A catalogue record for this book is available from the British Library.

Design by Newgen Imaging Systems (P) Ltd., Chennai, India.

First edition: May 2007

10 9 8 7 6 5 4 3 2 1

Printed in the United States of America.

For Sophia Kristen, born June 2, 2005

Contents

Acknowledgments

It has been said before but it is worth saying again, a book is never the work of just one person. I am indebted to many for the successful completion of this project. To those who I neglect to mention below, and there are no doubt a few, my sincere apologies.

My first thanks must go to God, without whom I would have no ability to think, let alone write and publish. All that I do is made possible through his creation. This book began its life as a doctoral dissertation at Duke University, North Carolina. I must thank the graduate school and the history department there for their generous financial support. In the history department, I owe my gratitude to the various Directors of Graduate Studies who served while I was there—Professors Ron Witt, Cynthia Herrup, Ed Balleisen, and Laura Edwards—as well as to the administrative staff, in particular Revonda Huppert. The late Professor John W. "Jack" Cell first pointed me in the direction of the Dublin Castle files and suggested I look at British governance in Ireland. Without his initial direction, it is doubtful I would have discovered this fascinating project. My dissertation supervisor Professor Alex Roland encouraged and shaped my understanding of those files, posing questions that I missed and providing insights that would have gone unnoticed. His handprint is on every page of this work. The other members of my dissertation committee—Professors Martin Miller, John Thompson, and John Richards—all provided their own unique reflections. I am particularly grateful to Professor Thompson for his thorough editorial and stylistic suggestions on several drafts of this work. I must also acknowledge Professor Susan Thorne for her helpful comments on my Master's Thesis, which eventually became Part 1 of this book.

At Duke University's Perkins Library, I am grateful for the assistance of the staff, particularly reference librarian Margaret Brill. My thanks also to the staff of the National Archives in Kew, Richmond-Upon-Thames. In preparing this book for publication, I am grateful for the staff at Palgrave Macmillan, particularly my editor, Alessandra Bastagli, her editorial assistant Emily Leithauser, and the production editor Elizabeth Sabo. I must also thank Maran Elancheran and the other staff at Newgen Publishing & Data Services for their copyediting and production assistance. My parents, Andy and Jane Fitz-Gibbon, have always listened to my ideas, and for that I give them thanks. Deserving of the highest acknowledgment is my wife, Amanda. Her patience and support has enabled me to complete this work. Finally, I have dedicated this book to my daughter, Sophia Kristen, born June 2, 2005. She was kind enough to share her nursery with me, my books, and my computer, and she listened to every word of this volume without complaint. This book is for her.

Introduction

At 12:45 p.m. on a sunny Easter Monday afternoon in 1916, Patrick Pearse, the headmaster of St. Enda's School in Dublin, appeared from behind the locked doors of the General Post Office on Lower Sackville Street. Protected by a lone guard, he paused on the top step and began to read from a single sheet of paper. An Irish republic had been proclaimed, he announced, and until legitimate democratic institutions were erected to represent it, the Irish Republican Brotherhood would act as its provisional government. This Irish republic was entitled to, and therefore claimed, the allegiance of all Irish men and women; it was the duty of Irishmen everywhere to fight for its existence. When he had finished his statement, Pearse disappeared back into the G.P.O. A perplexed crowd offered only a spattering of applause.[1]

Those who watched Pearse had no idea of the events that would unfold in Dublin in the days to come, nor of the violent guerilla war that would flow from his declaration. Yet the actions taken on that day were more momentous than the mere reading of a proclamation by a band of romantic nationalists.[2] The Irish Republican Brotherhood to which Pearse referred had come into existence in 1858. It was a secret, oath-bound society whose primary goal was to publicize the cause of Irish nationalism and bring about an Irish republic through the use of violence, not political negotiation.[3] It had attempted a general insurrection in 1867, but was quickly repressed, not to resurface until the early twentieth century.[4] The importance of the I.R.B., however, was not so much in its actions but in its words, for through its insurrection it had formulated an ideology of Irish nationalism based not on constitutional pressure exerted from within the British system, but on revolutionary violence brought to bear from without. Thus, although the I.R.B. as an organization had gone into decline following the 1867 rising, its ideas remained strong in the minds of some Irish nationalists. These men were only too happy to revive the brotherhood from its dormancy in 1907.[5]

It was to this new I.R.B. that Patrick Pearse devoted his life, and it was the I.R.B. that provided the core of volunteers for the rising that began on Easter Monday, April 24, 1916. Although the British government was taken unaware by these events, this rising was not the first seditious militancy to intrude upon Irish society in the early twentieth century. In December 1912, an illegal paramilitary army, the Ulster Volunteer Force, had formed in the north of Ireland, its sole purpose being to thwart the implementation of an Irish Home Rule parliament.[6] In response to the rapid growth of the U.V.F., a Catholic nationalist force, the Irish Volunteers, formed in November 1913.[7] Civil war between the increasingly agitated sides seemed inescapable, and was prevented only by the outbreak of the First World War, to which the leaders of both the U.V.F. and the Irish Volunteers pledged their service.[8] In September 1914, however, the Irish Volunteers split into two organizations, the National Volunteers, who supported the war effort, and the much smaller Irish Volunteers, who continued to agitate for the immediate implementation of Home Rule.[9] Within this latter group, the newly revived I.R.B. found its resting place, gradually persuading the leadership of the Irish Volunteers to abandon their calls for Home Rule and instead agitate for a fully independent Irish republic.[10]

When Patrick Pearse and his fellow insurrectionists entered the General Post Office and read their Easter Proclamation, therefore, they were doing so not as the first flicker of a new flame but as the culmination of a militancy that had been pervading Irish society for the previous three and a half years. Nevertheless, the Easter Rising was the first time that any of the militants had directly attacked the British state, and Easter Monday was the first day that a member of the British security forces was actually killed by Irish nationalists. This made the rising a far more real insurrection in the minds of the British government than the previous spates of armed drilling by the U.V.F. and Irish Volunteers. The government acted accordingly.

The rising began at about 11:45 a.m., when the combined forces of the I.R.B., the Irish Volunteers, and James Connolly's much smaller Citizen's Army formed a military column in front of Liberty Hall and marched on Dublin's city center.[11] They hoped to occupy several important buildings, including City Hall, Dublin Castle, the Four Courts judicial building, and the General Post Office, all symbols of the British presence in Ireland.[12] As the column moved off and split into smaller groups, each heading in a different direction, it was mocked by passersby.[13] Not until the first shot was fired and the first body dropped did the throngs of people who watched realize that anything was different from the marching and drilling of the previous three years.[14] The rising ended six days later, with Dublin in flames and under martial law, 450 people dead, and 1,836 interned. Of those who died,

250 were civilians and 132 were British soldiers or policemen; only 79 were rebels, including the 16 who were court-martialed and executed in its aftermath.[15]

This failure of the rising notwithstanding, Irish separatists had not issued their last call for Irish independence. Indeed, rather than being the grand finale of an overly optimistic insurgency, Easter Week 1916 was a sign of things to come. Following the rising, those who favored an independent Irish republic migrated to the Sinn Fein Party, as did the I.R.B., which eventually changed its name to the Irish Republican Army (I.R.A.).[16] Sinn Fein declared itself the organization best equipped to represent Pearse's proclaimed Irish republic, and asserted that the I.R.A. was this republic's only lawful security force. The party then participated in British elections, but declared that it would not take seats in the Westminster Parliament if elected. In the 1918 general election, largely through tactics of intimidation, Sinn Fein took 73 of the 105 Irish seats in the House of Commons. As promised, however, it did not send these members to Westminster. Instead, it set up an alternative parliament, the Dáil Éireann, an institution not recognized by the British government. From this body, Sinn Fein claimed to hold the rightful allegiance of the Irish people.[17]

With such an illegal institution present in Irish society, it was only a matter of time before a renewed insurgency would erupt. In 1919 a vicious guerilla war did indeed begin, a conflict that lasted until 1921. A truce was called when it became apparent to the Irish guerillas that they could not defeat the British security forces militarily and when it became equally apparent to the British government that rebellion within Irish society would not cease until some measure of autonomy was granted. In December 1921, the Anglo-Irish Treaty was signed between the warring parties. This partitioned Ireland into two countries, the 6-county Northern Ireland, which remained part of the United Kingdom, and the 26-county Irish Free State, which gained almost full independence from Great Britain.[18] The Irish separatists had waged a war against the most powerful empire in the world and, to all intents and purposes, they had won. The years 1912–1921 represented a colossal security failure for the British government.

The question this raises, of course, is how the British Empire, with all its political and military might, was unable to quell the insurgency in Ireland during these years. There are two parts to the answer currently given, as historians thus far have failed to view the years 1912–1921 as a single historical period.[19] First, they look at the rise of the Ulster Volunteer Force in the years 1912–1914, which they call the Ulster Crisis. Second, they look at the years 1916–1921, analyzing the Easter Rising and the Irish War of Independence, which together they call the Irish Revolution. Works on the Ulster Crisis do not reference the Irish Revolution, and vice versa. For those in the latter group, the beginning of the era was 1916, not 1912.

When looking at the first of these historiographies, that concerning the Ulster Crisis, it is important to ask two questions: what is the reason given for the British inability to quell the Ulster Volunteer Force, and why is the Ulster Crisis not viewed as part of the Irish Revolution? Historical studies of the Ulster Crisis are in no short supply. The first true monograph was published in 1967 and, still in print, its interpretation has yet to be overturned. A.T.Q. Stewart's *The Ulster Crisis: Resistance to Home Rule, 1912–1914* provides a step-by-step account of the formation and growth of the Ulster Volunteer Force. It concludes that had it not been for the outbreak of the First World War, there would almost certainly have been civil war in Ireland.[20] Despite the thoroughness of Stewart's work, other historians have continued to publish on the Ulster Crisis. Patricia Jalland has found that the militant resistance in Ulster brought the British government to "total deadlock" several months before the First World War began.[21] Eunan O'Halpin states that the U.V.F. was "of immense symbolic importance as the manifestation of Ulster unionism's resolution."[22] More recently, D. George Boyce and Alan O'Day have edited a volume devoted to the unionist defense of the Irish tie with Great Britain, reaching a general conclusion that Ulster had become its own nation by 1914, in character if not in name.[23]

Yet in all these works, an important question remains unanswered. What was the response of the British government to this paramilitary threat? The literature thus far suggests by omission that there was very little reaction. Stewart makes no mention whatsoever of any policing or other governmental response to the U.V.F.[24] Likewise, Patrick Buckland in his seminal work on Ulster unionism says little of a possible reaction to the Ulster militants.[25] Eunan O'Halpin perhaps best sums up the view of most historians. He writes: "A major problem facing [Augustine] Birrell [the Chief Secretary of Ireland] in dealing with Ulster was one of information. He simply was not in a position to give his cabinet colleagues an authoritative estimate of the intentions or the capabilities of the Ulster unionists, because the police were unable to brief him."[26] Birrell could not be expected to quell the militancy in Ulster, O'Halpin argues, because he was receiving no intelligence from the security forces. He had no idea of the extent of the threat. The consensus of historians who look at the Ulster Crisis, then, is that it occurred due to negligence on the part of British intelligence. As *Turning Points of the Irish Revolution* shows, however, this view is quite false. Furthermore, whilst historians of the Ulster Crisis tend to ignore its effect on later events in Ireland, and historians of the Irish Revolution choose not to examine the Ulster

Crisis, this book demonstrates that the Ulster Crisis was in fact central to the development of that later violence.

Within the historiography of the Irish Revolution, there are, broadly speaking, three schools of thought as to why the British failed to contain the insurgency. These I shall call the colony-to-nation school, the repressive-reaction school, and the inert-military school.[27] The colony-to-nation school holds that the British were defeated in Ireland because of the inevitability of a successful Irish nationalist struggle, an effort that had been intensifying for the previous two centuries. For those in this school, Irish nationalist history (and there is no other kind) follows a natural progression from the failed 1798 revolution of Wolfe Tone and his United Irishmen,[28] through the Young Irelanders' insurrection of 1848[29] and the 1867 rebellion of the I.R.B., to the eventual Easter Rising of 1916. Victory came to the Irish separatists in 1921 because revolutionary fervor had reached its pitch and the Irish people were ready for independence.

This school is largely the preserve of the popular historians (so-called). George Dangerfield offers the most accurate representation of its interpretation. In his work, *The Damnable Question*, he writes, "The Easter Rising of April 1916 rose up from the troubled depths of Irish history; it was even to some extent a product of the earthy spells of Irish mythology: it was also a bitter, exact and decisive gloss upon the long unhappy annals of Anglo-Irish relations."[30] Throughout Dangerfield's work, Irish history rushes inevitably towards an almost metaphysical state of perfect freedom and independence. The failure in 1921 to achieve a faultless united Irish republic, completely autonomous from Great Britain, is seen not as a compromise with reality, but as a disruption of providence.

Dangerfield himself, of course, would object to this characterization of inevitability, as is only proper and right for an historian to do. Indeed, Dangerfield even states (correctly) that the term "inevitability" has "no place" in history.[31] Yet his subsequent words betray him, as he suggests that the Easter Rising, although preventable, "*had* to happen."[32] Finally, he asserts, "the tragedy of the Irish Revolution which the Rising set in motion is that it was not allowed to complete itself."[33] The united Irish republic that should have been the perfect culmination of the Irish freedom struggle was never reached, and thus Irish history has been left unfulfilled. Despite this imperfection, however, the British security failure in Ireland in the years 1916–1921 was a direct cause of the seemingly inexorable march of the Irish nation towards independence.[34]

There is, indeed, some justification for the colony-to-nation school's interpretation. Underlying its thesis is the supposition that Ireland was a colony of England rather than its equal, and therefore could not reach its full potential until independence had been achieved. The first part of this argument, at least, holds water. Although the 1801 Act of Union had constitutionally joined Great Britain and Ireland together into a single state, there is much evidence to suggest that in reality Ireland was not as fully integrated into the United Kingdom as were England, Scotland, and Wales. It was, in fact, in a position more analogous to Britain's colonies than to its constituent nations. A number of key distinctions were made between Ireland and the British mainland.

Of prime importance was the difference in governmental administration. In Ireland, a Governor General was appointed to act as the king- or queen-in-person. This role had largely become ceremonial by 1912, but its significance should be seen not in its relative political power, but in what it represented. The Governor General, more commonly referred to as the Lord Lieutenant or Viceroy, was used to symbolize the omnipresence of monarchy throughout the British Empire.[35] He was always a peer, and often one of some standing. In Ireland, of the 34 Lord Lieutenants appointed between 1801 and 1921, 10 had been former cabinet members, one had previously been Viceroy of India, and another had commanded the British Army in France.[36] Ostensibly, as constitutional head of the Irish government, the Lord Lieutenant held wide authority, including full responsibility for the peace and security of the kingdom and the prerogative of mercy usually reserved for the sovereign. In reality, however, it was his political officer, the Chief Secretary, who held the reigns of power. The Lord Lieutenant's position was reserved as an embodiment of the dignity of the state, and, as such, he was in theory and practice positioned above partisan politics.[37]

Most colonies of any import had an equivalent of the Lord Lieutenant. England, Scotland, and Wales did not, however. This was because, constitutionally, the king or queen was ever-present within these countries, even when not physically so, since London, as the capital city of Great Britain, functioned as the seat of power. Under law, therefore, no one but the reigning sovereign could claim to be the king- or queen-in-person when in Great Britain without committing treason against the true monarch. Following the 1801 Act of Union, however, it was no longer Great Britain alone that provided the sovereign with his or her seat of power, but the newly created United Kingdom, of which Ireland was a part. Therefore, constitutionally, the king or queen should have been ever-present throughout the British Isles. Yet in Ireland, a Lord Lieutenant was appointed, indicating that the king or queen was somehow less present there than on the mainland. It seems, therefore, that Ireland held a lesser position within the union than that of England, Scotland, and Wales.

Ireland also received a Chief Secretary, who was the government's main representative in Ireland, often a member of the British cabinet. He was responsible for the civil administration of Ireland.[38] The Chief Secretary was in charge of the Irish civil service, which consisted of 29 separate departments dealing with all aspects of Irish life from revenue collection to agriculture. He also held direct control over the two Irish police forces, the prisons, and the judicial system.[39] The Chief Secretary was, therefore, essentially a provincial or colonial prime minister. He reported directly to the British Prime Minister and the Chancellor of the Exchequer rather than the British cabinet at large. By comparison, Scotland had a Secretary of State, but this minister held only an advisory position within the general cabinet; he did not have the sweeping powers of the Irish Chief Secretary.

The Chief Secretary was supported by an under secretary, who was responsible for the implementation of policy devised by the Chief Secretary. Whilst the former was usually based in London, the latter was continuously resident in Dublin, heading up the headquarters of Irish governmental administration at Dublin Castle. It was the Chief Secretary who laid out the blueprint for Irish government, but the under secretary who turned that blueprint into a tangible structure. In this sense, the under secretary truly ran the Irish government.[40] The under secretaries in the Scottish Office, in contrast, were usually responsible for only a very select piece of Scottish legislation, always under the supervision of their Secretary of State.

Not only did Ireland have a separate administrative structure from the rest of the United Kingdom, it also had different methods of state service, the most important of which was in policing. In England, Scotland, and Wales, the police service was under the sole control of local government, divided into county forces that were each responsible only to their county administration.[41] There was no national police force, and the Parliament at Westminster had no say in local policing matters.[42] In contrast, Ireland was policed by a national force, the Royal Irish Constabulary (R.I.C.), and a smaller city force, the Dublin Metropolitan Police (D.M.P.), both of which reported directly to the Chief Secretary's office, not to local government.

The D.M.P. operated much like London's Metropolitan Police. It was an unarmed force, whose officers had all risen through the ranks, starting in every case as a constable. Its members wore a blue civilian-style uniform and patrolled on foot.[43] The R.I.C., in contrast, had been established as a paramilitary force, its members wearing green, military-style uniforms and carrying rifles.[44] Unlike the British police forces, officers in the R.I.C. were commissioned directly rather than rising through the ranks. This had the result of creating a hierarchical force led by the Protestant gentry but manned by the Catholic lower classes.[45] Although the primary mission of the R.I.C. was to maintain law and order, it was also given the lead role in suppressing subversion and political crime. As such, it was closely tied to the Chief Secretary's office and the mainland British establishment.[46] It is perhaps unnecessary to state that such a force did not exist elsewhere in the United Kingdom.

There is, therefore, some legitimacy in the colony-to-nation school's assertion that Ireland was something other than equal to England, Scotland, and Wales. Ireland was both inside and outside the union, an integral part of the United Kingdom yet a colony of that same kingdom, a constitutional enigma that was neither British nor foreign; and where colonial institutions are placed over a subject people, there will always be the potential for disquiet, if not outright insurrection. The progression of Irish nationalism from the United Irishmen, to the Young Irelanders, to the I.R.B., and finally to independence does seem to carry with it a certain sense of inevitability. Yet there is nevertheless something unsettling for the historian about such seemingly unalterable progress.

The repressive-reaction school holds a more constricted view, choosing to focus primarily on the years 1916–1921. For those in this school, the British were ultimately unsuccessful in Ireland because they lost the battle for hearts and minds. This happened in the immediate aftermath of the Easter Rising, when the British security forces acted with undue force towards the rebels, turning them into popular heroes and swaying public opinion away from the British government and onto those who had revolted. This school is largely comprised of historians who study the events surrounding the 1916 Easter Rising. Sean Farrell Moran perhaps best sums up this interpretation, arguing, "While many of the public were angry at the rebels initially, the British execution of most of the leaders of the Rising galvanized public sympathy behind the rebels, making them into martyrs for Ireland and thereby legitimating the physical-force cause."[47] Hints of this interpretation can be found in each of the other schools of thought, lending it a certain weight of consensus. To take a familiar example, George Dangerfield, standard bearer of the colony-to-nation school, writes that although the rising was initially greeted with an "unwelcome notoriety," following courts-martial, executions, and "rumors of worse things to follow," public opinion swiftly turned and "the spirit of Dublin and the country at large underwent a profound and, as it turned out, a lasting change."[48] The rising, or more specifically the British response to it, became the catalyst for the violence that was to follow. Thus the primary reason for the eventual British security failure can be traced to British repressive reaction.[49]

Although initially appealing, this interpretation ultimately fails to provide a complete appraisal of the events that led to the British demise in Ireland. Indeed, on further examination more questions are raised than answered. How, for example, is the earlier emergence of the Ulster Volunteer Force to be accounted for, a paramilitary army that spurred the initial organization of the Irish Volunteers out of which the rising was born? If anything, it was inaction, not overreaction, that allowed the U.V.F. to form and grow. What sense, also, can be made of the continued service of Irishmen in the British Army to the end of the First World War, two years after the rising? If public opinion was so galvanized in 1916 that British failure in Ireland became a foregone conclusion, why did Irishmen continue to fight and die in droves for the same empire that they were supposedly rebelling against? Finally, if the rising and the subsequent British repression were the primary impetus for the later violence, why was there a period of almost three years between the end of the rising and the beginning of the guerrilla war? These are questions that the repressive-reaction school alone cannot answer. Although the British reaction to the rising undoubtedly played a part in the loss of British power, it is neither the beginning nor the end.

The inert-military school argues that the British suffered defeat in Ireland because they were unable to adapt their traditional order of battle to the new reality of a guerilla war. They had been schooled in the tactics of mass engagement and trench warfare, where the individual initiative of men and officers counted for very little. They were untrained, therefore, for the hit-and-run tactics of the Irish Republican Army. This school looks past the rising to the guerrilla war itself. It is best represented by Charles Townshend. Throughout his works, but most specifically in *The British Campaign in Ireland, 1919–1921*, Townshend argues that the British security forces were, quite simply, ill prepared to meet the new threat in Ireland. He writes: "The Republican guerrilla campaign proved too determined, too resilient, and too resourceful to be put down by the military force which was employed against it."[50] This military force was composed of two elements, the R.I.C. and the British Army. The former was untrained in military coercion and therefore proved no match for the newly formed and highly motivated I.R.A. The latter produced "only a very slow response to the challenge of guerilla warfare," delaying the implementation of martial law until November 1920, and even then imposing it on just a quarter of the country.[51] The inert-military school asserts that the British failed in Ireland because they were not ready for the guerilla campaign when it began.[52]

This is, perhaps, the most satisfactory of the three interpretations, yet still there are inconsistencies. It is true that the British were ill prepared for a guerilla war in 1919, but were they not equally ill prepared for a world war in 1914—or in 1939, for that matter? Had the British armed forces of 1982 any more experience in establishing a beachhead, which proved so effective during the Falklands War? Were the British any more schooled in the tactics of counterinsurgency when the recent conflict in Northern Ireland began, a clash that has successfully been brought to a close? To say that the British were unprepared at the beginning of the conflict seems, when placed against other military endeavors, nothing out of the ordinary. Such inexperience cannot in and of itself account for the failure that occurred, however. Furthermore, such an interpretation takes into account only the guerilla war of 1919–1921. It pays little attention to the Easter Rising, or to the Ulster Crisis before it.

Each of these three interpretations, of course, contains an element of truth. The colony-to-nation historians are correct to point out that each Irish insurrection built on the foundations laid by the previous one, and that Ireland was steadily gaining more and more autonomy. Likewise, the repressive-reaction historians are accurate when they claim that excessive British subjugation following the 1916 Easter Rising turned the tide of public opinion away from the government and towards the rebels. Finally, just as the inert-military historians argue, the British security forces were ill prepared to fight a guerilla war after four long years in the trenches of France. Yet each of these arguments taken alone is not enough to provide a comprehensive account of the security failure that began in 1912 and lasted until 1921. Furthermore, even if these three interpretations were merged—they are not mutually exclusive—there is still something missing from the picture. That something is intelligence. In none of these interpretations is the question of what the British did or did not know about the insurgents considered. Intelligence is simply not a variable.

Turning Points of the Irish Revolution makes a fresh examination of the British security failure in Ireland, looking for the first time at the Ulster Crisis and the Irish Revolution as a single historical phenomenon. It does not subscribe to any one of the interpretations outlined above. Indeed, it seeks to overturn the consensus surrounding the Ulster Crisis. It argues that there were three stages to this nine-year security failure, and in each stage the collection, dissemination, and use of intelligence by the British government contributed to that failure. The nature of intelligence in each of these stages varied greatly, however, providing for the historian three very different examples of British governance in Ireland. By conducting a close analysis of each of these stages, this book is able to evaluate not only the critical role that intelligence played in the British security failure, but also highlights the three crucial turning points of the Irish Revolution.

The first stage, the period of overt militancy (1912–1914), saw the rise of two opposing paramilitary armies, the Protestant Ulster Volunteer Force and the Catholic Irish Volunteers. Throughout this period, the British security forces collected precise and thorough intelligence, yet politicians at the highest levels of government refused to act on this intelligence, thus allowing the illegal armies to grow. The second stage, the period of clandestine organization (1914–1916), saw the resurgence and growth of the Irish Republican Brotherhood. During this stage, in contrast to the first, the British security forces collected very little intelligence: their attention was focused on the war in France rather than insurgency at home. When the I.R.B. led a rising against the British in 1916, therefore, the government was caught largely unaware. The third and final stage, the period of guerilla war (1916–1921), saw the I.R.B. (now known as the Irish Republican Army) launch a successful guerrilla war against the British forces in Ireland. Throughout this war, the British security forces once again began to produce sound intelligence and were able to assemble a working intelligence network. This intelligence came too late to be of much use to the British government in combating the insurgents, however. Each of these stages is inextricably linked. The Irish Volunteers formed in reaction to the threat posed by the Ulster Volunteer Force; the I.R.B. merged with the Irish Volunteers to lead the Easter Rising; and the I.R.A. evolved from the I.R.B. to fight the British in the years 1919–1921. In each of these stages, the collection, dissemination, and use of intelligence played a crucial role in the eventual British security failure, and provided a key turning point in the Irish Revolution.

Before proceeding further, it is perhaps necessary to explore the nature of intelligence in Ireland during these years, and to assess which security forces were most active in acquiring this intelligence for the British government. As discussed above, the constitutional nature of Ireland was somewhat of an enigma at this time. Although in theory an integral part of the United Kingdom, Ireland had always been a thorn in the side of England. Thus, whilst internal security was a low priority for the police forces in England, Scotland, and Wales, in Ireland it was placed on par with normal law and order. The Royal Irish Constabulary, therefore, was organized not as a neighborhood institution controlled by local government, as in Great Britain, but instead as a national force detached from society and living in closed barracks, as ready to quell a political riot as to arrest a criminal. It was this force, the R.I.C., which took the lead in counterinsurgency and in the collection of intelligence throughout the years 1912–1921.[53] Within the R.I.C., the Crimes Special Branch was most directly involved in the collection of intelligence and combating political insurgency. The Crimes Special Branch had been formed in 1872 and was housed at the R.I.C. headquarters in Dublin Castle. Its role was to investigate "crimes and outrages of a political and treasonable nature and [to be aware of] any activity which posed a threat to the security of the country."[54] Crimes Special Branch detectives, operating in plain clothes, were appointed throughout Ireland, two in each rural county or city. This number increased to twenty in Belfast following the 1886 riots, and remained higher in Belfast than other cities until 1921.[55]

The Crimes Special Branch was assisted in Dublin by the detectives division of the Dublin Metropolitan Police (G-Division). G-Division had been formed in 1843 to investigate violent crime in Dublin, and throughout most of its history was concerned more with normal, albeit serious, criminal offenses than with political crime.[56] Following the 1867 I.R.B. rising, however, G-Division was ordered to take a more active role in assisting the Crimes Special Branch in the collection of political intelligence.[57] After the 1916 Easter Rising, G-Division partnered directly with the Crimes Special Branch to combat insurgents in the capital city, an association that was maintained until the end of the guerrilla war in 1921. It was this combination of the Crimes Special Branch and G-Division that collected most of the intelligence used by the British government during the Irish insurgency. This intelligence was then transmitted to the Crimes Special Branch headquarters in Dublin. The Inspector General of the R.I.C. received copies of all such intelligence reports. When evaluating the security failure in Ireland, therefore, it is the collection of intelligence by these two organizations that is of primary concern.

This book is structured in three parts, each corresponding to one of the stages outlined above. A conclusion then offers a counterfactual argument and suggests that had the British government acted on the intelligence it received in a prompt and determined fashion, the rise of paramilitarism in Ireland could have been avoided and Ireland could have experienced a more peaceful twentieth century. The main source base used in this study is the Dublin Castle Records (Colonial Office 904), held at the National Archives in Kew, England. These records contain over 60, 000 pages of police reports, intelligence files, and judicial proceedings. These sources are supplemented by the Irish Confidential Print (Colonial Office 903), the Irish Office Records (Colonial Office 906), the War Office Records of the Army in Ireland (War Office 35), the Cabinet Papers (Cabinet Office 37), and the Cabinet Letters in the Royal Archives (Cabinet Office 41), also held at the National Archives in Kew. Taken together, these sources present an unparalleled insight into the world of intelligence in Ireland in the years 1912–1921. By viewing this, the historian can explore not only the causes of the colossal security failure that occurred in those years, but can gain something of far greater import. The turning points of the Irish Revolution can be seen, and with them, the cost of British indifference in the years 1912–1921 becomes clear.

PART I

The Period of Overt Militancy, 1912–1914

The Death of Constitutionalism in Ulster

On August 10, 1911, the British political landscape changed forever. On that date, the House of Lords reluctantly passed the Parliament Bill, which suspended their constitutional veto over the House of Commons.[1] Following passage of the bill, the Lords could only reject a Commons' bill twice. Upon a third successful reading, it would be sent to the king for his assent, with or without the support of the upper house. The British Prime Minister, Herbert Asquith, had introduced the bill following the Lords' rejection of his 1909 budget. It was, for him, the ultimate act of political vengeance against a recalcitrant aristocracy, but he also had more pragmatic motives. He was well aware that with the late nineteenth-century disintegration of the Whig Party, the Liberal Unionists had been swept into the ranks of the Conservatives, not the Liberals. This had resulted in a permanent Conservative majority in the House of Lords, placing any Commons' legislation proposed by the Liberals at the mercy of these Conservative peers. Thus, for the Liberal Party to be successful in the Commons, it first had to nullify the Lords.[2]

In order to push the Parliament Bill through the Commons, however, Asquith had no choice but to rely upon the support of the Irish Nationalist Party, which held the balance of power.[3] In return for their support, he promised that within the next parliamentary session he would introduce a new Irish Home Rule Bill. Such a bill had been introduced twice before by the Liberal Party, in 1886 and 1893. In the first instance, however, it had not passed the Commons, and in the second it had reached the Lords only to be vetoed.[4] Now though, with the passage of the Parliament Act, a Home

Rule bill would become law if successfully steered through the Commons three times, regardless of the Lords' position. This process would take two and a half years, as a single bill could be read only once in each parliamentary session, but with the Liberals reelected in January 1910, a new general election was not required until January 1915. There was, therefore, plenty of time for the Prime Minister to fulfill his promise to the Irish Nationalists. With the new Parliament Act, there was nothing the Conservative Unionists or the House of Lords could do to prevent it.

In February 1910, sensing the inevitability of the Parliament Act and fearing its consequences, the Ulster Party (a subset of the larger Conservative Unionist Party) replaced its elderly leader, Walter Long, with the younger and more charismatic Sir Edward Carson.[5] Carson, at first glance, seemed an unlikely candidate for the position, particularly at such a crucial time in unionist history. Only a second-generation Irishman, he had been born in Dublin and was raised in the Church of Ireland, not the Presbyterian Church that so dominated the more militant unionists. Whilst at Trinity College, Dublin, he had enjoyed the recently revived Irish sport of hurling, even gaining a mention in *The Irish Sportsman* for distinguished play on the field.[6] As a member of the College Historical Society, he had campaigned for the disestablishment of the Church of Ireland and had publicly denounced Oliver Cromwell's seventeenth-century subjugation of Ireland.[7] This early radicalism betrayed no hint of his later life as a unionist leader. Indeed, in 1877, he proudly took his place at the Irish Bar.[8]

Yet Carson had become a very different man in the 33 years between his call to the Irish Bar and his election as leader of the Ulster Party. As he had watched William Gladstone, Charles Stewart Parnell, and the newly formed Irish Home Rule Party attempt to sever the union with Great Britain, an attachment he held dear, Carson had become obsessed with preserving the union.[9] In 1892, he was elected to Parliament as the Unionist Member for Dublin University. That year, he symbolically transferred from the Irish to the English Bar.[10]

In February 1910, with Carson now at its head, the Ulster Party began to explore extralegal methods of thwarting Irish Home Rule, fully aware that with the imminent passage of the Parliament Act and a continuing Liberal majority in the Commons, all constitutional channels would soon be closed to them. Carson was joined in this task by several prominent unionists, chief amongst them Captain James Craig, a Belfast man born and raised. Craig had taken a commission with the Royal Irish Rifles at the outbreak of the South African War. Held captive by the Boers following the surrender at Lindley, he had hidden when the other officers were placed into ox-carts for transportation. He had then marched the 200 miles to the prison camp at Noightgedacht with his men, before being repatriated and rejoining the army at Durban.[11] He returned to Ulster a hero, and in 1906 entered Parliament as the Member for East Down.[12] It was Craig who introduced Carson to the more militant unionist politics in the north of Ireland, and Craig who suggested that the place to begin a campaign against Irish Home Rule was the northern province of Ulster.[13]

Nevertheless, Carson at first hesitated to follow Craig's advice. He knew that the Ulster Unionists had declared the will to fight numerous times since the first Irish Home Rule Bill of 1886. Indeed, the renowned unionist Lord Randolph Churchill had even declared, "Ulster will fight and Ulster will be right."[14] As yet, however, Ulster had not fought, and Carson had no interest in authoring what might become just another chapter of unionist talk with no action. In July 1911, therefore, he confessed to Craig: "What I am very anxious about is that the people over there really mean to resist. I am not for a mere game of bluff, and unless men are prepared to make great sacrifices which they clearly understand, the talk of resistance is of no use."[15]

Craig carefully measured Carson's concerns and determined that the best way to alleviate them was to organize a mass display of unionist loyalty to the cause of Ulster. On September 23, 1911, Craig gathered a crowd of 50,000 men from across the province. They met in Belfast and from the city center marched to Craig's estate at Craigavon, on the outskirts of the city. There, on the lawns that gently rolled from the main house to the shores of Belfast Lough, they demonstrated to Carson their determination to resist Home Rule. In such a show Carson found his confidence and pledged himself to their cause: "I know the responsibility you are putting on me today. In your presence I cheerfully accept it, grave as it is, and I now enter into a compact with you, and every one of you, and with the help of God you and I joined together . . . will yet defeat the most nefarious conspiracy that has ever been hatched against a free people." He then articulated what would become Ulster unionist policy for the next three years: "We must be prepared . . . the morning Home Rule passes, ourselves to become responsible for the government of the Protestant Province of Ulster."[16]

Of course, Carson's notion of the Ulster people existing alone, apart from the rest of Ireland, was not new. It formed the very basis of the political philosophy known as Orangeism, and it had been talked of in the Orange Halls and Lodges of the Loyal Orders for two centuries past. Indeed, Orangeism, a combination of Protestant exceptionalism and conditional loyalty to the British Crown, was a practice far older than the union itself. It had its roots in the tumultuous years of the eighteenth century, and it had been formed to commemorate the Protestant victory of King William III, Prince of Orange, over the Catholic King James II during the Glorious Revolution of 1688. To those in Ulster, and throughout the British Isles, this revolution was believed to be more religious than political, in large part due to the centrality of Protestantism to the emerging British national identity.[17]

There was one nation within the British Isles that did not share this Protestantism, however. That nation was Ireland. Before the sixteenth century, of course, there was no such thing as a Protestant Church and a Catholic Church. There was simply the Church, and all members of the Church swore allegiance to the Pope in Rome. Christians in England, Scotland, and Wales were, therefore, part of the same Church as Christians in Ireland. In 1536, however, King Henry VIII of England ushered in the English Protestant Reformation. It was as much political as religious, based on Henry's desire to annul his marriage, but a new Church of England was nevertheless established.[18] Initially, the Church of England showed few differences from the Catholic Church that preceded it. In Ireland, where Henry VIII had also established a Protestant Church of Ireland, the religious rituals and practices of the people remained largely unchanged.[19]

Edward VI succeeded Henry VIII in 1547 and attempted to consolidate many of the reforms that were introduced by the latter.[20] In 1553, however, Edward VI was succeeded by Mary I, who had remained Catholic. Upon ascension, in what has become known as the English Counter-Reformation, she attempted to restore ties with Rome and revive the Catholic Church in Great Britain. This she did through ruthless purges of the Protestant clergy, so much so that she received the appellation "Bloody Mary" from those under her rule.[21] Her reign created within the English people a loyalty to Protestantism that they previously did not have, together with a deep resentment of Catholicism. The schism between Rome and Great Britain thus became a division in practice, not merely in name. When Mary died in 1558, Elizabeth I restored the Protestant faith and introduced additional reforms, creating a distinct division between English Protestantism and Catholicism.[22] The lasting legacy of Mary's reign was that Catholicism was transformed from an accepted irritation to the unacceptable enemy within, and all Catholics were viewed as traitors. Catholic Ireland was seen as the greatest threat of all.[23]

Consequently, Elizabeth I sought to convert Ireland to Protestantism through a series of "plantations," which were launched in 1584. These sought to "plant" Protestants into Ireland, where they would form model English settlements to replace the communities of the Irish Catholic lords. In time, it was thought, the Irish Catholics would mimic the English, and Protestantism would spread by its own virtue. If it did not, it could be forcibly spread by the English settlers.[24] The first plantation was attempted in the province of Munster, but failed, lasting only until the 1590s, when it was violently expelled by the Irish populace during the Nine Years War (1594–1603).[25] In 1607, however, Elizabeth's successor, King James I, again attempted to plant

Protestants into Ireland, trying this time in the northern province of Ulster. Here he had more success than his predecessor, using a systematic regime of forced evictions to replace the Irish nobility with English and Scottish settlers.[26] In the face of such an onslaught, the chief Catholic earls fled to France, never to return. They left in their place a Protestant nobility precariously placed over a large Catholic peasantry.[27]

James I hoped to spread plantations from Ulster throughout Ireland, but as he became preoccupied with domestic events in England his interest in the scheme waned and no more plantations were introduced.[28] This resulted in a Protestant community that constituted a slight majority in the province of Ulster, but was a small minority in the island as a whole. In 1641, in the Ulster county of Armagh, the Catholic population rose up to overthrow these Protestant settlers. The rising quickly spread to the other Ulster counties, and more than 1,200 settlers were massacred. Rumors of these deaths quickly spread to England. The exaggerated death toll reached as high as 154,000.[29] In response to this rising, the English General Oliver Cromwell led an army of 12,000 to brutally suppress the Catholic population in Ireland.[30]

Despite this conquest, the Protestants remained only in Ulster. There they developed a garrison mentality, believing the Catholic population to be a constant threat to their safety and a challenge to their place at the upper strata of society. This fear seemed to be justified when, in 1689, the exiled King James II invaded Ireland from Catholic France. A year earlier, in 1688, James II had been forced to abdicate the English throne because of his Catholic faith, and the English Parliament had invited the Dutch Prince William of Orange to become King William III.[31] James II now returned to Ireland, hoping to gather support amongst Catholics there for a renewed assault on England. The newly crowned William crossed the narrow channel and defeated James II at the Battle of the Boyne, July 12, 1690. In defending his actions to the Bishop of Meath, he characterized his victory as a religious triumph, proclaiming, "I am come hither to deliver you from the tyranny of popery and slavery, to protect the Protestant religion, and restore you in your liberties and properties; and you may depend upon it."[32] With such words, William acquired an exalted status amongst the Protestants in Ulster.

In retribution for Catholic support for James II, the English Parliament passed a series of draconian laws that collectively have become known as the penal acts. These forbade Catholics from owning a weapon (a right of all citizens at the time), from gaining any education other than in Protestant schools, from inheriting or purchasing any property, and from leasing land for more than 31 years. They also banished all Catholic bishops, monks, nuns, and friars, and closed all Catholic churches. Finally, all Catholics were prohibited from entering the professions, taking an apprenticeship, voting, or gaining election to Parliament.[33] In England, the effect of these acts was negligible, as the Catholic population was small. In Ireland, however, it placed the majority in a constitutionally subservient position to the minority. Thus, the Protestants in Ulster, although constituting just one-eighth of the total population of Ireland, held complete power over the remaining seven-eighths. The consequences of these acts were quickly felt. In 1641 Catholics owned 60 percent of Irish land; by 1715 their ownership declined to just 5 percent.[34]

In 1714, in the aftermath of King William's victory, the first of the loyal orders was formed. That year, Colonel John Mitchelburne established the Apprentice Boys of Derry to honor the apprentice boys who had closed the gates on the besieging James II at the City of Derry. In so doing, these boys had demonstrated their loyalty to Protestant Britain over their Catholic neighbors. Each year, on the anniversary of the siege's end, the Apprentice Boys of Derry marched around the city walls, symbolically defeating the Catholics time and time again.[35]

The second and more significant of the loyal orders, the Orange Order, was established some years later, in the aftermath of a skirmish at the small hamlet of Diamond in 1795. In the years leading up to this scuffle, two secret societies had formed in Ulster, the Catholic Defenders and the Protestant Peep O'Day Boys.[36] In September 1795, a large contingent of the Defenders gathered at the crossroads in Diamond, where they marched through the village in a military formation. They were quickly set upon by the Peep O'Day Boys, together with other Protestant vigilante groups such as the Orange Boys and the Bleary Boys, who saw these Catholics as trespassing on Protestant land. Diamond was burned to the ground, and men on each side lost their lives, but the final victory was decisive in favor of the Protestants.[37] In the immediate aftermath of this victory, the Orange Order formed to consolidate the various Protestant groups who had fought. It was initially a vigilante para-military force, dedicated to further expelling Catholics from land in Ulster, but this aggressive organization gave way in 1798 to a reformed Orange Order, led by the Protestant gentry.[38]

This new Orange Order was a neo-Masonic institution devoted to remembering the victories of King William of Orange. With the 1801 Act of Union, the Orange Order expanded its mission to include protecting the union and ensuring its continuation. The Orange Order continued to grow throughout the nineteenth century, with the numerous Presbyterians joining its traditional Church of Ireland base.[39] In 1885, when British Prime Minister William Gladstone publicly declared his commitment to Irish Home Rule, prominent members of the Orange Order led the opposition.[40] Following the second Home Rule Bill of 1893, the Orange Order created a network throughout the province of Unionist Clubs, whose purpose was to systematize the opposition to Home Rule.[41] Two years later, in 1895, the Conservatives defeated the Liberals, thus ending the threat of Home Rule. Unionist action became dormant. With the Liberal victory ten years later, however, anti-Home Rule movements emerged once again. In 1905, the Ulster Unionist Council was established to unite all other unionist associations and to formulate a cohesive unionist policy against Home Rule. It quickly became the official voice of Ulster unionism.[42]

Thus, in September 1911, when Sir Edward Carson accepted leadership over the anti-Home Rule movement, there were already several prominent associations in Ulster, all committed to preserving the union with Great Britain and defeating Irish Home Rule. The primary method these organizations used was the circulation of propaganda to put pressure on the Parliament at Westminster, particularly the House of Lords, to vote against any Irish Home Rule Bill. With the passage of the Parliament Act, however, the Lords could no longer defend the interests of the Ulster Protestants with a veto. Carson, realizing that constitutional means were now useless, began to formulate a more aggressive unionist approach.

On September 25, the Monday after Carson's speech to the crowds at Craigavon, delegates from the various unionist associations met and formed the Commission of Five, whose purpose was to draft a constitution for the provisional government that Carson had called for. Chaired by Captain Craig, the commission soon found itself in verbal combat with an unlikely opponent.[43] Their adversary, Winston Churchill, had been born in 1874 into a staunchly Conservative and unionist family, son of Lord Randolph Churchill, the Member of Parliament best remembered for his infamous phrase, "Ulster will fight and Ulster will be right." Winston had initially followed in his father's footsteps, entering the Commons as a Conservative Member in 1900. Four years later, however, he crossed the floor to the Liberal Party on the issue of free trade and was brought into the cabinet by Asquith in 1908 as President of the Board of Trade. In 1910, he was moved to the Home Office and promoted to Home Secretary, a position he held for only a year before becoming First Lord of the Admiralty. It was in this position, as civilian head of the royal fleet, that he first drew swords against the Ulster Unionists.[44]

On Tuesday, September 26, 1911, Carson told a crowd at Portrush that unless they were in a position to take over all elements of the government in Ulster at the advent of Home Rule, they might be forced to take up arms against the army and navy. At this, a member of the audience shouted, "They are on our side," a charge that Carson did not correct.[45] Churchill, as First Lord of the Admiralty, was answerable for the idea that the navy was "on the side" of the unionists, and he responded to Carson's remarks during a constituency meeting at Dundee on October 3. He spent most of his speech discussing the ongoing labor struggles in Britain, recent price increases, and European unease about Germany. At one point he digressed, however, saying to the crowd, "I have spoken to you about the stormy outlook abroad and at home, but what of the squall which Sir Edward Carson is trying to raise in Ulster—or rather in that half of Ulster of which he has been elected commander-in-chief?"[46] Then, the first government minister to do so, he confirmed that the government would introduce a Home Rule bill in the next parliamentary session. Carson, he declared, was attempting to set up a "rebel government," but he assured his listeners that the cabinet would "not attach too much importance to these frothings of Sir Edward Carson."[47]

Churchill's words created an immediate uproar in Protestant Ulster. When he traveled to Belfast to address the Ulster Liberal Association on February 8, 1912, he was forced to move with a contingent of soldiers to protect him from unionist demonstrators.[48] Nevertheless, he boldly reiterated his claims, and then to the chagrin of unionists reused the famous words of his father in a very different context:

> Let Ulster fight for the dignity and honor of Ireland. Let her fight for the reconciliation of races and for the forgiveness of ancient wrongs. Let her fight for the unity and consolidation of the British Empire. Let her fight for the spread of charity, tolerance, and enlightenment among men. Then, indeed, "Ulster will fight and Ulster will be right."[49]

Into this charged climate, the parliamentary session opened on February 14, 1912. It did so in a state of bitterness between Conservatives, particularly those from Ulster, and Liberals. The Prime Minister had hoped to present his Home Rule Bill immediately, but was delayed from doing so until April due to labor trouble in England. This allowed the Ulster Unionists time for a planned response to Churchill's statement, a response they held on April 9 at the Agricultural Show Grounds in the Belfast suburb of Balmoral, just two days before Asquith was due to introduce his bill. Carson invited Andrew Bonar Law, leader of the Conservative and Unionist Party, to speak. When Bonar Law addressed the gathered crowd of 80,000, standing on a platform beside 70 British Conservative Members of Parliament, he officially committed his party to support the Ulster Unionists in whatever action they deemed necessary to resist Home Rule, and declared the following:

> Once again you hold the pass, the pass for the Empire. You are a besieged city. . . . The Government have erected by their Parliament Act a boom against you to shut you off from the help of the British people.

You will burst that boom. That help will come, and when the crisis is over men will say to you in words not unlike those used by Pitt—you have saved yourselves by your exertions, and you will save the Empire by your example.[50]

Despite this commitment, the Conservatives did not have the unionist strength in Parliament to oppose the government's agenda. On April 11, Asquith introduced his Home Rule bill at Westminster as planned. Officially called the Government of Ireland Bill, as the bills in 1886 and 1893 had been, its passage seemed all but certain. Under the provisions of the 1911 Parliament Act, it was on track to be signed into law in August 1914.[51] Thus, Carson had just two and a half years to organize an Ulster resistance, one he hoped would be strong enough to coerce the government into abandoning the bill.

He was given additional support for this task from Bonar Law on July 27. In a blunt speech delivered at Blenheim Palace, the Conservative leader declared, "[I]f the attempt be made under present conditions [to pass a Home Rule Bill] I can imagine no length of resistance to which Ulster will go in which I shall not be ready to support them and in which they will not be supported by the overwhelming majority of the British people."[52] As far as the Conservative Unionists were concerned, it was vital that Ulster remain British at all costs; constitutionalism be damned.[53]

Nevertheless, Carson was still concerned about the commitment of the Ulster people as a whole to such a resistance. Therefore, he discussed with Craig the possibility of drawing up a contract or oath pledging those who signed to give loyalty to Protestantism and the union, and promising to resist Home Rule by any means necessary. Craig consulted with the secretary of the Ulster Club in Belfast, B.W.D. Montgomery, who suggested that they model it on the old sixteenth-century Scottish covenant, which he said was "a fine old document, full of grand phrases, and thoroughly characteristic of the Ulster tone of mind at this day."[54] The men commissioned a special board to look at the ancient document and to alter its wording, making it more appropriate to the present situation. The commission determined, however, that the entire document was too archaic. One of the commission members, Thomas Sinclair, therefore drew up an entirely new document, which he titled Ulster's Solemn League and Covenant. Revised by Alexander McDowell, a delegate of the Presbyterian Church, the final document was ready by the end of the summer.[55] On August 17, the commission notified the Irish press that Saturday, September 28, 1912, would be "Ulster Day," when a campaign would begin throughout the province to get loyalists to sign the Covenant.[56]

When Ulster Day finally dawned, it brought with it a sense of great excitement. At a rally held in Belfast the night before, Colonel R.H. Wallace, the secretary of the Grand Orange Lodge of Ulster, had presented Carson with a yellow silk banner that he claimed had been carried before King William III at the Battle of the Boyne. Carson had unfurled the flag with great vigor, proclaiming, "May this flag ever float over a people that can boast of civil and religious liberty."[57] The following day, 218, 206 men signed the Covenant, together with 228, 991 women, who signed a declaration similar to the Covenant.[58] Carson declared that these signatures had "made a profound impression throughout the U.K.," and Bonar Law commented that the Covenant had "killed Home Rule, as I always felt sure it would."[59]

Bonar Law's contention did indeed seem to be the case. On November 11, 1912, the government held a snap division in the Commons to authorize payment to a future Irish Exchequer under the Home Rule Bill. When the House divided, the government was defeated by 227 votes to 206.[60] Two days later, Asquith commented that such a hasty division "did not represent the considered judgment of the House." At this, Captain Craig declared,

> I believe that my proper place, and the proper place of all other Ulster members, is among their own trusty friends in the North of Ireland, for I believe that this Government is not to be treated as a Government, but as a caucus, led by rebels. The only way to treat it is for us to go back quietly and assist our loyal friends there to make what preparations are necessary.

He then turned to Asquith and said, "Although you may do your worst here in the House, thank God the North of Ireland will be more than a match for you."[61]

Following this, the Conservative Sir William Bull rose from the benches to call Asquith a "traitor," breaking all parliamentary convention.[62] When called upon by the Speaker of the House to withdraw his insult, he refused, instead preferring to leave the chamber.[63] The opposition benches began to taunt Asquith, chanting "resign, resign," and "civil war, civil war." The Speaker felt compelled to adjourn the House, believing that "grave disorder had arisen."[64]

When the Commons reassembled an hour later, the fervor had not calmed, and the Speaker once again dissolved the House, only ten minutes into the sitting.[65] As the front bench left the chamber, the Ulster Unionist Ronald McNeill seized a bound copy of the parliamentary orders and threw it at Churchill, striking him on the head. Churchill had to be forcibly restrained from retaliating, and when the chamber finally emptied, the Commons did not meet again until the next morning.[66] On that dark November day, when civility and parliamentary propriety succumbed to partisan passions, constitutionalism in Ulster died its long awaited death.

The Rise of Militant Unionism

On September 18, 1912, ten days before the planned Ulster Day, Sir Edward Carson embarked on a ten-day tour of Ulster to promote the Covenant and explain its provisions. He decided to begin this excursion in the small town of Enniskillen, in County Fermanagh.[67] When he arrived, he was met at the train station by a squadron of mounted men carrying lances, who escorted him through the town. Although Carson did not know it at the time, this armed band was the beginning of a militancy that would pervade Ulster for the next two years.

Throughout 1912, an increasing number of trained militias had formed in Ulster. When Carson had first accepted leadership of the anti-Home Rule movement at Craigavon in September 1911, a contingent from a County Tyrone Orange Lodge had impressed those around them with their smart dress and strict marching routine. Upon investigation, Colonel R.H. Wallace, the secretary of the Grand Orange Lodge of Ulster, had discovered that for some months past they had been drilling on their own initiative.[68] Wallace had consulted with a prominent Ulster solicitor, J.H. Campbell, as to the legality of this. He was informed that an ancient law permitted military drill by civilian militias in Ireland, provided that it was authorized by two justices of the peace and was used "to make [the people] more efficient citizens for the purpose of maintaining and protecting their rights and liberties."[69] Wallace tested this law on January 5, 1912, before two Belfast magistrates, and found it to be sound. With few questions asked, he was issued a license for drill, to commence immediately at the local branch of the Orange Order.[70] By the following autumn, Orange Lodges and Unionist Clubs across Ulster had adopted this practice and were conducting military drill, all under licenses approved by law.

When the mounted squadron greeted Carson in Enniskillen, therefore, he could hardly have been surprised. After all, he had been witnessing such things for the previous nine months. The British government, however, was not so well informed. It first became aware of the growing trouble in Ireland only on October 14, 1912. Just after 2:00 p.m. that day, on an otherwise quiet Monday afternoon, Robert Harcourt, the Member for Montrose Burghs, rose from his seat in the Commons to question the Secretary of State for War, Colonel John Seely. Harcourt asked whether or not the War Secretary was aware of a political gathering that had occurred at the Ulster town of Enniskillen in County Fermanagh, where the honorable member for Dublin University, Sir Edward Carson, had been escorted by two squadrons of mounted men, each carrying a real lance bearing the pennon of the Inniskilling Dragoons. Was this not, Harcourt inquired, a formation usually known as a traveling escort, which was specifically proscribed for all but the reigning sovereign? Did "the King's Regulations permit the use of such escort by persons other than His Majesty within His Majesty's Dominions; and, if not, [would] the Regulations . . . now be altered?"[71]

Seely, receiving no counsel from his front bench colleagues, replied that his attention had not been drawn to the matter, but that the dragoons described did indeed appear to be similar to a traveling escort. As this body of men "formed no part of the recognized forces of the Crown," however, the latter question of whether or not the king's regulations would be altered was of no relevance. There was nothing more to be said on the matter.[72] Seely was not overly concerned with the situation that Harcourt described. After all, his cabinet colleagues, chief amongst them Winston Churchill, had assured him time and time again that Carson was nothing more than a minor irritant, his words mere bluff. The Secretary of State waited almost four months, therefore, until early February 1913, before requesting from the Irish Office any information about this mounted escort.[73]

This questioning of Seely in Parliament marked the first time that the government's intelligence about events in Ireland was publicly found wanting. It was a fateful introduction to a topic that would occupy the government for the better part of the next nine years. Despite what seemed to be clear evidence of trouble brewing in Ireland, the government seldom made the effort to investigate what was happening across the Irish Sea. Indeed, had Seely taken the time to contact the Irish Office earlier than February, he would have been told that the Royal Irish Constabulary (R.I.C.) was already keeping a close eye on such drilling, and had been doing so for several months. When Harcourt raised his question, the Inspector General of the R.I.C., Colonel Neville Chamberlain, had already read all about this squadron, known locally as the Enniskillen Horse. He was also well aware that a man named W. Copeland Trimble, the editor and owner of an Enniskillen newspaper, *The Impartial Reporter*, had distributed printed circulars throughout the county of Fermanagh claiming to be the commander of this force.[74] Yet Seely chose not to pursue Harcourt's inquiry. As a result, the War Office, and in turn the Prime Minister, were not informed of these events for some time to come.

The first hint that the R.I.C. received of such a force was from Sergeant Patrick Hughes, who submitted a report to his district inspector, J.W. Mahon, on September 4, 1912. The sergeant informed his superior that Trimble was attempting to get together a mounted escort for Carson's visit and was expected to raise over 150 men. He noted that several of the men being mobilized in his subdistrict already belonged to the armed forces. Two were sergeants in the Imperial Yeomanry, two others yeomen.[75] Mahon immediately forwarded this report to the Crimes Special Branch. Following requests for further information, Sergeant Henry Conway obtained copies of two circulars published by Trimble, dated August 30 and September 3 respectively, which urged men to join the Enniskillen Horse. These were also submitted to the Crimes Special Branch.[76]

In these publications, Trimble presented his reasons for forming the Enniskillen Horse. He said he wanted a "fine turn out" of "smart soldierly-looking men" and "well-groomed horses" to welcome Carson and to escort him whilst he was in Enniskillen. To assist in the training of this force, Trimble named seven volunteers, whom he called sergeants.[77] Conway reported that these drill sergeants were all, or had been at one time, professionally paid sergeants in the Imperial Yeomanry.[78] In his second circular, Trimble promised potential volunteers that they would be "proud in years to come to look back on the thought that [they] took part in this display of the young manhood of Fermanagh." He ended his pamphlet with a phrase that was common currency in Ulster: "God Save the King."[79]

Sergeant Joseph Ruddock also responded to the Crimes Special Branch's request for information about the Enniskillen Horse. On September 7, he submitted a report to his district inspector, C.E. Armstrong, explaining that a mounted drill had taken place on the public road at Croaghrim. Twenty-three men were involved, and Trimble was present.[80] Due to the loophole in the law that allowed two justices of the peace to permit drill, however, there was nothing Ruddock could do to break up the assembly. Trimble was a justice of the peace, as were other prominent members of the Enniskillen Horse. Unless the Royal Irish Constabulary could prove that Trimble's intentions were other than protecting the rights and liberties of his fellow Irishmen, the Enniskillen Horse could not be stopped.

Sergeant Hughes submitted a second report on September 8. He noted that drill had again taken place, this time with 37 mounted men in the village of Carrowkeel. Two serving sergeants of the Imperial Yeomanry had been in charge. Colonel Doran Brookeboro, whom Hughes did not identify further, was in overall command, and Trimble was again present.[81] Another sergeant of the R.I.C., William Agnew, also witnessed the Carrowkeel drill and submitted a list of the names and addresses of those involved from his subdistrict, Lisbellow. Of the seven names given, five were serving in the Imperial Yeomanry, and the remaining two had served earlier.[82]

On September 17, the Fermanagh county inspector submitted a report to Inspector General Neville Chamberlain. He described the drilling that had taken place but indicated that Trimble's men more than likely would be used only to provide a onetime escort for Carson's visit. After September 18, he suspected, the Enniskillen Horse would cease to exist. There was nothing in the reports of Hughes, Conway, Ruddock, or Agnew to suggest otherwise.

He confidently informed Chamberlain, therefore, that Trimble's mounted escort was in no way a threat to the security of the state or the peace of the county. The R.I.C. anticipated that the countryside would return to its normally peaceful state once Carson's visit passed. The Enniskillen Horse would be kept under observation but otherwise left to its own devices.[83]

As the constabulary expected, September 18 came and went with no great surprises. Carson spoke to a crowd of 40,000 people. Amongst other things, he told them that "if this unprovoked and wicked attack [on the union] is allowed to go on and this Bill [the Home Rule Bill] to become law . . . it is not only a right but a duty to prepare to resist it."[84] He was then escorted by the Enniskillen Horse back to the railway station, where he boarded a train bound for Belfast. For Carson, it was merely the first of a circuit of nightly meetings, culminating on September 28 with his signing of the Solemn League and Covenant.[85] For Trimble, however, September 18 was a day second to none in his life. It was on that date that Sir Edward Carson, albeit in an indirect way, gave him his orders to establish the Enniskillen Horse on a more permanent basis. Carson had preached that it was every Ulsterman's duty to prepare to resist Home Rule. Trimble intended to answer that summons.

Expecting a return to normal following Carson's visit, J. Cahill, the district inspector for Kesh, was somewhat surprised on October 27 to receive a note from Sergeant William McDowell regarding a mounted drill. The sergeant reported that a unionist troop was being formed at Ballinamallard, and that a "number of men on horseback" were planning to assemble there on October 31 to "ride through the town to practice some cavalry movements."[86] This concerned Cahill and he immediately asked if this troop was part of the supposedly defunct Enniskillen Horse.[87]

McDowell reported back on November 1, explaining that this squadron was indeed part of the Enniskillen Horse, with some new recruits added. The force was being drilled in preparation for a "general review of some kind which is to take place at Enniskillen on 26th December next," with Trimble still "at the head of the whole matter." According to McDowell, the Enniskillen Horse was growing quickly, spreading beyond the district lines of Enniskillen and Linaskea into Kesh. It was also clearly outlasting its stated purpose of a onetime escort to Carson.[88] In light of this new information, the Fermanagh county inspector wrote the next day to Chamberlain, providing the Inspector General with a fresh summary.[89]

Chamberlain took note of the information but decided to wait before taking further action. By now, Seely had given his reply in the House of Commons to Harcourt, confirming that this mounted guard was in no way part of the Crown forces. Nevertheless, Chamberlain was still uncertain which of the actions taken by the Enniskillen Horse could be considered illegal. As yet, the movement drilled without weapons. Furthermore, it was not in any way disturbing the peace because it paraded in purely unionist strongholds. Chamberlain therefore instructed the Crimes Special Branch to continue to watch the Enniskillen Horse and to collate reports, but to delay any proactive policing measures. Just as the policy had been prior to September 18, after this date it was thought best to merely observe and take notes, building up a steady intelligence dossier that could be used if ever the time came when Chamberlain judged the Enniskillen Horse to have moved beyond the bounds of legality.

Such observation was not difficult for the constabulary. The Enniskillen Horse paraded openly throughout County Fermanagh. On November 7, 39 turned out to drill in the town of Glassdrummond.[90] Two weeks later, they again drilled, this time with 35 men. Trimble was present and announced that "all the horsemen would assemble at Enniskillen on Boxing Day [December 26]" for a public display, after which "they would get lunch at the Royal Hotel."[91] On November 22, 9 men met for drill, under the command of William Bracken of Drumhack, who was a member of the Imperial Yeomanry.[92] On November 29, these men met again, and this time their number increased to 13.[93] They drilled again on December 2.[94] On December 5, 26 men assembled and drilled at Ballyreagh.[95] Thirty-three horsemen also assembled on that date at Glassdrummond.[96] The following day, 37 men met for drill in a field at Lurganbren, on the property of Colonel Brookeboro.[97] On each of these occasions, members of the R.I.C. witnessed the drills and submitted reports to their superiors.

The Crimes Special Branch, alarmed at these reports of an increasingly large and disciplined force, notified the Judicial Division of the Chief Secretary's Office. The division reviewed the reports, and, together with the Irish Attorney General and the Lord Chancellor, prepared a printed memo containing much needed legal counsel for the constabulary. The Attorney General advised that Trimble's role as a justice of the peace should be carefully considered when examining his conduct, for this added a semblance of legality to the drill. Furthermore, as no arms had yet been displayed, he did not think that action should be taken by the prosecution at this time. Nevertheless, he suggested that observation of the Enniskillen Horse be continued and all files relating to it be kept together for future reference.

The Lord Chancellor did not share his view, instead spurning the idea of collating the files. He felt that without the legal means to prosecute, any police investigation would be "futile" and would do more "to irritate and to increase the numbers of sympathizers." The Attorney General's conviction superceded the Lord Chancellor's, however, and a compromise was reached whereby any information that happened to be collected would be kept, but no special effort would be made to gather such information. At this time, they elected not to provoke the driller.[98]

The Boxing Day parade, like that of September 18, proceeded smoothly. A Dublin based newspaper, *The Evening Mail*, reported that Trimble had publicly chastised Robert Harcourt for calling into question the loyalty and good nature of the Enniskillen Horse. Trimble then recited a message from Buckingham Palace that had been sent in reply to a declaration of his loyalty. The message read as follows: "I am commanded to assure you that His Majesty has never had cause to doubt the loyalty and attachment to his Throne and Person of those on behalf of whom your letter was written." Finally, before finishing his speech, Trimble announced that he hoped each troop of the Enniskillen Horse would be armed and would partake in rifle practice by the spring.[99]

The Enniskillen district inspector, C.E. Armstrong, received this newspaper clipping, along with a report from the police who had been present at the parade. Taking these two items together, he was provided with evidence that 230 men on horseback had paraded, and that Trimble was sure they would be "responsive to [his] call whenever it may be thought right to summon [them] again." This body of men, clearly now a permanent formation, had been promised arms, and Trimble had given his guarantee that there would be "rifle practice in the months of May and June so that each man will be able to use a rifle as well as ride a horse."[100]

Armstrong forwarded these reports to the county inspector, who in turn wrote to Chamberlain. He confirmed that the Enniskillen Horse was now meeting regularly, and was being drilled in a professional manner by veterans of the armed forces and police service. He did not, however, believe that any of these drill sergeants had any active combat experience. Furthermore, he chose to ignore Trimble's promises to arm his men. Instead, he told Chamberlain that he did not expect the Enniskillen Horse to "meet again this summer" and reiterated the by-now ludicrous assertion that it had been formed only to provide an escort for Carson. Indeed, the county inspector even claimed that the Enniskillen Horse was now in the process of winding down.[101]

Trimble's men had drilled and paraded freely for the past four months, constantly increasing their numbers, yet the county inspector failed to see the significance of this. The constabulary had painstakingly watched their every move, yet the Chief Secretary's Judicial Office had forbidden them from taking any action to halt these displays of martial preparation. Now, Trimble was claiming that by the summer his body of men would be transformed from an unarmed, quasi-legal force into a fully armed, and therefore illegal, militia. Whilst the Chief Secretary and Prime Minister slept soundly in their beds, blissfully unaware of the developing threat in Ulster, the year 1912 ended for the Enniskillen Horse on a high note, with a toast to the sovereign, the singing of God Save the King, and a promise of guns.

Despite the growth of the Enniskillen Horse, and the continued drilling of the various Orange Lodges and Unionist Clubs throughout Ulster, there was still no central organization to the anti-Home Rule movement. There was also no coordinated plan for how to use these trained militias if and when an Irish Home Rule parliament was formed. Carson was cognizant of this fact, and it concerned him. He was well aware that if his followers wished to successfully resist Home Rule and set up an effective provisional government, they would need to do more than practice unsystematic and localized drilling. Serious military preparation was necessary, and such preparation could be done only by a well-trained, centrally led army.

On December 13, 1912, therefore, Carson called a special meeting of prominent members of the Ulster Unionist Council, including Captain James Craig and Ronald McNeill, the man who had hit Churchill with the parliamentary orders only a month before. There they discussed the possibility of establishing a more unified movement. Although nothing was immediately agreed upon, that evening a smaller and more extremist congregation of the Ulster Unionist Council met, including Colonel R.H. Wallace, the secretary of the Grand Orange Lodge of Ulster. Behind closed doors, these men agreed to form a centralized army to resist Home Rule. By December 23, they had made their decision known to the remainder of the Ulster Unionist Council, and by December 26, recruitment for the Ulster Volunteer Force (U.V.F.) had begun.

The R.I.C. became aware of this proposed formation within days of the council's meeting. In a five-page report to Belfast's detective department, Acting Sergeant Joseph Edwards noted that a "strictly private" meeting had been held on December 13 between prominent members of the Ulster Unionist Council, including Sir Edward Carson and Captain James Craig, both Members of Parliament. They had discussed a proposed deal between the Ulster Unionists and the Westminster government over the Irish Home Rule Bill. Two of the men, Carson and Craig, had proposed compromising, and suggested that a Home Rule bill might be allowed to proceed if Ulster was excluded and its people represented solely at Westminster. Their sentiment had been stoutly opposed by the majority present, however, and nothing was resolved at the meeting.

That evening, however, a smaller group gathered at the home of Colonel Wallace. In the safety of his private residence, they discussed the possibility of procuring and using arms should the Home Rule Bill become law. Although not all agreed to arm the general unionist population, everyone present agreed with the necessity to resist, in some way, the government's policy.[102] Although the R.I.C. did not know it at the time, Carson and Craig, whilst not present at this smaller gathering, had given their blessing to its deliberations.

Edwards' report was immediately forwarded to the Crimes Special Branch in Dublin. William O'Connell, the R.I.C. Deputy Inspector General, browsed its contents. Concerned by what he read, he sent Edwards' report to James Dougherty, the under secretary of Ireland.[103] Dougherty shared the report with the Chief Secretary, Augustine Birrell, on December 17.[104] Thus within two days of Edwards submitting his report, and four days of the conspiracy being hatched, the highest politician in Ireland, a man who held a place in the British cabinet, had been made aware of its existence. The Chief Secretary, however, did little to respond to the information he received.[105] Whilst acknowledging the sound investigative work of Edwards, he asked only that the sergeant "keep in touch with his informant and . . . report further from time to time any matters of importance that come to his knowledge."[106] Birrell gave no order to actually question those who had been named in the report, nor did he inform the cabinet of what was happening in Ulster.

Such a response in light of detailed intelligence seems startling. It calls into question the character and qualifications of Augustine Birrell. Who was this man who, as Ireland's highest politician, a colonial prime minister of sorts, failed to inform the British cabinet of such a crucial event occurring on his watch? Birrell was not an Ulsterman, nor did he have any particular connection to any other province in Ireland. Like most parliamentary Liberals, he was "a home ruler by conviction, but was pessimistic about its chances."[107] When appointed Chief Secretary, he admitted that he knew "little about the country save as a tourist."[108] It was not a position he had requested—indeed, he protested against his appointment—but once selected, "he approached his Irish work with good humored cynicism."[109]

For the first four years of his tenure, Birrell was a congenial if lackluster Chief Secretary. From 1911 onwards, however, just as the crisis in Ulster was beginning to brew, he came under tremendous stress as his wife was diagnosed with an inoperable brain tumor. She died on March 10, 1915.[110] Throughout this difficult period, Birrell "suffered intensely from the demands of a post which forced him to spend months in Ireland, away from his dying wife. Consequently, the Irish Secretary appeared increasingly ineffective and irrelevant as the [Ulster] crisis mounted from 1912 to 1914."[111] Birrell's private secretary, Andrew Philip Magill, wrote in his memoirs that this illness prompted a desire by Birrell to retire:

> [When I was offered the private secretaryship in 1913] Mr. Birrell was very insistent that it would only be for a few months, as he was anxious to retire. . . . I found out very soon after my appointment that Mr. Birrell

was quite serious when he spoke of his early retirement. Mrs. Birrell was very ill and died about a year after I joined him from some form of tumor on the brain. I never met her, but he was very attached to her, and when she had momentary spells of consciousness, she always asked for him and he was very often at the Irish Office or at the House, and could not be got at short notice. He felt this very much and had made up his mind to retire.[112]

Consequently, Birrell was loath to be drawn into any long-term dealings with Irish policy; it was his hope that he would remain Chief Secretary for only a few months more.

Magill, as the person in closest physical proximity to Birrell, offers other hints as to his behavior. Magill felt it "a pity" that Birrell had "abandoned literature for politics, to which he never really gave his heart," and often "felt ashamed" to interrupt Birrell, immersed in a book, simply "to distract his attention to deal with some dull problem connected with Ireland."[113] Birrell, he thought, continued to be more interested in literature than in politics. He also found Birrell to be idle at times and wrote,

I learnt very soon that it was hopeless to try and make Mr. Birrell do any work when he was not in the mood. I would spend half an hour with him in the morning and I would then see him beginning to yawn, and after another few minutes when I had got really important things finished, I would say that the rest of the files could wait until he had more leisure, when he would jump to his feet, grasp his hat and say to me, "I promise you, Magill, I'll come in at 10.30 tomorrow morning and we'll finish off these files then." Needless to say, he did no such thing.[114]

Such attitude to work, combined with his insistence on spending time each day with literature and the distraction he suffered due to his wife's illness, characterized the latter years of Birrell's time as Chief Secretary. When he received the police intelligence from Edwards, therefore, he was not in command of the situation on the ground in Ireland, and he was inclined to postpone any decisions to a later date beyond his anticipated retirement, perhaps hoping that the problems in Ulster would eventually dissipate without intervention.

Dissipate they did not, however. Edwards was not the only man to report on the proposed unionist resistance to Home Rule. R.I.C. Sergeant James English warned on December 23 that he had received reliable information about the formation of "an organization known as the 'Ulster Volunteer Movement.'" He explained that within this movement, 12 volunteers would form a squad, under the command of a leader. These squads would then be arranged by town-lands, and two or four squads would form a company. All correspondence concerning their formation was to be done in the utmost secrecy, and letters were to be written "in a prearranged code or cipher, and carried by hand, as the post office would not be trusted." The sergeant disclosed that forms had been sent from Belfast to the various Unionist Clubs throughout County Tyrone to be filled out by the secretary of each club and then returned to Belfast. The purpose of these forms was to ascertain the number of vehicles that could be used for troop transport, and the number of "shot guns, rifles, pistols, revolvers and ammunition in the possession of each [volunteer]."[115] Another sergeant, William James Blair, reported separately on the distribution of these forms,[116] and his district inspector, S.R. Livingstone, forwarded this report, along with a note of his own, to the Tyrone county inspector.[117]

Meanwhile, Deputy Inspector General O'Connell had clipped from the *Northern Whig* newspaper an article stating that during a meeting of the Bangor Unionist Club, Colonel Sharman Crawford, a prominent member of the Ulster Unionist Council, had asserted that the Ulster Unionists were "preparing for the whole of Ulster a new organization which all men who had signed the covenant would be asked to join." This, Crawford had claimed, was a "more forward movement than any that had taken place yet" and was the "only chance" the Ulster Unionists had of defeating Home Rule.[118]

On January 3, 1913, two reports submitted to Inspector General Chamberlain confirmed what had been reported in the newspaper. The first, from Belfast district inspector Robert Dunlop, stated simply, "I have heard that a movement is on foot to enroll members of a police force to be employed by the proposed Ulster provisional government. I understand that attestation forms are or will be provided, and it is proposed to arm this force with rifles."[119] The second, drafted by Antrim county inspector N.I. Marrion, included greater detail. It confirmed that the Ulster Unionist Council had begun to establish an armed volunteer corps, and that this organization would be "at least 2,000 strong." Until the passing of the Home Rule Bill, this force would "unofficially police" the unionist population. Once the bill passed, however, it would assume sole responsibility for the Ulster people in defiance of any established Home Rule government.[120]

The Inspector General immediately sent these two reports to the Chief Secretary's Office. Under Secretary Dougherty was neither impressed nor concerned by their content, however. He advised Birrell that Marrion had been "constantly alarmist on the Ulster Question," and added, "I am not disposed to take too seriously his latest contribution."[121] Although Dunlop "more or less" confirmed Marrion's report, Dougherty nevertheless remained "skeptical about this Volunteer Corps."[122] Birrell was wary of Dougherty's analysis. He had been in cabinet when Churchill had described the enraged unionist crowds that had protested against his visit to Belfast the previous February, and he had seen the raw passion of the Ulster Unionists when Parliament had erupted in November. He therefore wrote to Dougherty, saying, "It does not admit of doubt that a 'Force' is being organized as reported. . . . The real doubt is, What is behind it [?]—Are they playing at Treason [?] . . . Are they ready to die [?] If so, When [?]—this year, next year or the year after [?] It would be a mistake not to continue the closest observations."[123] Reluctantly, Dougherty did as his superior asked and requested that the R.I.C. continue its investigations.

Two days later, Birrell's concerns were justified. District Inspector Livingstone informed the Tyrone county inspector that on January 2, 50 more men from his district had enrolled in the Ulster volunteer movement.[124] The following day, Constable Henry Fyfe of Belfast confirmed that the Ulster Unionist Council had decided "to form a Volunteer Force for Ulster to act as a Police Force in the event of Home Rule becoming law."[125] Birrell received copies of both Livingstone's and Fyfe's reports on January 6. He could now be in no doubt that a new force was being formed across Ulster. The only question was how to deal with it.

Whilst Birrell and his under secretary considered their options, the constabulary continued to collect intelligence. Antrim County Inspector Marrion wrote again to Inspector General Chamberlain on January 8. He confirmed that a body of men was being formed to forcibly act against any Home Rule government, and that they would be armed with "carbines, swords, bayonets, and some kind of truncheon." Furthermore, he claimed, the Ulster Unionist Council believed that many of the Protestant members of the R.I.C. would "resign before 'the appointed day,' " which would "not only seriously reduce its numbers but [would] also render it less representative and thereby lessen its moral authority in Ulster." Without Protestants, it would be extremely difficult for the R.I.C. to police the northeastern counties of the island. Indeed, Marrion suspected that if the Protestant members of the force truly did leave, the R.I.C. would be "practically powerless to enforce the orders of an Irish Executive while confronted with an armed and disciplined force. . . . [I]ts position would be hopeless unless backed up all over the Province with an overpowering military force."[126]

It was now clear to the R.I.C., and conveyed to the Chief Secretary, that if the Home Rule Bill passed, the unionists would do all in their power to subvert the police in their efforts to support the new Irish government. An unauthorized army would sabotage a legitimate law, passed by a democrati- cally elected Parliament and given the assent of the king. If the Crown forces attempted to uphold the law, they might be resisted with force. Despite this knowledge, however, the Ulster Volunteer Force was permitted to grow beyond its infancy. The R.I.C. had precise intelligence showing what was forming, where it was taking place, and who was in charge, yet Birrell chose to ignore these threats. Without further instruction from the Chief Secretary's Office, all senior constabulary members could do was encourage their men to keep their eyes and ears open to new developments. No preventative policing could take place and the U.V.F. could not be shut down.

Such inaction characterized the government's response to the U.V.F. over the following ten months, from January to October 1913. The R.I.C. continued to collect and submit increasingly detailed and compelling evidence of the illegal nature of the force and the threat that it posed to the state, yet Birrell, encouraged by his under secretary, Dougherty, did nothing. Indeed, in the remaining days of January, whilst the movement was still small in size and stature, constables and sergeants of the R.I.C. submitted no less than 11 reports to their superiors,[127] and the county inspectors and Belfast commissioner updated the Inspector General of the R.I.C. six times.[128] Most important of these reports was the acquisition by Sergeant William Hall of a copy of the Ulster Volunteer Force's "Little Book" from a "very confidential friend." Hall made a copy of the book before returning it and forwarded this copy to the Crimes Special Branch.[129] The Little Book contained a wealth of information, including full descriptions of the objectives of the force, the duties of its volunteers, the qualifications needed to join, and its organizational structure. It confirmed in a single document, in words written by the leadership of the Ulster Volunteer Force, what the R.I.C. had been gradually pulling together from fragmentary reports over the past three weeks.

The reason that the Ulster Volunteer Force had been formed, according to the Little Book, was to act "for [the] self preservation and mutual protection of all Loyalists and generally to keep the peace." Any man between the ages of 18 and 60 could join. The force was organized on a county-by-county basis, with a county committee in each county or city in Ulster. That committee was directly responsible for the organization of the force in that area. The county was then divided into divisions, and each division nominated a divisional representative to sit on the county committee. The county committee also elected members to be county representatives, who would travel to Belfast whenever a meeting was summoned at headquarters. The divisional representatives divided their divisions into subdistricts and appointed district representatives. Together, the divisional representatives and the district representatives formed a divisional committee. This committee established separate localities within the subdistrict, headed by a locality leader.

It was these localities that enrolled individual volunteers. The locality leaders then divided their volunteers into squads of 11 men and one squad leader each. Two squads formed a section, which elected a section leader (or subleader). Two sections formed a half-company, under a half-company commander (or subcommander). Two half-companies formed a company, under the control of a commander. Thus, a company consisted of 3 officers (one commander and two subcommanders), 4 noncommissioned officers (the subleaders), and 96 men (including the squad leaders).[130] With Sergeant Hall's acquisition of the Little Book, the R.I.C. had all this information in hand.

Also significant was a discovery by District Inspector Vere Richard Gregory. He found that in addition to the policing component of the volunteer force, there was a rumor that there was a "sort of military force being started to include all persons over the age of 18 years of age willing to take up arms."[131] Four days later, he was able to confirm the existence of these distinct police and military wings. An informant had told him that the police wing was only, "to use his words, 'a tuppenny halfpenny thing that everyone was joining.' " The military wing, in contrast, was "much more secret," and "anyone joining it had to take an oath of secrecy."[132] Gregory's discovery confirmed for the R.I.C. that the U.V.F. was not only concerned with policing its own people but also had more militant ambitions. The police had this knowledge on January 26, 1913.

Inspector General Chamberlain was troubled by these new reports. He collated a file of all the information submitted to him and, on January 30, sent it to the Chief Secretary, Birrell, along with the usual monthly reports from the county inspectors. This file, combined with the monthly reports, showed that since mid-December, when the idea of organizing some form of Ulster army had first been discussed by the Ulster Unionist Council, the U.V.F. had grown steadily in strength and numbers. Perhaps more troubling, the force had gained such influence throughout the Protestant communities of Ulster that Chamberlain was worried about the loyalty of his own Protestant officers. He warned Birrell that in the event of the Home Rule Bill becoming law, "many Protestants [would] resign or retire."[133] If the volunteer force was allowed to grow, the Inspector General would be faced not only with treason amongst the people he was policing but also mutiny within his own ranks.

On reading these reports, however, Under Secretary Dougherty again dismissed the threat, telling the Chief Secretary: "This is the usual thing. . . . The greater part of this country [is] very peaceable."[134] When asked to clarify his comments, Dougherty explained to Birrell: "I place little reliance on the gossip of Orange Lodges and Unionists Clubs which our police officers in Ulster offer up so plentifully."[135] The Chief Secretary, heeding the advice of his under secretary over that of his Inspector General, chose to do nothing about the growing threat posed by the U.V.F. He failed even to mention it to the cabinet.

Throughout the months of February and March, the R.I.C. continued to testify in intelligence reports to the growing strength of the U.V.F. The force was now conducting military drill in public places throughout the northern counties of Ireland, some attended by more than 800 people. There were also rumors of arms importations, including one confirmed report of 10 cases of arms, containing between 200 and 300 rifles with bayonets. These rifles had been intercepted in Newcastle-upon-Tyne, England, on their way from Hamburg, Germany, to Belfast.[136]

Still, Dougherty counseled caution. In a memo to Birrell dated March 10, he cited numerous reasons for dismissing the police intelligence. He first claimed that the police constables were inherently biased, holding an "evident desire" to "impress their superiors with the seriousness and extent of the Ulster preparations for resistance to Home Rule." He also questioned their competence, claiming that many of the officers merely repeated "the gossip of Orange Lodges and the wild talk of the Unionist Clubs apparently without any attempt to verify the statements of anonymous informants." Even those reports that could be confirmed, he argued, were not representative of the greater Protestant community. The drill participants were "mostly prominent members of the Orange Society or Rectors of the late established Church who are neither the natural leaders of, nor possess any influence with, a large section of Ulster Protestants." As to the drilling itself, Dougherty dismissed it as "nothing but a piece of 'bluff' on the part of the leaders, however serious may be the intentions of some of their ignorant followers." Finally, he assured Birrell, the reports of arms importations were "purely imaginary."[137]

Birrell, as he had done before, prioritized the advice of his under secretary over the advice of the Inspector General. This raises the question of why he would continue to do so in light of such compelling intelligence. Why would Birrell accept the advice of a bureaucrat over that of a trained and experienced police commander? By 1913, the Chief Secretary had become a weak man, distracted by the illness of his wife. He had neither the time nor the energy to deal with the worsening situation in Ulster, and he spent increasing amounts of time in London, rather than Dublin. He was content to allow others to make the important decisions in his absence. Dougherty, being his closest colleague and a reliable intermediary between London and Dublin, seems to have held greater influence with Birrell than the written police reports arriving daily on his desk. Birrell relied on his under secretary to perform many of his more mundane duties during his wife's illness. It is not unreasonable, therefore, to suspect that just as he relied on Dougherty for practical implementation of

Irish policy, he also relied on him for interpretation and understanding of the intelligence he received.

Furthermore, Dougherty's judgment was supported by other men close to Birrell. Andrew Magill, the Chief Secretary's private secretary, blamed Birrell's unfortunate position on the Irish Nationalist Party, which he claimed was "doubly the cause of [Birrell's] debacle":

> [I]n the first place because they insisted on him staying at his post—they would have no one else—and secondly by urging him on every occasion to do nothing, to take no notice of the murmurs of discontent which they attributed to a small number of Adullamites. I remember well, when all the members of the Cabinet handed in their resignations to Asquith during the [First World] war so as to leave him free to reconstitute the government, Mr. Birrell saying to me, "It's a curious thing, Magill, I believe I am the only member of the Cabinet who is really anxious to clear out, and I am the only one who will not be let go." This was perfectly true as Redmond and Dillon refused to consider anyone else. I sometimes made a feeble remonstrance as to Mr. Birrell's *vis inertiae*, but his invariable answer was "Dillon assures me it is all right and Dillon knows the country."[138]

It is easy to understand why John Dillon would have been so keen to discredit the power of the U.V.F. in his conversations with Birrell. Dillon, as the deputy leader of the Irish Nationalist Party, had a stake in seeing the implementation of an Irish Home Rule Parliament. Any acknowledgment by the Nationalist Party of the growing strength of the Ulster Unionist movement might have caused the government to reconsider the wisdom of seeking home rule for all 32 counties of Ireland, including those in Ulster. It was best, therefore, for the Irish Nationalist Party to downplay the significance of the U.V.F. and thus ensure the continuation of the government's Irish policy. Birrell received such political counsel from Dillon whilst at the same time relying on Dougherty for his analysis of the police intelligence.

The question remains, however: why would Dougherty fail to communicate that intelligence to his boss? This is a more difficult question to answer. When he first took over the post of under secretary in 1908, Dougherty was 64 years old. He was by all accounts a "safe, sensible, level-headed man,"[139] not the sort to distort police reports in pursuit of a personal agenda. Unlike Birrell, he was an Ulsterman, but he was not a career politician and had been a Presbyterian minister when appointed, and a professor of philosophy at Magee College in Londonderry before that.[140] He was not a typical Ulster Unionist Protestant, though. Rather, he was a confirmed Liberal and Home Ruler, even standing (unsuccessfully) for the Derry City House of Commons seat as a Liberal in 1895.[141] Following his resignation as under secretary in October 1914, he was elected as Liberal M.P. for Londonderry and sat in the House throughout the years of the First World War.[142]

What, then, can be made of this Protestant minister who was in favor of a Home Rule parliament for Ireland? Why would Dougherty go to such lengths to persuade the Chief Secretary that the police were exaggerating the strength of the U.V.F. and that the best course of action was to leave the paramilitaries alone? Without a diary, journal, or series of personal letters laying out his innermost thoughts, and without the memoirs of a private secretary, it is impossible to answer this question with any certainty. Several points suggest themselves, though. Initially, Dougherty seems to have had genuine difficulty believing that his fellow Protestant countrymen, usually law-abiding and upstanding members of the community, could display such violence towards the government as the police were reporting. It seems to have been quite inconceivable to him that Protestant Ulstermen could act in such a treasonable fashion.

As an avid Home Ruler, however, Dougherty was not typical of his Ulster brethren, and thus perhaps could not judge their character, motivations, or capabilities. As the months progressed and the intelligence on the U.V.F. mounted, it became impossible for him to mistake the threat that the force presented. Why, then, would he continue to persuade the Chief Secretary otherwise? The answer to this question may again lie with Dougherty's political convictions. Dougherty, as a committed Home Ruler, may have arrived at the same conclusion as Dillon. He may have found it difficult to admit to anything that could lead the British government to reconsider the implementation of Irish self-government. Had he concurred with the police reports of a growing threat in Ulster, and agreed that when the Home Rule Bill passed there would be a large outbreak of violence in the province, the government may have stalled a Home Rule parliament until Ulster Unionists could be appeased. Dougherty, committed to the ideal of an Irish parliament, may not have wished to provide any evidence that could hinder the process of attaining such self-government. As a result, it is possible that he continued to cast doubt on the accuracy of the police intelligence that was being collated in accordance with his political agenda.

In spite of Dougherty's doubt, the U.V.F. continued to grow in April 1913. That month, Inspector General Chamberlain reported to Birrell that the force was by far the greatest concern of the R.I.C.: there was reason to believe that many rifles had been smuggled into Ulster for immediate use against Home Rule.[143] In response to this, Birrell convened a meeting with Asquith and the cabinet on April 22. Rather than relate Chamberlain's concerns, however, he instead circulated an anonymous document that had been sent to the king on March 23 with a cover letter stating that it was from "a magistrate in the north of Ireland who was for many years in the public service."

This magistrate stated that there were 100,000 Orangemen, in addition to 100,000 men in 381 Unionist Clubs across Ulster, most of whom owned revolvers and all of whom were committed to defeating Irish Home Rule. The leaders had not yet distributed arms, but they had established rifle clubs. The magistrate had personally witnessed the practice there and reported that "the accuracy of the shooting came as a great surprise to me." The unionists carried out drill across the province, and trained instructors taught signaling at night, with signals "given and taken from the hill-tops between club members located 3 or 4 miles apart." Unionist leaders had also divided each county in Ulster into military districts and had established a "police force," the U.V.F., in each military district.

The magistrate admitted that "for a long time I laughed at all the tall talk that one heard; I laughed at the same old speeches and harangues; I laughed at the local newspapers." He could not now, however, bring himself "to believe that all these precautions and preparations are mere bluff." He explained that it would be impossible "for the leaders to restrain the rank and file if this Bill becomes law":

> Too many boats have been burnt. The men are being drilled and prepared very seriously and very completely. It would be very difficult if not an entirely impossible task to persuade these men that all their shooting practice, all their drill, and the arms and ammunition and money spent is all for nothing—merely bluff—and that they must disband and take the Home Rule Act lying down.[144]

The U.V.F., he assured the king in his letter, was serious in its intentions.

For many members of the cabinet, it was the first they had heard of the U.V.F. If they were alarmed by what they read, Birrell soon assuaged their fear. He assured them that the document "contains nothing new to me; in fact, it does no more than re-state as confidential information what has been common talk on Ulster political platforms." He told them that the claims of 200,000 able-bodied men ready to reject Home Rule were "simply ridiculous," and that, "as a matter of fact, there is very little evidence to show that the movement has taken any real hold. . . . [T]hough the more fiery spirits of the Orange lodges are undoubtedly ready for any extreme measures, they are in a very substantial minority even of the Protestants in Ulster." He admitted that the idea of a provisional government in Ulster was "no doubt discussed much" but did not believe there was much to it:

> [T]hough by no means an impossible supposition, the business men of
> Belfast—who are just as fond of money as every other commercial-minded
> population—will think a great many times before they strike so heavy a
> blow at their business undertakings. Ulster is not in the least cut off from the
> rest of Ireland; it is intensely Irish in feeling. . . . The material prosperity of
> Ulster largely depends upon the maintenance of close business relations
> with all parts of Catholic Ireland.[145]

Despite the concern of the Inspector General, the cabinet was assured by
Birrell that Ulster would remain calm when the Home Rule Bill finally passed.

In May, Chamberlain reported that the situation in Ulster had become a
"matter of grave anxiety." Drilling was now "practiced with more enthusiasm
in every county of the province," and on May 16 a private meeting of
the Ulster Unionist Council had taken place, during which the strength of the
Ulster Volunteer Force had been confirmed at 30, 000 men and growing.[146]
The Crimes Special Branch reported that 326 drills had taken place in
123 separate locations that month.[147] Military drill continued throughout
June and July, with 402 drills in 164 locations in June, and 442 drills in
174 locations in July.[148] In several counties, the U.V.F. also established a signaling corps that, together with other companies of the force, practiced
signaling, dispatch carrying, ambulance drill, tent pitching, and cooking.[149]
In August, the number of drills rose to 456 in 181 locations.[150]

The Crimes Special Branch sent each of these monthly reports to
Dougherty, who in turn forwarded them to Birrell. Attached to each of these
files, however, was a note from the under secretary telling the Chief Secretary
such things as, "There is nothing very interesting in these reports."[151] Birrell,
therefore, chose to ignore the information provided by the police, listening
instead to the analysis of his under secretary. Such neglect concerned
Chamberlain, who believed that the Chief Secretary's Office was not paying
the attention due to the R.I.C.'s intelligence. Accordingly, he set about
writing a "special report" on the situation in Ulster, which he completed on
August 26 and sent immediately to Birrell, by way of Dougherty.

Chamberlain reported that between 40,000 and 50,000 men were
enrolled in the U.V.F., all of whom had received some training in military
drill from ex-British Army instructors. He estimated that if and when the
Home Rule Bill became law, "this number would probably be augmented by
most of the adult male population in Ulster who are Protestants." Although
there had been no widespread importation of rifles yet, Chamberlain
reported, large sections of the population in Ulster carried personal revolvers.

He also stated that the two religious communities in Ulster had become polarized over the past year, and warned, "So bitter is the feeling against Home Rule, particularly in Belfast and the North Eastern Counties, where the Unionists are in a majority, that it is believed large numbers would respond to the call to arms." He concluded, "If trouble breaks out in Belfast, it will assuredly spread rapidly to other parts of the Province, and the Royal Irish Constabulary, distributed as they are in small parties, throughout each county in Ulster, will be quite powerless to deal with the situation. The question will, from the very commencement of disorder, become a military one, and one of considerable gravity."[152]

Dougherty dismissed the report with his usual contempt and delayed almost a month, until September 23, before forwarding it to the Chief Secretary. When Birrell finally did see the report, Dougherty had attached his own comments in front, so that the Chief Secretary would consider his opinion before the Inspector General's. Dougherty acknowledged that "the situation in Ulster is difficult and may develop dangerously, if not from a Military at least from a Police point of view." He warned, however, that "in reading these reports it is perhaps necessary to remember that these officers are more closely associated with Unionist politicians and with the better classes of society in Ulster than they are with the masses." He assured Birrell, therefore, that the R.I.C. was "a little inclined to over-rate the importance of the drilling and other military operations which have been carried on and the readiness of the Protestant population to resist in the field the establishment of a Home Rule Government." He concluded that whilst "the great majority of the Protestant population of Ulster dislike the prospect of Home Rule, their expressed intention of resisting it has not the significance which some of these reports attach to it."[153]

Four days before Dougherty forwarded his comments to Birrell, on September 19, the under secretary received more intelligence from the R.I.C., informing him that the police had finally established the identity of the staff officers of the U.V.F. The General Officer Commanding was Lieutenant General Sir George Richardson, who had retired from the Indian Army in 1906. The Chief Staff Officer was Colonel Hackett Paine, who had retired from the British Army in 1901. This information, however, was not included in Dougherty's report to the Chief Secretary.[154]

On the same day that Birrell received Dougherty's report, 500 delegates of the Ulster Unionist Council gathered at the Ulster Hall in Belfast and officially approved the establishment of a provisional government should the Home Rule Bill be passed. In that event, the council would delegate all its powers to this provisional government. In the meantime, 77 members were selected to act as representatives of this provisional government, with Carson as the chairman of the central authority. A military council was also set up to administer and issue orders to the Ulster Volunteer Force, its powers effective immediately.[155] The Ulster Unionists had now formalized the organization of their rebellion against Westminster.

The following week, the R.I.C. supplemented its knowledge of the U.V.F. still further. On September 27, the force held a regimental parade through the streets of Belfast, ending at the Balmoral Agricultural Show Grounds where Bonar Law had committed the Conservative Unionist Party to the anti-Home Rule cause in April 1912. The parade had been announced not in secret, but in two newspapers in their September 12 editions: the *News Letter* and the *Northern Whig*. The parade would begin at 4:00 p.m., they stated, and the volunteers would be inspected by Carson and Richardson, the General Officer Commanding the U.V.F.[156]

On September 18, one week before the parade, the R.I.C. received another vital piece of intelligence. T.J. Smith, a justice of the peace, had obtained copies of the orders that were given for the parade, and these he immediately gave to the Crimes Special Branch.[157] The orders stated that the parade would be made up of the four U.V.F. regiments that formed the Belfast Division, each numbering 800 men. With a total of 14 battalions, the division was expected to parade with 11,200 men. Each battalion would carry a colored flag indicating its regimental designation and battalion number (the colors specified in the orders), and each had an assigned location and time to begin the parade.[158] With such information, all the R.I.C. had to do to gain an accurate picture of the U.V.F.'s Belfast Division was place police constables and sergeants at selected places along the indicated routes, at the correct times, and have them note how many men were in each battalion, how (if at all) these men were armed, and who was leading them. With the help of the numbered, colored banners, it would be a simple but critical intelligence coup for the police.

On September 26, the day before the parade, the R.I.C. received a further piece of intelligence to aid them in their task. An anonymous source gave to the Crimes Special Branch an official U.V.F. pamphlet that listed all those in leadership positions in the Belfast Division, from the General Officer Commanding right down to the battalion commanders. In all, the source named 26 men, with their respective ranks and titles. Significantly, of those listed, 12 had formerly served as officers in the British Army and one was a sitting Member of Parliament.[159]

When the U.V.F. began to march the following day, the R.I.C. had all it needed to identify those who were involved. Acting Sergeant Joseph Edwards submitted the final report on October 4, together with the inspection orders and the rank designations that the Crimes Special Branch had obtained. These were immediately given to the Inspector General, who in turn forwarded them to the Chief Secretary's Office. Both Birrell and Dougherty initialed reading these reports.[160] That same week, the Crimes Special Branch also reported to the Chief Secretary that in September, the number of drills practiced by the U.V.F. had risen dramatically to 757, carried out in 289 separate locations.[161] At the end of October, Chamberlain wrote again to Birrell, declaring that "a very serious state of unrest prevails throughout the province of Ulster." He reported that the membership of the U.V.F. had now reached 88,000 men. There were also at least 10,000 rifles ready for use by the volunteers in Belfast alone, with more reported throughout the countryside.[162]

The Ulster Volunteer Force was growing rapidly, had defiantly paraded through the City of Belfast en mass, and now appeared to be arming. But still, Birrell did nothing. Only at the end of October, and then only at the specific request of some fellow members of the cabinet, did he begin circulating to his colleagues any sort of regular report on the situation in Ulster. He simply did not believe the crisis deserved the attention of the British government; indeed, for Birrell, there was no crisis.[163]

An Irish Nationalist Response

It was almost by chance that "The North Began" was published in *An Claidheamh Soluis* on November 1, 1913. Eoin MacNeill, professor of early and medieval Irish history at University College, Dublin, had been in bed with a cold when Michael O'Rahilly, business manager of the Gaelic League's official magazine, paid him a visit. O'Rahilly suggested that since he was incapacitated from university work, MacNeill might wish to direct his efforts towards writing a more "popular" article for the magazine. MacNeill, one of the original founders of the Gaelic League and still its vice president, happily agreed. He decided to compose a commentary on the political situation in Ireland, above all focused on events in Ulster. He did so in a lighthearted manner, whilst still recovering from his illness. When he penned "The North Began," therefore, he had no idea of the political storm that his words would create.[164]

He began the article with a dismissal of the unionist community in Ulster, accusing it of being little more than a feudal system upheld by the British establishment. He then turned to the Ulster Volunteer Force, noting in particular the lack of response it had elicited from Westminster. He suggested that this political reticence by the British government was because the U.V.F. claimed to be drilling "for the Empire," and he noted that "it appears that the British Army cannot now be used to prevent the enrolment, drilling, and reviewing of Volunteers in Ireland." With such a policy in effect, he advised, "[t]here is nothing to prevent the other twenty-eight counties [outside Ulster] from calling into existence citizen forces to hold Ireland 'for the Empire.' "[165] It was only a single sentence amidst 60 others, but those 22 words were seized upon quickly by the nationalist population of Ireland. If the north could organize, why not the south?

One who read MacNeill's piece was Bulmer Hobson, a member of the Supreme Council of the illegal Irish Republican Brotherhood (I.R.B.) and Chairman of the I.R.B.'s Dublin Centres Board. Previously, Hobson had held a meeting with the board in July to discuss the possibility of arming the I.R.B. and forming some sort of Irish volunteer movement in response to the U.V.F. At that time, however, the board had decided that it should delay public drilling, as renewed activity by the I.R.B. would arouse British suspicion and bring unwanted attention from the police.[166] Now, though, with the publication of MacNeill's article, Hobson believed the time had come to form an Irish Volunteer Force. He immediately went to O'Rahilly to seek his opinion. O'Rahilly agreed, on the condition that Eoin MacNeill lead the movement. This was a stipulation that Hobson was only too happy to meet, as he believed that "the I.R.B. must not show its hand."[167] Two days later, O'Rahilly went with Hobson to MacNeill's house to see if the professor truly held the sentiments he had expressed in the article. MacNeill assured them that he did, and the three men decided to form a committee with the sole purpose of organizing an Irish Volunteer Force.[168]

MacNeill knew that he was being used as a front of respectability for the illegal I.R.B. He later wrote, "I had no doubt in my mind that both these men came to me from the old physical force party whose organization was the I.R.B., and I also had little doubt of the part I was expected to play."[169] Nevertheless, he acquiesced with Hobson's plan, and O'Rahilly immediately sent out invitations for those interested to meet with MacNeill. On November 11, of the eleven men invited, ten gathered at Wynn's Hotel on Lower Abbey Street in Dublin. O'Rahilly, not yet an official member of the I.R.B., made great efforts to ensure that those who came represented not only the I.R.B. but also less militant factions of the Irish nationalist community. Of the eleven invited, therefore, only five were members of the I.R.B. The leader of the Sinn Fein Party, Arthur Griffith, had been specifically forbidden to attend.[170] Bulmer Hobson likewise stayed away, hoping that his absence would keep police attention from their first meeting.[171] Other well-known members of the I.R.B. were told not to join.[172]

Even so, and despite the care O'Rahilly had taken with invitations, when the ten met they agreed they still were not politically diverse enough. They feared that, as constituted, they would not be truly accepted by the greater Irish population. They decided, therefore, to expand the committee to thirty, and to meet again in three days with a more representative membership.[173] This they did, and on November 14, again at Wynn's Hotel, thirty men met to form the Provisional Committee of the Irish Volunteers.[174]

One of the primary concerns of the committee was that the movement be accepted by John Redmond and his Irish Parliamentary Party (also known as the Irish Nationalist Party and the Irish Home Rule Party). Redmond came from a distinguished line of moderate politicians. His great uncle, John Edward Redmond, had entered Parliament as a Liberal in 1859 and his father, William Archer Redmond, had been a Member of Parliament for the newly formed Irish Home Rule Party from 1872 onwards. His mother had been born into a Protestant family and had converted to Catholicism only upon marriage. She had retained her unionist politics to her death, even though happily married to an avid Home Ruler. The younger John Redmond, therefore, although raised a Catholic nationalist, did not have boiling within him the fiery blood of some of the more revolutionary and sectarian Irishmen.[175]

Redmond studied law at Trinity College, Dublin, receiving his degree from the same institution as Sir Edward Carson, but he postponed his call to the bar upon graduation. Instead, he moved to London in 1876 to work as a clerk in the House of Commons.[176] As a young clerk, he was thrown into the world of Charles Stewart Parnell and his unconventional political practices. Parnell soon began to use obstructionist tactics never before seen in the Commons to make his small Irish Home Rule Party a force to be reckoned with. Redmond's father, with his son watching, was center stage throughout this parliamentary drama.[177] When his father died unexpectedly in 1880, John hoped to succeed him as the Member of Parliament for Wexford, but Parnell instead offered the seat to Tim Healy, a prominent member of the Irish Catholic community. Redmond graciously stepped aside, and, as a reward, Parnell supported him as the Home Rule candidate for New Ross, a seat he won in 1881, at just 25 years of age.[178] Thus, John Redmond embarked upon his long parliamentary career, entering the Commons at the height of the Irish Land Wars and just five years before Gladstone's first Irish Home Rule Bill.

From 1882 to 1889, Parnell led a strong Irish Home Rule Party, and John Redmond's stature rose with that of the party, both amongst his colleagues in the Commons and with his constituents back home in Ireland. In 1889, however, Parnell became embroiled in a prominent divorce scandal.[179] The affair proved too shocking for the more orthodox Catholics within Ireland, and Parnell's colleagues began to fear the effect it would have on their constituents when election time came. In November 1890, therefore, these members approached the Prime Minister and informed him that either Parnell must be replaced as leader of the Irish Home Rule Party or the Liberal alliance would fall, together with Gladstone's majority in the Commons. Gladstone, fearful of loosing power, put pressure on the Home Rule M.P.'s to choose a new leader. On December 6, 1890, the party split, with most prominent members opposing Parnell. Redmond was one of the few to remain loyal.[180] When Parnell died the following year, Redmond took leadership of the Parnellite faction of the party. Over the next few years he impressed many of his former colleagues with his political skill and wit, particularly during the 1893 Home Rule debates. Ten years after the split, in 1900, the party reunited and Redmond became its sole leader.[181]

During the political upheavals in Ulster 12 years later, the Home Rule Party was in much the same position as it had been during the 1886 and 1893 debates. The Prime Minister was reliant upon Redmond for the Liberal majority in the Commons, and he was thus more inclined to support the Irish Nationalists than the Ulster Unionists. Redmond's party held 73 of Ireland's 105 seats; the Sinn Fein Party, which represented the physical-force tradition of the I.R.B., held none. It was absolutely essential for the success and legitimacy of the newly formed Irish Volunteers in November 1913, therefore, that they gain Redmond's support. The addition of four members of the Irish Nationalist Party to the provisional committee, whilst not as many as they had hoped for, was seen by MacNeill, O'Rahilly, and Hobson as an important first step.[182]

The newly formed provisional committee, now numbering 30, decided to put the idea of establishing an Irish Volunteer Force before a larger audience at a public meeting, which they planned to hold at the Rotunda Park in Dublin.[183] Initially, the committee booked only the small concert room, but as interest in their planning grew, they also booked the large concert hall.[184] On November 21, the committee ran an advertisement in the *Freeman's Journal*: "A public meeting for the purpose of establishing a corps of Irish Volunteers will be held in the large Concert Hall of the Rotunda at 8 p.m. Eoin MacNeill, B.A., will preside." As the day neared, and yet more interest was shown, the committee decided that it had better also book the largest venue at the Rotunda Park, the rink, to supplement the large concert hall.[185]

On Tuesday, November 25, the meeting was held as planned. Eoin MacNeill, Patrick Pearse, Alderman Kelly, and Luke O'Toole each took their turn at the podium.[186] To the surprise of the organizers, over 3,500 men showed up, and three additional overflow rooms close to the main rink had to be opened.[187] Enrollment forms were handed out by stewards, most of whom were members of the I.R.B. On its first day, the Irish Volunteer Force enrolled 3,000 men.[188]

The R.I.C. proved far less concerned with the formation of the Irish Volunteers than it had been with the U.V.F. The police were well aware of what was taking place; MacNeill's meeting in the Rotunda Park had hardly been kept secret. On that November day, the provisional committee had even openly distributed copies of the Irish Volunteer Force's *Manifesto*, written by

MacNeill, which was readily available to the police. The *Manifesto* cited the Ulster Volunteer Force as the root cause of Ireland's current problems, claiming that it was attempting "to make the display of military force and the menace of armed violence the determining factor in the future relations between this country and Great Britain." It asked if, in light of the U.V.F., the Irish nationalist population could afford "to rest inactive, in the hope that the course of politics in Great Britain may save us from the degradation openly threatened against us?" It concluded that they could not, as "[i]n a crisis of this kind, the duty of safeguarding our own rights is our duty first and foremost." Therefore, the *Manifesto* continued, the Irish Volunteers were being formed to protect the cause of Irish Home Rule; "the Nation" had an obligation to "maintain its Volunteer organization as a guarantee of the liberties which the Irish people shall have secured."[189]

In their planning, MacNeill and O'Rahilly did not fear a conspiracy being uncovered, nor did they want to hide from the government the events of the Rotunda Park. Indeed, it was their hope that as large a segment of Irish and British society as possible would know of the Irish Volunteers. In contrast to the intimate reporting that had taken place in Ulster, therefore, the police reports detailing the organization of the Irish Volunteers were slim. They told the Chief Secretary only that "attempts have been made to spread the Irish Volunteer movement, which was inaugurated in Dublin on 25th November, to the provinces." This movement, however, "had not met with general support," and the only cities outside Dublin in which branches had been formed were Cork and Galway. In Galway, 230 volunteers had enrolled, and in Cork, 250. Meetings were also held in Roscommon, Omagh, Tralee, Annascaul, Dunmor, and Duagh, but no branches had been formed in any of these places. The names of those enrolled had been collected by the police for future reference, but it was not thought that they would be needed.[190] As the new year dawned, for the R.I.C. the most pressing problem remained the Ulster Volunteer Force. Indeed, most of those who wore the uniform expected that the Irish Volunteers would simply fade away.

Enter the Politicians

King George V was a troubled man. His natural sympathies lay with the unionists, but, being a firm believer in the virtues of constitutional monarchy, he was more than willing to defer on this occasion to the wisdom of Parliament. Nevertheless, he was still king, and throughout 1913 he had been receiving letters in the thousands from his subjects pleading for their head of state to intervene in the crisis in Ulster. Furthermore, Bonar Law and other prominent Conservatives had pressed him to dissolve parliament and dismiss his ministers, arguing that to do so would be well within his constitutional rights. These Conservatives claimed that the British people had been misled at the 1910 general election, that Home Rule had not been an issue in the Liberal manifesto, and that now the Liberals were usurping power that they had won only by deceit. They assured him that if the people were given the vote again, now fully aware of the Liberal agenda in Ireland, they would not return a Liberal government and would instead side with the Ulster Unionists. It was an argument that held great sway with the king.[191]

In August 1913, therefore, George V summoned Asquith to the palace, where he suggested to him that a general election ought to be held before a Home Rule bill was finally passed. Mindful of his constitutional position, however, he acknowledged that a British monarch could only dissolve parliament at the request of the Prime Minister, and thus the final decision lay with Asquith. The Prime Minister listened carefully to what his sovereign had to say, but in his reply, he left the king with no doubt that if he forced an election now, it would be held on one issue alone: "Is the country governed by the King or by the people?" He suggested, therefore, that parliament be allowed to continue in its present constitution, and asserted that he, as Prime Minister, had the support of the greater population of the United Kingdom for the passage of an Irish Home Rule bill. Despite his misgivings, there was little the king could do to protest.[192]

Although he had displayed confidence before George V, Asquith was concerned about the constitutional problems raised by the king. He thus composed a "most secret" memorandum for the cabinet, titled "The Constitutional Position of the Sovereign." This he circulated in September, shortly after his meeting. He began by reminding the cabinet of the history of the relationship between the Crown and Parliament:

> In old days, before our present Constitution was completely evolved, the Crown was a real and effective, and often dominating, factor in legislation. . . . The [Glorious] Revolution [, however,] put the title to the Throne and its prerogatives on a Parliamentary basis, and, since a comparatively early date in the reign of Queen Anne, the Sovereign has never attempted to withhold his assent from a Bill which had received Parliamentary sanction.

No sovereign, he assured the cabinet, has "ever dreamt of reviving the ancient veto of the Crown. We have now a well-established tradition of 200 years, that, in the last resort, the occupant of the Throne accepts and acts upon the advice of the Ministers." He reiterated this point, feeling it to be important: "[T]he rights and duties of a constitutional monarch in this country in regard to legislation are confined within determined and strictly circumscribed limits." The king, he told the cabinet, "is entitled and bound to give his Ministers all relevant information which comes to him; to point out objections which seem to him valid against the course which they advise; to suggest (if he thinks fit) an alternative policy. . . . But, in the end, the Sovereign always acts upon the advice which Ministers, after full deliberation and (if need be) reconsideration, feel it their duty to offer."

Asquith then turned to the Parliament Act, claiming that it "was not intended in any way to affect, and it is submitted has not affected, the Constitutional position of the Sovereign. It deals only with differences between the two Houses." The passage of the Parliament Act, therefore, was irrelevant to the Home Rule Bill as far as the king was concerned. It was essential, Asquith argued, that the king remained above politics, without the ability to contradict his ministers' policies:

> [To do so] frees the occupant of the Throne from all personal responsibility for the acts of the Executive and the Legislature. It gives force and meaning to the old maxim that "the King can do no wrong." So long as it prevails, however objectionable particular Acts may be to a large section of his subjects, they cannot hold him in any way accountable, and their loyalty is (or ought to be) wholly unaffected.

If the sovereign intervened to stop the passage of the Home Rule Bill, or to force the present cabinet to resign, his elevated position would be destroyed, and he would be expected to pick sides in every subsequent debate, "dragged into the arena of party politics." If that happened, Asquith contended, "the Crown would become the football of contending factions." The suggestion that the king actively involve himself in politics was "a Constitutional catastrophe which it is the duty of every wise statesman to do the utmost in his power to avert."[193] It was imperative for Asquith, and for the sanctity of the British state, that the Conservatives not succeed in their efforts to involve George V in the debates over Irish Home Rule.

Meanwhile, the problems in Ireland grew only more complex. On August 26, 1913, the Irish Transport and General Workers Union launched a strike against the Dublin Tramway Company. The company's owner, William Martin Murphy, immediately ordered a lockout of any worker in sympathy with the strikers. By September 22, 25,000 workers had been locked out.[194] The man leading the union at this time was James Larkin. Originally part of the Irish diaspora in Liverpool, Larkin had come to Belfast in 1907 as general organizer of the National Union of Dock Labourers. He was suspended by the Dock Laborers after only one year on account of his extreme socialist views, but in 1908 he founded his own union, the Irish Transport and General Workers Union.[195] When the August strike began, Larkin immediately sent for his friend, the Scottish labor organizer James Connolly, who arrived in Belfast on August 29.[196] Connolly was promptly arrested for seditious speech and sentenced to three months in jail. On September 6, however, he began a hunger strike to protest against his imprisonment. He was released after only seven days, weary but victorious. Such was the persuasive power of Connelly's methods of political action.[197]

In October, Larkin himself was arrested for seditious speech and was sentenced to seven months imprisonment. Connelly took over leadership of the strike. On November 3, he held a protest meeting at the Albert Hall to petition against Larkin's captivity. There he claimed that it was Carson and the unionists in Ulster who should be arrested for sedition, for it was they who were arming themselves against Parliament, not the striking tramway workers. Ten days later, on November 13, Larkin was released. Connelly, warming to his theme of comparison with the U.V.F., held a celebration rally on Larkin's release and called for the formation of a citizen's army to mirror the Ulster Volunteers, saying to the crowd,

> Listen to me. I am going to talk sedition. The next time we set out for a route march, I want to be accompanied by four battalions of trained men. I want them to come out with their corporals and their sergeants and people to form fours [a common British military formation, with rows of men four deep]. Why should we not drill and train in Dublin as they are drilling and training in Ulster?[198]

Thus, the Irish Citizen Army was born, 13 days before MacNeill formed the Irish Volunteer Force. The two armies worked side by side until 1916.

In response to this "ever-simmering cauldron of unrest," the Secretary of State for War, Colonel Seely, sent on October 21 for one of his highest-ranking generals and the Director of the War Office, General Sir Nevil Macready. He requested that Macready leave the War Office and go at once to Ireland to take over a division there.[199] Macready refused, citing personal reasons. Sixteen months earlier, in April 1912, Birrell had summoned him, requesting troops to quell the riots that were expected when the Home Rule Bill was introduced in the House of Commons on April 11. Macready had replied that as troops had been constantly withdrawn from their training stations to quell striking miners in Wales, "nothing but the most urgent necessity should interfere with the summer training," and that the "rioting in Belfast was not of a nature that could not be controlled by the Royal Irish Constabulary." The Chief Secretary had responded that "he did not care whether the troops were trained to fight Germany or not, but he wanted them for police work and intended to have them." Unwilling to work under such a man, Macready declined Seely's request. He later commented that his memory of this first meeting with Birrell "lessened my surprise when later on I saw the fruits of his rule in Ireland."[200]

Seely accepted Macready's rebuff, but three weeks later asked him again to go to Dublin and Belfast, this time to report on "the failure of the police during the late disturbances in the two cities, and on other matters connected with the military administration of the command." Macready duly left for Ireland and composed his report. When he attempted to submit it to Seely on November 24, however, he was told that it was no longer necessary, for the "Government intended to do nothing—in fact would 'wait and see'—but that possibly there might be a compromise."[201] The warning that Macready had been prepared to give of the deteriorating situation in Ireland was never received by the cabinet, therefore.

On December 5, looking at the recent labor struggles in Dublin, at the formation of both the Irish Citizen Army and the Irish Volunteers, and at the continuing growth of the U.V.F., the British cabinet recommended to the king that he issue two royal proclamations, one banning the importation of arms and ammunition into Ireland, the second banning the coastwise transport of any arms and ammunition within the waters of the United Kingdom.[202] The Attorney General, John Allsebrook Simon, had recommended this course of action to the cabinet a week earlier, on November 26, just two days after Macready's report was rejected. Citing section 8 of the Customs and Inland Revenue Act of 1879, Simon had explained to his colleagues that the king could prohibit any items that might be used for a military purpose from being exported to Ireland. It was for this reason that the proclamations were issued.[203]

Immediately, the proclamations were condemned by Irish nationalists, coming as they did less than two weeks after the formation of the Irish Volunteers. Why, they asked, had the proclamations not been issued 12 months earlier, when the U.V.F. first began to march?[204] To the king, already conscious of his unionist sympathies and concerned that they should interfere with his constitutional duties, the timing of the proclamations and the criticism they received could not have been more unfortunate.

To make matters worse, there was something to the nationalist critique. The nationalists argued that the government had allowed the U.V.F. to arm but were now preventing the Irish Volunteers from doing the same. Guns had been coming into Ulster for some time. These importations had been organized primarily by Major Frederick Crawford, a retired artillery officer who had signed the Ulster Covenant in his own blood, claiming that his ancestors had done the same in Scotland in 1638. He had since been appointed Director of Ordnance on the U.V.F.'s headquarters staff.[205]

In 1907, ironically the same year that the I.R.B. was reforming, Crawford, as secretary of the Ulster Reform Club, had run an advertisement in the national newspapers of France, Belgium, Germany, and Russia requesting the sale of 10,000 secondhand rifles and 2 million rounds of ammunition.[206] That same year, with the Liberals newly in office after a ten-year absence, the Ulster Unionist Standing Committee had formed a smaller committee to consider the use of force to prevent the possible establishment of a Home Rule government in Ulster. After Crawford showed the committee members samples of the weapons he could obtain, many in the committee had lost their enthusiasm for the scheme.[207] Nevertheless, they ordered Crawford to obtain 1,000 rifles, a shipment that was sent from Hamburg, Germany, via the English industrial cities of West Hartlepool and Newcastle-upon-Tyne disguised as zinc plates. Over the next few years, other rifles were imported via Manchester, Glasgow, Liverpool, and Fleetwood.[208]

Despite the secrecy that Crawford attempted to impose on these shipments, there was little the British government could do to seize the rifles, even on those occasions when they became aware of his activities.[209] This was because Augustine Birrell, in his first year as Chief Secretary, had failed to renew the Peace Preservation (Ireland) Act when it expired in 1907. This act had originally been drafted by Gladstone in 1881, giving the government complete control over the importation, sale, and carrying of arms in Ireland.[210] It had been intended for a single year only, in an attempt to bring stability to Ireland during the Land Wars, but had been renewed without question each year since. In 1907, however, John Redmond persuaded Birrell against renewal of the act, claiming that it was redundant as there was no longer any active threat in Ireland. Besides, Redmond argued, the act was used in a discriminating fashion against Catholics only. Birrell, sympathizing with Redmond's arguments, allowed the act to lapse.[211] Crawford's shipments, coming after the act had fallen from the statute books, were therefore perfectly legal.

Because of Birrell's lack of judgment and foresight, arms importations flooded into Ireland after 1907; there was no legal recourse to prevent them. The government, fearful that to renew the Peace Preservation Act after it had lapsed would cause an outcry in the nationalist community, explored alternative means of stopping the shipments. A loophole in the law was finally found in 1911 when Crawford ordered 7,000 rifles from Hamburg via the Lewes & Lewes Gun Company in London. All were seized upon arrival in Dublin. Crawford immediately crossed to London to protest the seizure, but was informed by Winston Churchill, Home Secretary at the time, that an act passed in 1860 allowed the London and Birmingham Gun Makers' Guild to prohibit the importation of any gun barrels that were not specifically tested by this guild. If Crawford claimed the rifles, he would be liable to a fine of £2 for each barrel, totaling £14,000 for the shipment.[212] He approached the Ulster Unionist Committee, therefore, and recommended that they suspend further shipments until they were able to import a large quantity of arms in a single consignment that could be cleverly disguised.[213] In the meantime, Crawford clandestinely continued to smuggle small packages of rifles into Ireland whenever the opportunity arose.[214]

By the time George V issued his proclamations in December 1913, therefore, the Ulster Volunteer Force already had several thousand arms stored and ready for use throughout the province. The 10,000 rifles that the R.I.C. had noted in its October 1913 reports had been steadily brought into Ulster in small shipments over the previous two years. With few exceptions, the police had informed the Chief Secretary's Office of each of these shipments. Indeed, in 1913, between October 31 and November 14 alone, Birrell received almost daily reports that together catalogued the importation of 805 rifles, 1,506 bayonets, and 50 revolvers.[215] Following the proclamations, coming just two weeks after these reports, such importations were illegal.

Gunrunning was not the only illegal action for which the government could prosecute the U.V.F. In December 1913, Attorney General Simon prepared a second report for the cabinet, this time examining specific breaches of the law in Ulster. He discovered five such areas. The first charge upon which a conviction could be brought, he explained, was treason-felony:

> The avowed objects of the Ulster Volunteer Force make those who are actively responsible for it liable to be prosecuted for treason-felony, for that crime consists in conspiring to make rebellion in order by force to compel the King to change his counsels, or in order to put constraint upon and intimidate either House of Parliament.

The second charge was illegal drilling. Under the Unlawful Drilling Act of 1819, the "training of persons to the use of arms and to the practice of military evolutions and exercise" was illegal, with a penalty of seven years' penal servitude for the drill master and two years' imprisonment for each participant. Section 1 of the act did allow drilling when conducted under "lawful authority" from the king, a lieutenant, or two justices of the peace; it was this section that had been used by the U.V.F. to gain licenses for drill thus far. The Attorney General, however, did not think that justices of the peace could give lawful authority when "the whole proceeding is a seditious conspiracy." Indeed, he continued, "I think the Justices of the Peace who gave such authority would be accessories to the crime." He also pointed out that section 2 "expressly authorizes justices, constables, and other persons acting on their behalf, to disperse people who are unlawfully drilling and to arrest any person present or aiding at the meeting."

The third charge that could be brought against the U.V.F. was for engaging in unlawful assemblies, defined by law as "meetings organized for the purpose of preparing or threatening armed resistance to lawful authority." Any person organizing or attending such a meeting could be imprisoned, and in Ireland, under sections 2 and 3 of the 1887 Coercion Act, such persons could be prosecuted summarily before a court of summary jurisdiction, without a conviction by jury. The fourth charge was for the illegal storing of ammunition, which was prohibited by the Explosive Act of 1875, which placed specific limits on the amount of ammunition that could be kept in any one place. Finally, since the king issued his royal proclamations, any arms importations into Ireland were illegal. The arms could be seized, and those involved in the smuggling could be arrested.

Simon also mentioned a sixth possible area where the government could act, and recommended that the cabinet carefully consider "whether retired [military] Officers and Reservists should be permitted to draw pensions while assisting the Ulster movement."[216] Taken as a whole, the Attorney General's report declared that any volunteer could be arrested for being a member of the U.V.F. (which he determined to be treason), for drilling, for unlawfully assembling, for storing ammunition, and for importing weaponry. If the cabinet acted upon his advice, it would be practically impossible for the U.V.F. to continue to exist.

John Allsebrook Simon was not the only man to report to the cabinet that December. John Seely, the Secretary of State for War, also prepared a memorandum, examining the position of the army in Ulster. He at first acknowledged that the law allowed for a soldier to obey an unreasonable order, such as an order to massacre Orangemen participating in a demonstration that presented no danger to the community. What the army might be required to do in Ulster, however, was quite different, Seely continued. On the contrary, the army now faced not a military situation but rather "the possibility of action being required by His Majesty's troops in supporting the civil power in protecting life and property when the police were unable to hold their own." In such a situation, he explained, the assistance required by the army was "quite as likely to be wanted in England as in any part of Ireland." No allowances, therefore, could be made for the personal politics of officer or man.

To suggest that the army might opt out of military action in Ulster, Seely argued, "amounted to a suggestion that officers or men could pick and choose between lawful and reasonable orders, saying that in one case they would obey and not in another." For example, Seely went on, "one man would say he would shoot an Ulsterman, but not a Trades Unionist or a Socialist; another would shoot a Trades Unionist or a Socialist, but not an Ulsterman; another would shoot a Socialist, but not an Ulsterman or a Trades Unionist." Such a situation was, for a professional army, completely unacceptable. Seely wanted the cabinet to know, therefore, that "any such conduct would be dealt with forthwith under the King's Regulations."[217] As far as the Secretary of State for War was concerned, the army could be used to support the police in Ireland. Any soldier who refused to obey an order requiring such would be punished.

As 1913 came to a close, then, Birrell could not have been in a better position to interrupt the actions of the paramilitary forces in Ireland, particularly the threatening and well-organized Ulster Volunteer Force. The Attorney General had provided five concrete situations in which charges could be brought against the force; collectively these could prevent any further action by the U.V.F. The Secretary of State for War had committed his troops to support the police in suppressing the paramilitaries if required. Even the king had issued two royal proclamations, albeit at the insistence of the cabinet, which specifically forbade the importation of arms into Ireland. Yet for the first three months of 1914, drilling continued uninterrupted.

Indeed, in January, despite the new ability to crack down on the paramilitaries, the government actually considered meeting the demands of the U.V.F. by giving Ulster special consideration within the Home Rule Bill. Asquith circulated a memorandum to the cabinet suggesting that Ulster (the exact geographic boundaries of which would be determined at a later time) be regarded as its own statutory unit, with the police force and Board of Trade inspections continuing as they were presently constituted, education administered by a special Ulster board responsible not to an Irish Home Rule Parliament but to the Parliament at Westminster, and local government administered by a local government board in Ulster, also responsible to the Westminster Parliament, not that in Dublin. Ulster would still have representation in the Home Rule Parliament, but its members would have a right of dissent. This would allow a majority of representatives from Ulster who disagreed with any home rule legislation that imposed new taxes or increased existing taxes, or that affected religion, land tenure, education, or industrial matters, to prevent that legislation from taking effect in Ulster.[218] In effect, Asquith was suggesting that Ulster be given a form of provincial home rule within the larger Irish Home Rule, with distinct Ulster institutions responsible only to Westminster, and with Ulster Home Rule parliamentarians given a veto over most legislation proposed by the Irish Home Rule parliament.

This was not the first time that the concept of Ulster's being treated differently within the Home Rule Bill had been raised. On returning from his trip to Belfast in February 1912, Winston Churchill, despite his strong words, had been greatly impressed with the passion displayed by both sides of the political and religious divide in Ulster. He soon thereafter became convinced that Protestant Ulster would be more trouble within an Irish Home Rule parliament than without. Together with his cabinet colleague David Lloyd George, therefore, he suggested that Ulster be excluded from the Home Rule Bill, with an Irish parliament only covering the Catholic-majority counties of the other three Irish provinces. Churchill and Lloyd George were immediately rebuked by the cabinet for suggesting compromise, particularly by the Lord Chancellor, Lord Loreburn. Full Irish Home Rule could not be compromised or watered down to appease a vocal minority in Ulster, Loreburn argued. No more was said of the matter.[219] Almost two years later, however, in September 1913, Loreburn, no longer Lord Chancellor, published a letter in the *Times* advocating separate treatment for Ulster and suggesting that in light of the growing threat of the U.V.F., a conference should be called by the Prime Minister to discuss Ulster.[220] In public, the government dismissed Loreburn's suggestion outright as an unacceptable compromise, but behind closed doors they had no choice but to take it seriously.

In October 1913, therefore, Asquith called a cabinet meeting to discuss the problem of Ulster. He began by stating emphatically that no concession should be given to the U.V.F., and that the government could not be seen to bow before threats. He had seen the king, he told the cabinet, who had at first argued for negotiation and had hinted that if this was not forthcoming, he might intervene. Asquith had been prepared for this, however, and at first mention of intervention, he had read for the king the memorandum he had earlier circulated to the cabinet regarding the constitutional position of the monarch. On hearing it, the king had quickly changed his tone, and Asquith believed that the cabinet would now have no more obstruction from Buckingham Palace.

Birrell spoke next, saying that Loreburn's letter had created quite a stir in Ireland, the majority of its populace believing that it had come from within the cabinet, "instead of being the output of an always disgruntled ex-colleague." The cabinet discussed this problem, and although stating that they would not be intimidated, all agreed that "if the Tories [the Conservative Unionist Party] wanted concessions, and would in exchange offer a permanent settlement based on an Irish Parliament and Executive, we [the cabinet] would go any lengths to meet them."[221]

From this point on, members of the government sought to meet with the Conservative leader Bonar Law and with Carson to see if any form of compromise was possible. Churchill was sent by Asquith to discuss their options with Bonar Law over a game of golf, and he later reported to Asquith that the Conservative leader "recoils from these desperate measures [the setting up of a provisional government in Ulster]." Churchill added that "the remarkable conversation of which I have given you some account has altered my views about a conference considerably. . . . I have always wished to see Ulster provided for, and you will remember how Lloyd George and I pressed its exclusion upon the Cabinet."[222] Churchill was now ready to again consider excluding Ulster from the Home Rule Bill.

Bonar Law told Carson of his meeting with Churchill, and Carson was encouraged by the news, telling Bonar Law: "As regards the position here I am of opinion that on the whole things are shaping towards a desire to settle on the terms of leaving 'Ulster' out." He was, however, concerned about how Ulster would be defined, and conscious of the fact that to agree to a Home Rule parliament with Ulster excluded would be to abandon those unionists who lived in the southern part of Ireland. He and James Craig, therefore, called a meeting of the southern unionists at Carson's home in London, where they asked the southern delegation to join with the northern under a single leadership. When the southern delegation refused, Carson asked them, "Is it your decision that I am to go on fighting for Ulster?" They told him "yes." He then asked, "Will my fight in Ulster interfere in any way with your fight in the south." They told him "no." Finally, Carson asked, "If I win in Ulster, am I to refuse the fruits of victory because you have lost?" The southern unionists, driven by Carson's logic, replied "no." Carson was thus satisfied that to gain exclusion for Ulster from the Home Rule Bill would not be traitorous to the unionists in the south, and he informed Bonar Law that henceforth he would be concerned only with Ulster.[223]

On October 14, therefore, Bonar Law met secretly with Asquith at the house of a mutual acquaintance, Sir Max Aitken. Little was achieved, however. They met again on November 10, but again did not reach a compromise. Asquith reported to the cabinet that Bonar Law had said the minimum he would accept was "the exclusion of Ulster, and the reservation of legislation relating to it, to the Imperial Parliament, and not even to an Ulster Assembly." Bonar Law had also demanded that the counties of Antrim, Down, Armagh, Derry, and Fermanagh be included as Ulster "beyond question," and Donegal, Tyrone, Cavan, and Monaghan also be considered likely for inclusion. Asquith had replied that Donegal, Tyrone, and Monaghan, due to their large Catholic populations, could not possibly be excluded from Home Rule. The meeting had ended with a request by Bonar Law for a general election before any Home Rule measure was finally agreed upon, a request that the Prime Minister turned down.[224]

In December, Asquith met again twice with Bonar Law, and once with Carson. Both told him that the only settlement the Protestants in Ulster would accept was the complete exclusion of Ulster from any Home Rule parliament, a request that again Asquith told them he was unable to meet. He therefore wrote to Bonar Law and Carson on December 23, enclosing for them a copy of the proposals that he would later detail for the cabinet in the January memorandum mentioned above, promising a statutory Ulster that would be represented in the Irish Parliament, with a veto over any Irish legislation concerning finance, police, education, religion, and local government.

On December 27, Asquith received his reply from Carson, who said that "these proposals were useless to his friends in Ulster," but if Ulster could be excluded from the Irish parliament, "he was ready to accept Home Rule for the rest of Ireland." The Prime Minister met Carson in person on January 2, where his proposals were again rejected, followed by further rejections by letter on January 8 and 9. Finally, on January 10, Carson wrote to the Prime Minister bringing an end to any negotiations that would not consider the complete exclusion of Ulster.[225] It was following this letter that Asquith circulated his proposals to the cabinet and asked for their advice. He was told by all involved that such obstinacy by Carson "put an end to all further conversations."[226] At no time during these three months of negotiations did Asquith consider simply moving against the U.V.F., preventing them from organizing and seizing their weapons. Such action does not appear to have crossed his mind. He seems to have been far more comfortable with the notion of a compromise that would appease the Ulster militants than with a confrontation that would directly target these militants. Certainly he made no mention in cabinet of shutting down the Ulster Volunteers.

Meanwhile, as these fruitless talks were taking place in London, the U.V.F. in Ulster continued to organize and grow. The R.I.C., ever vigilant, watched and reported upon its movements. In September 1913, they reported that the strength of the U.V.F. was 56,651 men, only 15,000 more than the 41,000 reported in April of that year.[227] By November, however, whilst Asquith was attempting to reach compromise with Bonar Law and Carson, the police reported that the political situation in Ulster had become "more serious," and that the strength of the U.V.F. had been "considerably augmented." Its numbers now sat at 76,757, with 17,051 serviceable rifles and enough revolvers to arm each and every volunteer.[228]

This growth continued into the new year, and by the end of March 1914, the R.I.C. had information that showed the strength of the U.V.F. to be 84,540 men, armed with 24,874 serviceable rifles, "considerable quantities of military equipment [such as] haversacks, bandoliers, etc," and an ambulance and nursing corps that had "medical stores in considerable quantities."[229]

The U.V.F. seemed to be preparing for such widespread casualties as might be expected in major combat; at any rate, they had made the appropriate arrangements for such.

Still, the government did nothing to put a stop to the illegal force. Instead, it again attempted to placate the volunteers. On March 9, Asquith reintroduced the Home Rule Bill to parliament, with one major amendment. The new bill stated that the Ulster counties could opt out of the Home Rule parliament, on a county-by-county basis determined by referenda, for a period of six years, at the end of which their representatives would be transferred from Westminster to the new Irish Parliament. It was the government's final offer.[230] Carson immediately rejected the amendment, claiming that it was nothing more than "a sentence of death with a stay of execution for six years."[231] The government had sought to appease but had been greeted for their efforts with outright rejection. For the Ulster militants, there would be no compromise.

Following this rebuff, the cabinet became concerned that the U.V.F. might try to seize British Army and police weaponry, aware that negotiation was now over. Recent reports from the police had indicated as much.[232] On March 11, therefore, Asquith set up a cabinet committee, chaired by Winston Churchill and including in its membership Lord Crewe, Birrell, Seely, and John Allsebrook Simon. Its purpose was to consider how the government would react to such a seizure.[233] Three days later, Churchill warned the unionists against any direct confrontation.[234] Then, on March 17, he recommended to the committee that they reinforce the garrisons in Ulster as a show of strength against the U.V.F.[235] It was the first proactive step the government had taken against the U.V.F. in the face of 15 months of illegal militancy.

On March 18, Major General Edward Gleichen, commander of the 15th Infantry Division, headquartered at Belfast but stationed throughout Ireland, received a telegram from the Secretary of State for War informing him that the Carrickfergus garrison was to be strengthened, the gates of all barracks throughout Ireland were to be shut, and the number of guards on duty was to be doubled. Gleichen received no explanation for this order, but he nevertheless did as commanded.[236] The following day, he was further ordered to send two infantry companies to Enniskillen, one to Omagh, and one to Armagh. An infantry company already stationed at Enniskillen was to move to Derry, and the battalion stationed at Victoria Barracks in Belfast was to cross the Lough to the barracks at Holywood. Again, no explanation was given for these orders, and Gleichen did not know why he was moving his men.[237]

Meanwhile, General Hubert Gough, commander of the 3rd Cavalry Brigade stationed at the Curragh, just outside Dublin, received an order from the Commander-in-Chief in Ireland, Sir Arthur Paget, that ball ammunition was to be given to all guards at the Curragh. An hour later, Gough was ordered to give this ammunition to every man stationed there.[238] The following day, March 20, Gough, together with "every general within reach," was ordered to Paget's headquarters in Dublin. There, the Commander-in-Chief told those gathered that "active operations were about to commence against Ulster." Although he was "not expecting any bloodshed [because] we are too strong," several ships of the fleet had nevertheless been brought to Belfast harbor in support. Paget then gave the generals an ultimatum: either their officers follow the action through "to the bitter end," whatever that may be, or they resign their commissions.[239]

Gough, a born Ulsterman, immediately decided to resign, and telegraphed his brother to tell him so: "[I have] [t]he alternative of marching against Ulster, or resigning from the Service just offered me by Paget. Am accepting second alternative."[240] He then went to see General Gerald Friend, the Director of Administration on Paget's staff, to inform him of his decision. Friend attempted to persuade him otherwise, but seeing that this was impossible, told Gough to "carry on as usual, but send me a letter requesting to retire."[241] Gough returned to the Curragh, where, upon hearing the ultimatum presented by Paget, 57 other officers immediately tendered their resignations. Paget traveled to the Curragh and pleaded with them to withdraw their resignations but to no avail.[242] The Curragh mutiny had begun.[243]

On March 23, after two days of defiance, Gough traveled to London to meet with Seely at the War Office, together with General Sir John French, the Chief of the Imperial General Staff, and Major General J.S. Ewart, the Adjutant General. After several hours of negotiation, Gough extracted from them a document that stated,

> His Majesty's Government must retain their right to use all the forces of the Crown in Ireland or elsewhere to maintain law and order and to support the civil power in the execution of its duty. But they have no intention whatsoever of taking advantage of this right to crush political opposition to the policy or the principles of the Home Rule Bill.[244]

Following these negotiations, and with his document in hand, Gough returned to the Curragh triumphant and his men withdrew their resignations.[245]

When the contents of the document were leaked to the press the following day, Churchill was outraged. He declared to the cabinet that "whatever might be the indiscipline in the Army, the Navy was prepared for anything." He further informed them that Admiral Sir Lewis Bayly had been ordered to court-martial on the spot the first officer who so much as hesitated to obey.[246]

There was little he could do alone, however, and ultimately no action was taken by the fleet. Seely, French, and Ewart all resigned over the incident, their last days in government coming on March 31.[247] Their resignations did little to alter the promises they had given to Gough, however.[248] General Macready, Director of the War Office, traveled to Belfast shortly after the Curragh mutiny to see for himself the situation on the ground. His conclusions were damning, and deserve to be quoted at length:

> During my visit to Belfast in March, 1914, I was convinced that through a policy of drift the Government had lost all control of the situation, which was entirely in the hands of Carson and his followers. Every Government service was either effete or unreliable, results due on the one hand to the policy of Dublin Castle, and on the other to sympathy with the Orangemen. . . . With regard to the Royal Irish Constabulary I was sorry to be obliged to come to a conclusion which I had no occasion to modify during the years which followed when I was in close touch with that force. This once magnificent body of men had undoubtedly deteriorated into what was almost a state of supine lethargy, and had lost even the semblance of energy or initiative when a crisis demanded vigorous and resolute action. The immediate reason was not far to seek. If an officer of whatever rank took it upon himself to enforce the law, especially during the faction fights which are the popular pastime of the Irish, his action would as often as not be disavowed by the authorities at Dublin, on complaint being made to them by the Irish politicians by whose favor the Government held office. This is no idle assertion on my part.[249]

The government had decided not to intervene in Ulster and the leadership of the U.V.F. knew it. They now saw before them the opportunity they had been craving since the royal proclamations had been passed the previous December. It was time to resurrect Major Frederick Crawford's plan for a large-scale arms-smuggling operation.

To the Edge of the Abyss

On the evening of March 31, 1914, a telegram was sent from Sir Henry Lowther, the British ambassador to Denmark in Copenhagen, to Sir Edward Grey, the British Foreign Secretary. Lowther had just received information from a vice consul at Svendborg that a Norwegian steamer named the *Fanny* was bound ostensibly for Iceland but was in reality heading for Ireland, fully laden with 300 tons of rifles for use by the U.V.F.[250] The Foreign Secretary immediately forwarded the telegram to Birrell. He sent a second letter from

Lowther on April 1, and a letter from Walter Hearn, the British consul general in Hamburg, on April 3, both of which provided more detail about the *Fanny*.[251]

The government heard nothing more about the ship for another three weeks, and, without additional information, there was little the cabinet could do to keep track of it. The movements of the *Fanny*, however, can be traced from the memoirs of Major Frederick Crawford: Ulster's primary gunrunner sailed on board in charge of the shipment. From Denmark, where the ship illegally left port without any papers, it headed straight for England, where it docked at Great Yarmouth. After being moored for an evening, it set out into the English Channel and sailed past Lundy Island to Cardiff, in Wales. There it stayed for several days, before docking at Tenby, still in Wales. At this point, Crawford left the ship and traveled to Belfast, where he met with Craig, Carson, and the other members of the Ulster Unionist Military Committee. At this meeting, there was some concern over how Crawford wished to manage the gunrunning operation, but Carson told the committee, "We had better leave the details to him. I feel sure he will see his way to carry out his plans." The committee then gave Crawford its blessing to do as he saw fit.[252]

This meeting was held in mid-April. The police and British government were unaware of it. On the afternoon of April 24, however, the R.I.C. received information from an informant that Crawford's rifles would be landed at the Queen's Quay in Belfast that evening. Together with the customs authorities and the coast guard, members of the R.I.C. lined the dockside and watched as a large ship, the S.S. *Balmarino*, sailed silently up Musgrave Channel into Belfast, cutting from one bank to the other, flashing strange signals and lights towards the shore. The uniformed men watched in anticipation, preparing to make what they thought would be the largest arms seizure in Irish history. Unbeknownst to them, however, they had been deliberately led astray by the informant and were in fact witnessing an elaborate decoy set up by Crawford and the U.V.F.[253] The real rifles were being off-loaded at various points away from the main Belfast harbor—from the *Roma* at the Workman & Clark wharf across the river, from the *Fanny* at Larne, the *Mountjoy* at Bangor, and the *Innismurray* at Donaghadee. Here, at these isolated wharfs and piers, only a few members of the R.I.C., customs service, and coast guard were left to watch, with no available backup, as 30,000 rifles were handed over to the U.V.F. Because of their small numbers they could do nothing to prevent the rifles from being brought ashore, but they made efforts to keep the shipments at the docks. This was to no avail, however, as the U.V.F. used threatening and illegal actions to prevent the police from carrying out their duty. Looking at just one of these landing sites, at Larne, can illustrate the difficulties the police faced.

At 7:40 p.m. on the evening of the landings, Customs Officer George Goodman was patrolling the sea coast towards Glenarm when he saw on the road ahead of him members of the U.V.F., along with two lorries and several motor cars, all with their lights turned off, facing the waterfront. As he came closer, their lights began to flash signals out to sea. It was then that he saw a ship, unlit and with no distinguishing marks, silently moving into the harbor. He hurried along the coast road in its direction, but was stopped by members of the U.V.F. When he demanded to be let through, informing the volunteers that they were interfering with official business, he was told, "No, not even the King should pass nor the police." He demanded again to be allowed to pass, but was forcibly prevented from going any further. Unable to do anything alone, he headed back to the town to summon the police.[254]

Once in Larne, Goodman went immediately to the R.I.C. barracks, where he found Head Constable James McHugh. Goodman informed McHugh that a mobilization of the U.V.F. had begun along the coast road and that they were not letting anyone in authority pass through their cordon. McHugh summoned Constable Charles Roberts and, together with Goodman, headed back towards the harbor. When they reached the junction between the Bay Road and the Curran Road, they were stopped from proceeding any further. A man whom McHugh knew, Thomas Robinson, approached him, swinging a baton larger than those carried by the police. He bluntly told the head constable, "We have orders not to let any one past, and we have better batons than you have." Seeing that this was no bluff, McHugh left to find his district inspector.[255]

District Inspector William Moore was already on his way to the harbor, having been told by Acting Sergeant Robert Gordon and Constable Quinlan that something was afoot. Whilst on the move, Moore noticed several lights along the coast road and sent Gordon to investigate. Meanwhile, he and Quinlan continued towards the harbor, where they were stopped by 40 or 50 Ulster Volunteers wearing identifying white armlets. He could see beyond them that there were two ships moored off Barr Point. The men would not let him and Quinlan through, so they began to cut across a field to the Bay Road.[256] Whilst crossing the field, Sergeant Gordon returned to Moore and informed him that the lights on the coast road had come from 11 motor cars that were signaling out to sea. He had attempted to get close to them but was threatened by a gang of 20 Ulster Volunteers who served as a protection guard to the signalers.[257] As the three men arrived at the Bay Road, they were met by McHugh and Roberts, who requested their assistance at the corner of the Bay and Curran roads.[258]

Moore confidently approached the cordon at the Bay Road, certain that the volunteers would not forbid a district inspector to pass. He was surprised, therefore, to find his passage blocked. He demanded to speak with Thomas Robinson, the man who had threatened McHugh. When Robinson arrived, still swinging his baton, he told Moore that he had been ordered by Major Calmont, a Member of Parliament, not to allow any person of authority down to the harbor. Robinson then said that Calmont would arrive shortly, if the district inspector wanted to wait. Moore did so, and in the meantime sent Head Constable McHugh back to the barracks to call Belfast to request help.[259] When McHugh tried to put through the call, however, he found that the line had been cut. He then tried to send a telegram, but found that the telegraph line was also out of order. All communication between Larne and the outside world had been sabotaged by the U.V.F.[260]

Whilst McHugh was at the barracks, Major Calmont returned to the harbor. Moore demanded to be given an explanation for the cordons, but was told only that Calmont had orders "from Sir William Adair to block the roads leading to the harbor against every one and particularly the police and Customs officers." Moore asked if Calmont was willing to uphold the cordons by force, at which he was told that Calmont's intention was to block the roads at any cost, and that the major had 700 men to support him in his efforts.[261] There was little Moore, with his head constable, sergeant, and two constables, could do to stop the landings.

At the other harbors, the police encountered similar resistance. In Bangor, the U.V.F. established cordons with guards who were armed with rifles.[262] At Donaghadee, two members of the constabulary, District Inspector John Shankey and Sergeant Orr, managed to sneak past the cordon and hide behind some coal wagons in the harbor. When they were discovered, however, they were surrounded by two gangs of men carrying ash sticks. They were then held captive at the coal wagons until the rifles had been completely unloaded, at about 9:00 a.m. the following morning.[263]

Despite such obstruction, at each harbor the police were able to note who had been involved in the smuggling and track where the rifles had gone upon leaving ship. Even when faced with considerable danger and threats to their own lives, the police, customs officers, and coast guard refused to leave the scene of the arms shipment. They were able to compile detailed reports of what had taken place. All of these reports were forwarded to the Crimes Special Branch, who in turn sent them to the Chief Secretary.[264] Within days of the landings, Birrell knew exactly who was responsible and where the rifles were being stored. He also had the opportunity to read in detail of the illegal activities of the U.V.F, of their threatening and intimidating behavior towards the police, and of their total disregard for the royal proclamations, which forbade such arms importations.

In the months that followed April 1914, few extra rifles were brought into Ulster. There was little need for them. In an end-of-year memo to the Chief Secretary, the R.I.C. reported that the U.V.F. had 55, 166 rifles ready for use against any potential Home Rule government.[265] No more than a few thousand of these had been brought in through small-scale smuggling operations after April; the rest had been accumulated on the night of April 24 or before. Following the gunrunning operation, the U.V.F. was fully armed and, after 16 months of undisturbed drilling and target practice, well trained and disciplined. The police knew from their actions on that April night that the volunteers were ready and willing to use illegal force to achieve their goals.

Still, however, Birrell chose to do nothing. In a remarkable statement, his private secretary, Andrew Magill, claimed that the gunrunning was the "first thing" that showed the "seriousness of the situation," and wrote that it "gave us a nasty surprise."[266] On April 26, just two days after the gunrunning had been completed, Birrell confessed to the Prime Minister, "the more I think of *Arrest* the more objections occur."[267] Although he did not list for Asquith these objections, it is clear from earlier statements that Birrell lacked the political will and the courage to directly confront the Ulster Volunteer Force, fearful of aggravating a threat that he naively believed might fade away without government intervention. Thus, he expressly ruled out a policy of arresting the leaders and recovering the arms. The Prime Minister supported him in this decision. In his memoirs, Magill wrote,

> The leaders [of the U.V.F.] were perfectly well known, and the only proper course for the government to have followed was to have put them on trial. . . . Instead of taking any action, [however,] the government did nothing. The Attorney-General at the time, Serjeant Moriarty—afterwards Lord Justice Moriarty—had the courage of his convictions and drew up the indictment against the leaders. But Redmond and Dillon went to Asquith and asked him not to proceed which, they said, would only make martyrs of these men, and Asquith as usual decided to do nothing.[268]

With no action from the government, the police were forced to stand back and watch helplessly as Ulster descended towards anarchy.[269]

A future of lawlessness did indeed seem to be the unavoidable fate not only of Ulster but of all Ireland as the Irish Volunteers, like those in the north, continued to grow. On March 31, 1914, the police reported to the Chief Secretary that the volunteers' numbers had reached 14,171. Whilst nowhere near the strength of the U.V.F., the Irish Volunteers could no longer be ignored, particularly as their drill was perfected by former British Army sergeants and officers and route marches were becoming a common sight, especially in Dublin, Cork, Limerick, and Galway.[270] In April, the Irish Volunteers continued to draw support. By the end of May, their numbers had reached 69, 641 men.[271] They would continue to recruit members until their peak in September 1914, when the strength of the Irish Volunteers was 181, 732 men.[272]

On May 19, having returned from another trip to Belfast, General Macready met with the Prime Minister and "impressed upon him the drift events were taking, especially the fears of the Lord Mayor of Belfast for the safety of his city." Asquith informed Macready, however, that "in case of serious faction fighting between Orangemen and Nationalists, troops should not intervene and run the risk of having to be extricated, but should isolate the area of the fighting until reinforcements arrived. If Carson proclaimed his Provisional Government the only course was to remain on the defensive and do nothing." If the U.V.F. dispatched units to the smaller towns and outlying villages, "Mr. Asquith was of opinion that there was no power to prevent it." Macready noted sarcastically in his memoirs that with "these heroic instructions in my pocket I returned to Belfast that night." He was thoroughly discouraged.[273]

Later that month, as the Irish Volunteers continued to grow, Eoin MacNeill contacted John Redmond. MacNeill saw that Redmond was close to securing an Irish Home Rule Bill in Parliament and was well aware that Redmond's party represented the vast majority of the Irish people. He therefore believed that it was important to get Redmond's blessing on the movement. Throughout late May and the early part of June, MacNeill and Redmond negotiated. On June 9, Redmond issued a statement to the Irish press, saying that he was willing to work with the Irish Volunteers if they would add 25 persons, nominated by him, to the existing committee of 30.[274] On June 16, a week later, the provisional committee acceded to Redmond's demand and granted him his nominees. John Redmond was now in charge of the Irish Volunteers, a force that had come to match the U.V.F. in strength and determination.[275]

On July 4, just two weeks after Redmond took the leadership, the top-ranking military officers of the British Army Council wrote an urgent memorandum to the Prime Minister and cabinet. They warned of "two opposing forces," with more than 200,000 men between them, that were being "systematically and deliberately raised, trained, equipped and organized on a military basis" within Ireland. They noted that if these two forces came into conflict, a situation would arise where "it might be necessary to employ the whole of [the British] Expeditionary Force to restore order." This could "involve general mobilization, placing Special Reserve troops in the ports, and assembling the Local and Central Forces now composed of Territorial troops." This would have the very serious consequence of making the British Army "quite incapable of meeting [its] obligations abroad." Under such a situation, the army would be "an inadequate security against invasion." They complained, however, that "no plan for military operations" to meet this danger had yet been prepared "or even considered" by the War Office.[276]

The British Army Council had identified for the cabinet a distinct breakdown in its security planning. Who, though, was responsible for this failure? Since Seely's resignation as War Secretary in March, Asquith had taken the position of Secretary of State for War. Already Prime Minister, however, he neglected his obligations in the War Office and instead concentrated on his larger responsibilities as head of the British government. The day-to-day running of the navy and army was therefore left to the respective service chiefs, and the broader questions of policy were left to those in other offices of state; to the Colonial Secretary in the Empire, and to Birrell in Ireland.[277] It was Birrell, therefore, who was ultimately responsible for remedying the situation described in this memorandum. The concerns of the British Army Council, like those of the R.I.C., fell upon deaf ears, however.

On July 21, two weeks after the British Army Council issued its warning, Redmond and Carson met with Asquith at a hastily called conference at Buckingham Palace, an attempt to reach compromise, but to no avail. Redmond was insistent on the immediate implementation of home rule; Carson was equally insistent that there could be no such thing in Ulster. General Macready warned Asquith that when "the Home Rule Bill became law, disturbances, if they occurred, would be more in the nature of civil war than of faction fights." On July 24, therefore, three days after the failed conference, Asquith ordered Macready to Belfast on a permanent basis. Macready was told, however, that there was "to be no change from the former policy, troops were to 'sit tight' and make no moves of any kind." In his memoirs, Macready wrote that "[a] more thoroughly unsatisfactory position for any soldier it is hard to imagine."[278] If the U.V.F. rebelled against an Irish Home Rule government, and violence between it and the Irish Volunteers erupted, the British forces were to do nothing.[279]

For the previous two years, the threat had been growing, the peril increasing, yet it had been ignored by the government. More remarkable, perhaps, was the fact that this was not happening in India, or Africa, or one of the more far-flung outposts of the empire, but within the borders of the United Kingdom itself. But then, just when it seemed that Ireland was about to erupt into civil war, the threat was suddenly diverted, not by the stroke of a British bureaucrat's pen or the strike of a police constable's truncheon, but by the bullet of a Serbian assassin.[280]

A Failure of Governance

The men of the Ulster Volunteer Force finally got their fight, but it was not the battle they had been expecting. As they stood side by side, armed with rifles and ammunition, they did so not in a light rain on the fields of the Boyne valley or amongst the brick buildings of Belfast's shipyards but rather on the riverbank of the Ancre in France, nestled between the gentle slopes of Thiepval. Unlike in Ulster, the sky was an almost perfect blue and sunshine glistened off the water beside the main contingent of the 36th Ulster Division, X Corps.[281] The vast majority of the men who waited there had served in the U.V.F., leaving Belfast for the last time on May 8, 1915. Amidst the spectacle of bunting and flags, crowds and jingoistic brass bands, they had departed for the First World War, not so much to fight Germany as to validate Ulster's position as an integral part of the British Empire.[282]

On July 1, 1916, the men felt ready for battle. It was a special day for the Ulstermen, the original anniversary of the Battle of the Boyne (using the Julian calendar) when in 1690 King William III had defeated King James II. The evening before, Sir Oliver Nugent, Commanding Officer of the Ulster Division, had written to his friend Sir George Richardson, still commanding those Ulster Volunteers left in Ireland. He boasted that his division "could hardly have a date better calculated to inspire national traditions amongst our men of the North."[283]

And, indeed, the significance of the day did rouse his men. At 7:10 a.m., the leading wave rose from its trenches and clambered over the parapets, followed at 7.15 a.m., 7:20 a.m., and 7:30 a.m. by the second, third, and fourth waves respectively. The First Battle of the Somme had begun.[284] As the men rushed forward, a sergeant of the Royal Inniskillings donned the Orange Order Sash that he had brought from home.[285] A captain pulled out an orange handkerchief and, waving it around his head, shouted, "Come on, boys, this is the first of July."[286] Many others in the Ulster Division wore orange ribbons or lilies on their breasts. Most cried out "Remember the Boyne" and "No surrender, boys," the famed answer given by the Protestant Apprentice Boys of Derry to their Catholic besieger in 1689.[287]

In the eyes of these Ulstermen, their charge was the ultimate act of loyalty to the union between Great Britain and Ireland. In the name of that union, they had been willing to subvert the law and possibly kill those tasked with policing; now they were willing to die for that union. Yet Thiepval and the Somme were far different from the mythical image of the Battle of the Boyne that most carried with them. There was no King William III riding upon a white horse, no Catholic menace to strike down with pike and sword. They found only mud, bullets, and barbed wire. Although their assault began courageously, even the spirit of 1690 was not enough to ensure the survival of these men against the harsh realities of modern warfare. As they overran trench after trench, they lost more and more of their own men and became further separated from other British troops. Finding themselves cut off from all support, they had no choice but to retreat under fire, their uniforms reduced to rags as they traversed the rugged terrain of no-man's land.[288] By the end of the day, X Corps had suffered over 9,000 casualties, 5,500 of whom were Ulstermen.[289] In all, there were 60,695 British casualties on the Somme that day; 19,240 were left dead on the battlefield.[290]

These men were in France at the bequest of their master and commander, Sir Edward Carson. He had rallied the U.V.F. shortly after the outbreak of the war, mimicking the old Irish nationalist cry of "England's difficulty is Ireland's opportunity" with the emendation that "England's difficultly is not Ulster's opportunity."[291] He had done so because John Redmond had offered up the services of the Irish Volunteers to the Crown on August 11, claiming that even though the nationalists sought Irish Home Rule, they were still loyal subjects of the British Empire. Redmond, however, had offered the troops only on the condition that the Commons first pass the Home Rule Bill. Carson, seeing his opportunity, declared that the loyalty of the Ulstermen was not conditional upon anything, and his men would serve regardless of the political situation in Ulster. It was his hope that as a reward, Ulster would be exempted from any future Irish Home Rule parliament.[292]

The cabinet met on September 9 to resolve the Irish Home Rule problem once and for all. The war in France was heating up and Lord Kitchener, the new Secretary of State for War, had told them that whilst recruits in Ulster were plentiful, outside of Ulster he had been forced to rely upon English troops to fill gaps in the Irish regiments. As a result, they needed Redmond's Irish Volunteers. These men would join only with their leader's blessing, however.[293] Prime Minister Asquith offered two suggestions: either the Home Rule Bill could be passed immediately, with its implementation suspended for 12 months or to the end of the war, whichever was later; or, the Home Rule Bill could be passed and implemented immediately, but with Ulster excluded until some still-to-be-determined later date.[294]

He proposed each of these solutions to Redmond and Bonar Law, and both agreed upon the first. Redmond preferred postponement because he did not wish to see Ulster separated from the rest of Ireland in legislation. Bonar Law, for his part, believed that after a victorious war fighting for the British Empire, the Irish nationalists would no longer want Home Rule and thus Ulster's exclusion would become a nonissue. Nine days later, therefore, on September 18, the Commons passed the Irish Home Rule Bill, along with a second bill suspending its operation until after the war.[295] In Ulster, many of the men who had pledged to oppose such a move had already left their homes and enlisted at Carson's command in the British Army, training to fight for a very different cause. The passing of the Home Rule Bill was greeted with very little fanfare, therefore. Indeed, September 18 saw considerably less militarism than had been displayed on many other days over the previous two years.[296] The period of overt militancy was finally over.

Despite its peaceful resolution, the situation in Ulster had presented the gravest threat to the safety, security, and constitutional sanctity of the United Kingdom since the revolutionary years of the seventeenth century. Not since the 1640s had a civil war on British soil seemed so imminent. Only events abroad, completely out of the hands of the British government, had prevented the unthinkable. The Ulster Volunteer Force was the root cause of the political problems during this time. Had there been no U.V.F., there would have been no reason for the Irish Volunteers to form. Had there been no U.V.F, there would have been no need for the government to compromise the Irish Home Rule Bill, leading to a postponement of Home Rule that would prove fatal to future hopes of peace in Ireland. During the period of overt militancy, the government failed, and failed dramatically, in its security efforts. The consensus of historians thus far is that this failure occurred because the government lacked information, particularly on the Ulster Volunteer Force. The police, it is claimed, collected no intelligence during this crucial two-year period. The Chief Secretary, therefore, had no idea of the extent of the threat.[297]

Such reasoning can be seen when looking at historical accounts of the gunrunning operation of April 1914, to take just one of many events. Patricia Jalland has asserted that the operation was conducted in "secret," that "the Volunteers encountered no effective resistance," and that news of the landing "did not reach Dublin Castle until the following morning."[298] Likewise, Leon Ó Broin has argued that once the illegal cargo was unloaded, it was "rapidly dispatched to Volunteer units throughout the province or hidden away near at hand in places where the police could not find it."[299] Even A.T.Q. Stewart, in his extremely detailed account of the operation, stated that "[f]rom the beginning to the end there had been no interference from the police, coastguard, or Customs. The naval and military authorities knew nothing of what had occurred."[300] As has been shown, however, this was simply not the case. The police had the information in hand and continually provided it to the government. The government chose not to act.

There was clearly a security failure in Ireland during these years. This failure was, first and foremost, one of intelligence. It was a failure not in the collection of intelligence, however, but in the implementation of government policy based on that intelligence. Who is culpable for this failure? Who was responsible for formulating Irish policy based on the information received?

Although Asquith was Prime Minister, Ireland was Birrell's responsibility, and it was the Chief Secretary's obligation to propose a course of action that would deal with the Ulster Volunteer Force. It was, above all else then, a failure of Augustine Birrell's leadership.

Birrell, of course, was not acting in a vacuum. The decisions he provided for the cabinet were, more often than not, decisions made by his under secretary. Dougherty's reticence in the face of compelling intelligence, coupled with Birrell's weakness, acted together to allow a grave and treasonous threat to be born, to grow, and to remain unchallenged for the better part of two years. During this time, a competing paramilitary army, the Irish Volunteers, rose to challenge the influence of the U.V.F. Only the outbreak of the First World War prevented a civil war between the two, one whose blame could have been laid substantially at the feet of the Chief Secretary and his under secretary.

But although the period of overt militancy had come to an end, there was a far greater threat to the British state brewing in Ireland. For whilst Redmond's Irish Volunteers sought to ensure that an Irish Home Rule dominion would be established within the British Empire, a new and more clandestine group of Irish Volunteers formed, with the Irish Republican Brotherhood at its core. This new organization would settle for nothing less than a fully independent Irish republic. It was more than willing to use violence to achieve its aim.

PART II

The Period of Clandestine Organization, 1914–1916

The Arming of the Irish Volunteers

In many respects, for the police in Ireland there was very little to distinguish July 26, 1914, from any other Sunday that summer. In County Armagh, they watched as orders were given by the Ulster Unionist Council for a general mobilization of the Ulster Volunteer Force (U.V.F.).[1] On Captain James Craig's estate at Craigavon, they witnessed two six-pounder field guns being taken into the main yard, where they were placed alongside the large quantity of arms and ammunition already there.[2] In Londonderry, Sir Henry Hill spent the day commanding a contingent of the U.V.F. to arrange 1,000 sandbags in a barricade around his house, again observed by the police.[3] Such events were by now commonplace in Ulster, and the Royal Irish Constabulary (R.I.C.) had watched as the militancy in Ireland had become ever bolder and more open over the previous 18 months. Yet July 26 differed in one important respect. Whilst the police concentrated their efforts on the U.V.F. in the north, at the southern Irish harbor of Howth, just to the north of Dublin, the Irish Volunteers responded to the Ulster gunrunning with an arms shipment of their own.

Bulmer Hobson of the Irish Republican Brotherhood's (I.R.B.) Supreme Council first became aware of the plan in early June 1914. That month, Sir Roger Casement had approached him to see whether he was willing to make arrangements for the landing of two shipments of arms for the Irish Volunteers. Casement had already been to see Eoin MacNeill and Michael O'Rahilly, but both were men of ideology rather than action; they had yet to come up with a practical plan. Casement, therefore, turned to Hobson and the I.R.B.[4] That he should have done so surprised some people. Indeed, at first glance, it seemed highly unusual that Casement would be involved with the Irish Volunteers at all, let alone devising a scheme for importing illegal arms on their behalf.

Casement did not fit the common mold of Irish nationalists. Although born in the Irish port town of Kingstown in 1864, he had left Ireland early in life, moving to Liverpool in 1880 to live with Edward Bannister, a foster-parent of sorts who was responsible for the West African interests of a Liverpool trading company. Casement immediately took a clerkship in the company, where he worked for three years. In 1883, however, he left to become a purser on board the SS *Bonny*, a ship that traded with West Africa. Casement undertook three voyages on the *Bonny*, and then, in 1884, traveled to Africa on a more permanent basis, serving in Leopold III's International Association in Congo. He remained with the association for two years, before joining the Sanford Expedition in 1886, which was led by an American, General Henry S. Sanford, for the purpose of opening up the upper Congo for scientific and commercial discovery. In 1888, he resigned from the expedition to join an elephant-hunting party, after which he became general manager of all railway construction in Congo, a private position contracted out by the British government. In 1892, he entered the service of that government permanently, gaining appointment as a staff member of the Survey Department in the Oil Rivers Protectorate (present-day Nigeria). Within a few months, just shy of his twenty-ninth birthday, he became assistant director general of customs at Old Calabar.[5]

Casement remained in British service for the next 20 years. In 1895, he received a waiver of the consular examination on account of his experience in Africa and was appointed British consul at Delagoa Bay in Portuguese East Africa, a neutral port on the edge of the Transvaal. He found the bureaucracy there trying, however, and in 1897, he transferred to become British consul for Portuguese West Africa, where he oversaw British interests in Congo and French Congo. He remained in this position until 1900 when at the height of the Boer War he volunteered to take part in a commando operation, the aim of which was to destroy a bridge on the Netherlands railway line between Lorenzo Marques and Pretoria. At the last moment, the operation was called off, and Casement returned to London for a well-deserved break. In 1901, however, he was sent back to Africa to set up a new consulate at Kinchasa in the newly formed Congo State, where he remained until 1903. He was then promoted to a staff appointment at Lisburn.

Unsuited for staff work, Casement lasted only three months at Lisburn and then, unable to secure another operational posting, took a two-year leave of absence from the Foreign Service. In 1906, however, he was offered the consular post of Santos, in Brazil, which he readily accepted. Two years later, he became British consul at Pará, in northern Brazil, and in 1909, he became consul general of the Rio consulate. His career in the Foreign Service ended a year later, and he left Brazil for the last time in late 1910. He continued to work for the British government in London, however, overseeing two special commissions for the Foreign Office. In 1912, he left British imperial life forever, but not before receiving a knighthood in 1911 for his loyal service.

Having worked for the British Empire for the better part of his life, Casement was, therefore, an improbable acquaintance of Bulmer Hobson. Yet whilst in Africa and South America, he had developed a loathing for imperialism, seeing first hand the consequences of colonialism abroad. In particular, he had become disturbed at the torture and mutilation of slaves used in the rubber trade in Congo, which he believed was a direct consequence of European intrusion in Africa. He had, therefore, become involved with the Africa movement, run by Mary Kingsley, the purpose of which was to promote an independent Africa, free of all colonialism.[6] Kingsley introduced him to Alice Stopford Green, widow of an English historian and daughter of a County Meath archdeacon, who suggested that he revisit the home of his youth. At her invitation, Casement returned to Ireland in 1904.[7] He found twentieth-century Ireland very different from the nation of his birth, and immediately became enthralled with the Irish cultural movements, particularly the Gaelic League.[8] Through this, he first met Eoin MacNeill and, ultimately, Bulmer Hobson. In 1905, he and Hobson began working on some anti-English, Irish separatist pamphlets. In 1907, he secretly joined the Sinn Fein Party.[9]

Although freshly knighted in 1914, it was not out of the ordinary, therefore, for Casement to seek out Hobson. He had been collaborating with him for the better part of the previous nine years. This was, however, the first time that he had proposed importing arms for use by the Irish Volunteers, and the first time that he was ready to actively engage his previous masters in a violent way. It was, therefore, a significant step for him to take, one from which there could be no going back.

The scheme began when Casement traveled to London to meet with Alice Stopford Green in May 1914. Stopford Green had been in close contact with her friend, Mary Spring Rice, who believed that following the U.V.F.'s gunrunning operation in the north, the Irish Volunteers needed to arm themselves also. Spring Rice visited her friend Erskine Childers and his wife, Molly, at their home in London's Embankment Gardens, where she suggested that a committee be formed to raise funds for arming the Irish Volunteers.[10] Like Casement, Erskine Childers was not a natural Irish nationalist. Born in London and educated at Haileybury and Trinity College, Cambridge, he had worked as a clerk in the House of Commons from 1895 to 1910. During the Boer War, he volunteered for military service and later wrote two popular books about his experiences there.[11] With the formation of the Ulster Volunteer Force, however, he had become more and more sympathetic to the Irish nationalist cause. Following the successful gunrunning by the U.V.F., he had, like Spring Rice, become convinced of the need to arm the Irish Volunteers.[12]

The Childers therefore agreed to meet with Spring Rice at Stopford Green's larger home on Grosvenor Street in Mayfair, their purpose being to form an arms committee. At this meeting, the Childers, Spring Rice, Stopford Green, Casement, and Spring Rice's cousin, Conor O'Brien, pledged £1,500 to purchase arms.[13] They then commissioned Darrell Figgis, an Englishman who lived in Ireland, to travel to Antwerp to collect the rifles. Childers and O'Brien agreed to smuggle the arms back to Ireland in their private yachts, the *Asgard* and the *Kelpie*.[14] With the money the committee gave him, Figgis was able to purchase 1,500 rifles and 45,000 rounds of ammunition. By June, the cargo was ready to be transported. All Figgis needed was a detailed plan explaining how and where the rifles would be landed.[15] It was at this point that Casement turned to the I.R.B. Bulmer Hobson, as a member of the Supreme Council and the head of the I.R.B.'s Dublin Centres Board, was only too ready to help.

The I.R.B. had been increasing in strength since its rebirth in 1907. Nevertheless, it had yet to make much of an impression on the Irish nationalist community as a whole, which still put its faith in the constitutional practices of John Redmond's parliamentary party. This was in part due to the stigma that had become attached to the old Fenian tradition of violence following the advent of the Irish Home Rule Party in the 1870s. Charles Stuart Parnell had shown that nonviolent methods could bring the British to the negotiating table. Most Irish nationalists now believed that with an Irish Home Rule parliament seemingly imminent, open revolutionary violence was no longer an acceptable means to use against the British government.

In response to this shift in public opinion, prominent advocates of the physical-force tradition began to develop the concept of "moral insurgency," which held that Irish nationalists could pursue a moral insurgency by establishing institutions independent of Great Britain. These could then be protected by a physical-force insurgency if later required. This philosophy was best encapsulated by the formation of the Sinn Fein Party in 1905, its name literally meaning "Ourselves Alone."[16] It was from within Sinn Fein that the I.R.B. reformed in 1907.

Four years after Sinn Fein's birth, in August 1909, Bulmer Hobson formed an additional militant organization, the Fianna, which was to act as a Boy Scouts group for Irish separatists. Its object, as stated in its handbook, was "[t]o re-establish the Independence of Ireland." The method was "[t]he training of the youth of Ireland, mentally and physically . . . by teaching scouting and military exercises, Irish history, and the Irish language." Before being sworn in, each member of the Fianna had to declare, "I promise to work for the Independence of Ireland, never to join England's armed forces, and to obey my superior officers."[17] When the Fianna boys reached the age of 17, the best amongst them were recruited into the I.R.B. In 1912, Hobson also established a special Fianna Circle of the I.R.B. for those who were too young to join the regular I.R.B. but wished to do more to oppose British rule than the Fianna allowed.[18] This youth movement, together with the Fianna Circle, proved to be an important recruiting ground for the I.R.B. and the Irish Volunteers throughout the subsequent years.

Hobson, with all his organizational experience in the I.R.B. and the Fianna, was considered by Casement the best man to arrange the arms landing. He developed an extravagant plan for doing so. Well aware that the U.V.F. had smuggled in 30 times as many rifles as the Irish Volunteers were now planning, and seeing that this had been done without any impediment from the police, Hobson believed that the shipments should be made in "a sufficiently spectacular manner" so that they would inspire others throughout Ireland to donate money to the Irish nationalist cause, thus giving the Irish Volunteers additional funds to buy more rifles. He suggested, therefore, that they land the rifles in broad daylight, "in the most open manner and as near to Dublin as possible." If 30,000 rifles could be brought to Ulster free of police interference, surely the Irish Volunteers could import just over a thousand in a similar manner. Hobson surveyed "every harbor between Greystones and Balbriggan," and eventually settled on Howth, a small fishing village on the peninsula at the north end of Dublin Bay.[19]

Hobson met with Casement and Childers at Buswell's Hotel in Dublin at the end of June. He outlined for them his plan, which called for a large number of Irish Volunteers to meet Childers' yacht, unload the rifles, and carry them away from Howth in an orderly formation. The volunteers would not be given any ammunition, as they were "too raw and undisciplined to be entrusted with ammunition on that occasion," but a select number of the Fianna would be given 200 oak batons, crafted by I.R.B. carpenters, to use in the event of police interference. Hobson set the date for this landing as Sunday, July 26, and he arranged with Eoin MacNeill to have large Irish Volunteer route marches every Sunday for the three weeks preceding that date. The first was to Lucan, the second to the harbor at Kingstown, and the third to Clondalkin. Finally, on the fourth Sunday—the day of the landings—the volunteers marched to Howth. Hobson recalled,

The police were enormously interested in the first [route march] and followed in strength. At the second they were not so active, and the third week they were indifferent. When we finally marched to Howth on the 26th July they assumed that it was just another route march and were not present at all.[20]

As Hobson suspected, in their monthly reports for July the R.I.C. made little mention of the Irish Volunteers. They did note that on July 26, volunteer units had paraded in four separate locations in County Cork, and that route marches had taken place in Dublin on July 8.[21] They also reported that drill had been conducted in 13 of the 32 Irish counties (Fermanagh, Londonderry, Kerry, King's, Limerick, Mayo, Monaghan, Roscommon, Sligo, Tyrone, Waterford, Westmeath, and Wicklow). Little was said of the route march to Howth, however, despite the fact that the Irish Volunteers openly paraded through numerous Dublin districts. Indeed, the only police to mention it were those actually stationed in Howth who witnessed the landing.[22] The Irish police as a whole had become so used to paramilitary drilling that an orderly, unarmed procession was not important enough for comment. After all, the government had set a precedent in Ulster that they were unwilling to act against illegal drilling. There was, therefore, little reason for the police to file reports if no disturbance to the peace had been caused.

When July 26 dawned, Hobson dispatched 20 members of the I.R.B. to Howth under the command of Cathal Brugha, where they were tasked with helping to moor the yacht when it arrived. He also arranged for several taxis to transport I.R.B. members, together with their girlfriends, to lunch at the local hotel beside the harbor, paid for by I.R.B. funds. It was his intent that the taxis would then be used to convey ammunition back to safe houses in Dublin.[23] The larger contingent of the Irish Volunteers, numbering about 800, met at Father Matthew Park in Dublin's Fairview district, where they were commanded by an ex-army sergeant. Eoin MacNeill ordered this sergeant to assist Hobson in any way required.[24]

The Irish Volunteers arrived at Howth just as the yacht was being moored. The rifles were fully unloaded within half an hour, and the ammunition taken away in the taxis, with the exception of 2,000 rounds kept by I.R.B. guards. The men then began the long march back to Dublin, each carrying an unloaded rifle. Members of the Dublin Metropolitan Police (D.M.P.) along the route notified their superiors, and at Clontarf, in the north of Dublin, the Irish Volunteers encountered a company of British soldiers blocking the road, two-deep and armed with rifles and bayonets. In front of them, standing at right angles along each side of the road, were 80 police constables from the Dublin Metropolitan Police. The Assistant Commissioner of the D.M.P., William Harrell, had called out the military, acting on his own initiative, for he had received no counsel from Dublin Castle.[25] Hobson, at the head of the Irish Volunteers' column, approached the army company. As he did so, Harrell stepped forward. He informed Hobson that the volunteers were "an illegal body, illegally importing arms" and that the police would exercise their duty to confiscate the rifles. He then ordered his officers to seize the weapons, at which a fist fight broke out between the volunteers and the police.[26]

Harrell and Hobson stood aside and watched this skirmish, neither man attempting to control his forces. They instead occupied themselves with a debate over the legality of the landings. As this conversation continued, however, a sergeant of the D.M.P. approached Harrell and pointed out that most of the volunteers, together with their rifles, had disappeared into the surrounding fields. Only a small contingent remained to fight the police. Realizing that he had failed to prevent the arms from entering Dublin, Harrell dismissed the gathered soldiers, telling them that they were no longer needed, and called his men away. In all, the police seized only 19 rifles.[27]

The soldiers, a company of the King's Own Scottish Borderers, marched back to their barracks, pursued by a small crowd of civilians, not associated with the Irish Volunteers, who pelted them with stones along the way. As they moved onto the quays at Bachelor's Walk, the company commander ordered his men to disperse the crowd. Untrained in riot duty, the soldiers fired on their pursuers, killing 3 instantly and injuring a further 38, 1 of whom subsequently died from his wounds.[28] To the nationalist community in Ireland, the contrast between the British response to the U.V.F.'s gunrunning in April and the Irish Volunteers' venture in July could not have been starker. In Ulster, 30,000 rifles had been landed without interference; in Howth, 1,500 rifles came ashore and four people lost their lives. It proved to be an instant recruitment coup for the Irish Volunteers. Their numbers rose dramatically to 184,000 by the end of August.[29]

The debacle in Dublin embarrassed and infuriated the British government: embarrassed it because four people had been killed and, to the general public, the government seemed inconsistent in its treatment of paramilitaries in Ireland; infuriated it because Assistant Commissioner Harrell had acted without orders or permission from the Chief Secretary's Office. The cabinet immediately appointed a commission to look into the shootings. At the committee's recommendation, Harrell was censured and dismissed from the D.M.P. for calling up the military and confronting the volunteers.[30]

There was much unease about the committee's findings, however. General Macready, writing in his memoirs, commented, "[I]t was not upon the soldiers, but upon Mr. Harrell that the Government, egged on by their Irish supporters, vented their spleen." He scornfully noted that Harrell should not have been held accountable because Dougherty, "the responsible authority," had issued no instructions. The commission, however, "found the scapegoat for the Government, and Mr. Harrell was dismissed from his appointment for having exceeded his powers in calling out the military." The general opined that it would be hard to find in history a "more disgraceful exhibition of weakness on the part of a Government," the result of which was that the "already shaken morale of the Irish Police" became "broken for all time." Such consequences were felt long after Harrell's dismissal: "Years afterwards I saw evidences of this, the Harrell case being pointed to as the reward of an official who endeavored to carry out an obvious duty."[31]

Andrew Magill, Birrell's private secretary, shared Macready's opinion. He noted:

> I could never understand why a circular sent to every junior district inspector of constabulary throughout Ireland, instructing him in the event of anyone attempting to land arms, to do exactly as Mr. Harrel [sic] did— viz., to call out the military and stop the landing by force if necessary— was not referred to in the report of the Commission, as I believe the Commissioners had a copy before them. . . . In my opinion the dismissal of Mr. Harrel [sic] was a crucial factor in disheartening the police through- out the whole of Ireland. They saw that if they did their duty they would not be supported and being human beings and not being angels, they took the safest course from that date, and refused to do anything without an order from their superior officers.[32]

Magill was present with Birrell in the House of Commons when he sent the wire suspending Harrell. He protested against the Chief Secretary's actions, but was told by Birrell, "It's no use, Magill, we must send it. Redmond and Dillon have been round at Downing St to see Asquith and he has agreed to suspend Harrel [sic]."[33] As he had been throughout the period of overt militancy, Birrell was more concerned to placate Irish Nationalist Party politicians than to actively address the security situation in Ireland.[34]

The members of the cabinet, too, were angrier at Augustine Birrell than at Harrell, feeling that the Chief Secretary had once again allowed the situation in Ireland to get out of hand. Charles Hobhouse, commenting on the cabinet meeting of July 27, noted in his diary,

> Birrell gave us the most lame and unconvincing account of Mr. Harrell's action. In the first place Birrell had not, save for a few days, been in Dublin for months, nor did it occur to him to go there now. Secondly, he had made up his mind on an *ex parte* statement of Dougherty that Harrell was willfully guilty.

He finished his diary entry, noting, "The whole of the present difficulties in Ulster and Dublin are due to Birrell's own negligence of duties, and his habitual absence from Ireland."[35]

Despite this criticism, there was little Birrell could have done to prevent the Howth gunrunning. Unlike in Ulster, the police had not suspected that the landings were forthcoming and were thus not as prepared as they had been in Belfast and the surrounding towns. In contrast to the gunrunning in April, the government had not received warnings from a British ambassador abroad, nor had the Foreign Secretary communicated with the Chief Secretary that an arms shipment was imminent. In Ulster, the R.I.C. had provided the government with solid intelligence; the government had merely chosen not to act. In Dublin, the R.I.C. had no such intelligence to provide. In his monthly report to the Chief Secretary, Inspector General Chamberlain simply wrote that the landings had been "unknown" to the police, and that "there were only a few R.I.C. at Howth, who could not prevent the landing."[36]

The Dublin county inspector provided more detail, explaining that the R.I.C. contingent in Howth consisted of only one head constable and eleven men. When the volunteers marched into the harbor, "Head Constable Walton and the police attempted to get on to the pier, but they were not allowed and having regard to the overwhelming force, the police did not attempt to force their way." Walton had telephoned the county inspector for advice, but the county inspector, "seeing that the police, owing to their numbers, were powerless to prevent the actual landing of the arms," did not allow his men "to interfere in any way with the Volunteers."[37]

Despite this, the county inspector did direct his men "to count the number of rifles, note the number and marks on motor cars conveying arms from the pier, note as many persons as possible, especially those taking a prominent post for identification purposes, and accompany the main body in whatever direction they went." The R.I.C., therefore, followed the volunteers back to Dublin. Upon meeting the D.M.P. in Clontarf, however, they returned to their station at Howth, leaving the Dublin police to trace the weapons. Unlike the R.I.C., the D.M.P. had not been issued with orders to follow the shipment, and the R.I.C.'s order was not communicated to the Dublin police constables. The D.M.P. thus failed to follow the volunteers and did not note the final destination of the rifles.[38] A police operation that could have produced similar intelligence as in Ulster came to naught, therefore, largely because of ill communication between the different police forces.

The Irish Volunteers had broken the law and, under the royal proclamations that forbade arms importations, could have been prosecuted for their actions. The police, however, had taken insufficient steps to track the arms, and thus the British government had no knowledge of where these imported arms were stored. They could, of course, have actively sought out these weapons. To an uninspired and uninspiring Chief Secretary, however, to actually encourage further intelligence gathering and action required too much effort. Birrell, therefore, did nothing.

On August 5, only a week after the landings had taken place, the Chief Secretary had the royal proclamations revoked.[39] The day before, the British government had declared war on Germany. The leader of the Irish Nationalist Party, John Redmond, immediately pledged the support of Irishmen everywhere to the cause of the British Empire. Birrell, trusting Redmond's authority to speak for those in Ireland and believing that any armed Irishman would use his weapon against Germany only, convinced the cabinet that the proclamations no longer held any utility.[40]

From that day forth, arms could once again be brought legally into Ireland. Almost immediately, the Crimes Special Branch noted that police reports sent to them "disclosed a renewal of activity on the part of the Ulster Volunteers to add to their stores, while for the first time the Irish Volunteers (Sinn Fein Section) began to purchase rifles in the English market."[41] The main impediment to paramilitary arming in Ireland had now been removed. Not only could the U.V.F. and the Irish Volunteers take advantage of this. The clandestine I.R.B., already becoming an ever more important if unacknowledged part of the Irish Volunteer movement, could also arm at will. There was little the police could do to stop them.

A War Distracts from Trouble in Ireland

R.I.C. Inspector General Neville Chamberlain made a telling remark to the Chief Secretary in his report on the shootings at Bachelor's Walk, which had followed the gunrunning at Howth. He noted that whilst the incident had "aroused much resentment in the Country" and had given "at once a great stimulus to the Volunteer Movement," this resentment was "soon eclipsed by events on the Continent." The sympathies of the Irish Volunteers, he assured Birrell, were now "on the side of England."[42]

The "events on the Continent" to which Chamberlain referred were, of course, the assassination of Archduke Franz Ferdinand, Germany's invasion of neutral Belgium, and the subsequent outbreak of the First World War, which Ireland, as part of the United Kingdom, had entered with the British declaration of war on August 4. It was these same events that provoked Birrell to revoke the royal proclamations prohibiting arms importations. And, indeed, it did seem like the European conflict had overshadowed all else. The R.I.C.'s county inspector for Antrim confirmed in his August report that "for the time being all parties appear to have forgotten their differences," a sentiment shared by other county inspectors. In Cavan, the county inspector reported that "feeling between the Ulster Volunteers and Irish National Volunteers [is] much better since the outbreak of the war." The Monaghan county inspector proclaimed that "much of the bitterness existing between Unionist and Nationalists has been obliterated by the outbreak of the War and all danger of a collision between rival parties has disappeared for the present." The Tyrone county inspector even went so far as to say that the war had "worked a revolution in the state of party feeling in the county," in essence preventing a civil war in Ireland.[43]

It was little wonder that the war seemed to achieve such unity. For the first time since the Boer War of 1899–1901, unionist and nationalist leaders called on their followers to join together in support of the same cause. On August 1, three days before Britain entered the war, Sir Edward Carson wrote a letter to the *Times* pledging the Ulster Volunteer Force for home defense and encouraging all who felt able to join the British armed forces for service abroad.[44] Two days later, on August 3, John Redmond offered the same exhortation in a speech to the Commons, declaring that "the coast of Ireland will be defended from foreign invasion by her armed sons, and for this purpose armed Nationalist Catholics in the South will be only too glad to join arms with the armed Protestant Ulstermen in the North."[45] When Britain declared war on August 4, both Carson and Redmond renewed their offers, hoping that their volunteer armies would be brought into the British order of battle.

The new Secretary of State for War, however, had other ideas. Lord Kitchener was a professional soldier who, although born in Ireland, had little time for private Irish militias, particularly those formed for political purposes.[46] When appointed Secretary of State on August 5, he immediately shocked the British cabinet by warning them to prepare for a war of at least three years' duration and recommended that the British Army be expanded to seventy divisions. The cabinet accepted his recommendation and recruitment for Kitchener's "New Army" began immediately.[47] On August 7, Carson and Redmond each met individually with Kitchener to suggest that the Ulster and Irish Volunteers be kept as separate formations within the British Army. Kitchener, consistent with his disdain for private armies, declined in both cases.[48]

The following day, Redmond wrote to the Prime Minister, warning that if Kitchener would not consent to using the Irish Volunteers as a separate force, Redmond would not support other recruitment efforts amongst Catholics in Ireland. Despite this threat, Kitchener remained steadfast in his opposition to the idea, believing that incorporating existing private militias into the Crown forces would only encourage the growth of others.[49] On August 11, both Carson and Redmond again publicly offered their volunteer forces to Kitchener. Redmond's offer was conditional on the successful passage of the

Home Rule Bill, but Carson's attached no strings.[50] Kitchener met with the cabinet to discuss these offers, but all present agreed that they could not accept any sort of conditional offer; furthermore, for political reasons, they could not take one volunteer force whilst leaving the other. They decided therefore that traditional recruitment for Kitchener's New Army should continue as before, with both volunteer forces left out.[51]

Within a month, recruitment in Ireland began to decline. Kitchener met with the cabinet on September 9 to suggest that they resolve the Home Rule question. Irish troops were sorely needed, and without Redmond's support, it was increasingly difficult to recruit any.[52] As a result, the cabinet reached a dual compromise with Carson and Redmond. The Home Rule Bill would be passed, but its implementation would be suspended until the end of the war.[53] In accordance with this agreement, the House of Commons finally passed the Home Rule Bill on September 18 and sent it to the king for his assent.[54] Two days later, on September 20, in a speech at Woodenbridge, Redmond urged the Irish Volunteers to join the British war effort: "[A]ccount yourselves as men not only in Ireland itself, but wherever the firing line extends, in defense of right, of freedom and religion in this war."[55] Following Redmond's speech, the men of both the Ulster Volunteer Force and the Irish Volunteers were united in their support for the British Empire. The War Office formed the 36th (Ulster) Division and the 16th (Irish) Division shortly thereafter.[56]

Sinister undertones lurked beneath the surface of this triumphant unity, however, brief warning signs of things to come. The R.I.C. county inspector for Cork's West Riding cautioned that the attitude of those within his area was very much "influenced by party politics," with a substantial number of Sinn Fein members "very extreme in their views and opposed to England." The Wexford county inspector likewise reported that opposition to the war had been shown "by a small though aggressive body of Sinn Feiners who are circulating anti-English pamphlets." Anti-enlistment posters had been displayed in Tipperary's South Riding, and "seditious leaflets" circulated in County Roscommon. More alarming, the Irish Volunteers seemed divided amongst themselves about the war. In Limerick, the members of the city branch were at odds with each other "owing to the action of Sinn Fein members," and the County Dublin Swords branch had actually split into two distinct sections formed from those who supported the war and those who sided with Sinn Fein.[57]

Bulmer Hobson fell into the latter category. He had been wary of John Redmond's influence over the Irish Volunteers ever since the parliamentarian gained control in June. When the provisional committee had surrendered to Redmond's request to add 25 of his chosen delegates to the committee, it had done so only reluctantly, and it had issued a public protest at Redmond's actions. In a memorandum written by Hobson and issued to the Irish press on June 16, the committee had stated that following Redmond's demand, it recognized that

> for the time being, in view of the new situation created by Mr. Redmond's attitude, it is no longer possible to preserve the unity of the Irish Volunteers and at the same time to maintain the non-party and non-sectarian principle of the organization. . . . This being the case, the Committee, under a deep and painful sense of responsibility, feel it their duty to accept the alternative which appears to them the lesser evil. In the interest of National unity, and in that interest only, the Provisional Committee now . . . accede[s] to Mr. Redmond's demand to add to their number twenty-five persons nominated at the instance of the Irish Party.[58]

The committee, for the sake of keeping intact the Irish Volunteers as a single organization, had allowed the Irish Nationalist Party to dominate it, but they had done so only grudgingly. Redmond's declaration of support for the British war effort, and his willingness to use the Irish Volunteers in that fight, made the original members of the provisional committee, including Bulmer Hobson and Eoin MacNeill, yet more restless under Redmond's leadership.

Despite this, however, and despite the concerns expressed by some of his county inspectors, the Inspector General reported to the Chief Secretary in his monthly summary for August that "[p]opular feeling is undoubtedly in sympathy with Great Britain and hostile to Germany." He did acknowledge that "Sinn Feiners, and other extremists, are here and there making efforts to stir up anti-English feeling by the dissemination of seditious literature," but he held that this had "not yet affected the public mind to any serious extent."[59] With the outbreak of war, Chamberlain believed, political trouble in Ireland had come to an end.

The Irish Republican Brotherhood thought otherwise. Indeed, adopting the age-old Irish mantra that "England's difficultly is Ireland's opportunity," the leadership of the I.R.B. saw the outbreak of war as a unique opportunity to make a final push for Irish independence. The Irish Volunteers, a large body of men already trained and to a certain extent armed, seemed the natural starting place to begin such a campaign. John Redmond's support for the British war effort complicated things, however. The I.R.B. had to make a break from Redmond, therefore, and take as many Irish Volunteers with them as possible.

On September 24, just four days after Redmond's speech at Woodenbridge, the original members of the provisional committee published an open letter to the Irish Volunteers, signed by Eoin MacNeill and 19 others. The letter began with a denouncement of the tactics used by Redmond in June to take control of the movement, and reminded its readers that the committee had accepted his proposals only as "the lesser evil," preferable to the breakup of the Irish Volunteers. Following the Woodenbridge speech, however, Redmond had now

> announced for the Irish Volunteers a policy and programme fundamentally at variance with their own published and accepted aims and objects. . . . He has declared it to be the duty of the Irish Volunteers to take foreign service under a Government which is not Irish. He has made this announcement without consulting the Provisional Committee, the Volunteers themselves, or the people of Ireland, to whose service alone they are devoted.

That being the case, the letter stated, the provisional committee was now reverting to its original membership, with neither Redmond nor his 25 nominees entitled to any place within the organization. The letter closed with an announcement that on November 25 of that year, the provisional committee would hold a convention to renew its original manifesto and to publicly declare that no Irishman should ever serve the British Empire whilst Ireland had no legislative body of its own.[60]

John Redmond, perhaps predictably, refused to acknowledge the sentiments expressed in this letter. Following its publication, however, the provisional committee ceased to meet as a unified body; instead, one committee met composed of John Redmond and his 25 nominees and a second met composed of the original members of the provisional committee. The individual volunteers were left to decide which committee they would support.[61] Two weeks after the letter was published, on October 10, the original committee drafted a "Proposed Constitution of the Irish Volunteers," which was accepted by 160 delegates at the First Convention of the Irish Volunteers on October 25, one month earlier than planned.[62] Immediately after this convention, Redmond announced that his army would henceforth be known as the National Volunteers to avoid confusion. Following the split, the vast majority of volunteers remained loyal to Redmond and the National Volunteers; only 3,000 of the more than 180,000 volunteers joined Eoin MacNeill's newly formed Irish Volunteers.[63]

The British government, in stark contrast to its thorough and up-to-date intelligence on the Ulster Volunteer Force, was not aware of this split until the following month, in November 1914.[64] Even after this date, the government continued to refer to the National Volunteers haphazardly as the Irish

National Volunteers, the Irish Volunteers, the Irish Volunteers (Redmondite Section), and the Irish National Volunteers (Redmondite Section). The Irish Volunteers were referred to, again without pattern, as the Irish National Volunteers, the Irish Volunteers, the Irish National Volunteers (Sinn Fein Section), the Irish Volunteers (Sinn Fein Section), and the Irish Volunteers (MacNeill Section). No distinct terminology was established in the police reports to differentiate the two forces. The reports were, therefore, often confused, in several cases reporting on the same incident yet attributing it to different organizations.[65] Only beginning in May 1915, did the police become consistent in designating two separate organizations, which they called the Irish National Volunteer Force and the Irish Volunteers (Sinn Fein).[66] Consequently, for the first seven months of its existence, the more extreme Irish Volunteers was largely ignored by the police.

In early October 1914, for example, despite Redmond's speech at Woodenbridge on September 20 and the provisional committee's open letter denouncing Redmond four days later, Chamberlain reported to the Chief Secretary that whilst the Irish Volunteers numbered "about 184,000 men, and are spread over the whole country from North to South," there had been "no progress [in their organization] whatsoever" during September, and there was nothing more of interest to report.[67] It is apparent that at this point, and until May 1915, both the police and the British government were less clear about the organizational structure of the National Volunteers and the Irish Volunteers than they had been about the Ulster Volunteer Force. They did not, therefore, give the smaller and more extremist Irish Volunteers organization the attention that it deserved, instead concentrating on the larger National Volunteers.

The reason for this ignorance was the police and government's fixation, bordering on obsession, with army recruiting and reporting signs of pro-British sentiment within Ireland. Beginning with his September 1914 monthly report, the R.I.C. Inspector General ceased to include a special section on the Ulster and Irish volunteers (as he had been doing since early 1913) and instead included a section on "the State of public feeling in Ireland in connection with the War." Chamberlain's special report made no note of the growing discontent within certain factions of the Irish Volunteers. In County Antrim, for example, he reported that the Irish Volunteers were "distinctly anti-German in feeling" and that there had been "no attempt" by extremists to "change the feeling of sympathy with the Allies in the war." The "main point of interest" in County Carlow was "the attitude of Irish National Volunteers towards England: there does not appear to be any spirit of disloyalty existing amongst them." In County Longford, the Irish Volunteers were reported as "strongly in favor of England and the Allies" and "on the side of the Empire in its present struggle," and in County Mayo, the Inspector General reported that "the sympathies of the people are practically entirely with England."[68] Throughout the country, Chamberlain assured Birrell, the Irish citizenry, and those enrolled in the Irish Volunteers, supported the British war effort.

Only in counties Dublin, Limerick, and Wexford (3 out of 32 Irish counties) was Sinn Fein cited as a problem. In the first, Chamberlain noted that Sinn Fein was "doing all they can to sow dissention amongst the National Volunteers and endeavoring by all means in their power to prevent enlistment in the British Army." They were doing likewise in Limerick. In Wexford, there was a "growing spirit of dissension" within the Irish Volunteers "due to the action of Sinn Feiners in opposing the policy of Mr. Redmond." Despite these comments, however, Chamberlain hastened to add that in County Wexford "the majority support Mr. Redmond," and in Limerick, Sinn Fein had "not met with much success as the sympathies of the people are with the Allies."[69]

Indeed, the main problem in Ireland, the Inspector General told Birrell, was in County Waterford, where although support for the war was strong, "when it comes to the point of doing anything definite they [the people of Waterford] are too lazy to do anything for themselves; they think the war is far away and in this County they are quite comfortable in the idea that the fighting will be done for them."[70] Overall, the reports showed Ireland to be in a satisfactory state and gave the impression that for the first time since the Ulster Volunteer Force had been formed, there was the possibility for peace in Ireland. No comment was made on the provisional committee's letter condemning the war and expelling John Redmond from its body.

In the significant month of October 1914, when the Irish Volunteers formally split into the pro-war National Volunteers and the anti-war Irish Volunteers, little was said by the Inspector General to cause alarm in the British government. The country, he told Birrell, was "generally quiet," and all of Ireland was caught up in an "absorbing interest in the war." The Irish Volunteers were "steadily on the decline," partly due to the end of their raison d' être with the passage of the Home Rule Bill, and partly due to their drill instructors and prominent members leaving Ireland for British war service. Chamberlain did note that "the Sinn Feiners who founded the Volunteers resent control by the Redmondites," but nowhere in his report did he suggest that there had been a split in the movement.[71]

As in September, the reason for this neglect was an all-encompassing focus on the war effort. In his monthly report for October, the Inspector General again included a special section on the state of public feeling towards the war. There was a more noticeable presence of Sinn Fein in the reports than there had been in September. In County Kilkenny, for example, Chamberlain stated that the "large majority of eligible young men are not inclined to take their part in fighting, this spirit being to some extent fostered by the subtle influence which is being exercised by Sinn Fein." In County Kerry, the Union Jack had been burned and an Irish Nationalist member of parliament had been shouted down when delivering a pro-war speech. In County Tipperary, the "more advanced Nationalists" had turned against the war, and in County Clare, the "feeling regarding the war has undergone a great change since it began. . . . [T]here is decidedly a much greater anti-English feeling than there was at the beginning of August." Nevertheless, the other 28 counties were said to be loyal to Great Britain and to the British war effort, and those four that had displayed disquiet appeared to be doing so more as "an excuse . . . [to] do nothing to defend their country" than as a distinct stance against the war.[72] As in the September report, there was no mention of a concerted Sinn Fein position against the war.

Finally, in his November monthly report, written and submitted to the Chief Secretary in early December, Chamberlain acknowledged the divide within the Irish Volunteers. He noted that since the outbreak of the war, "the split between the followers of Mr. Redmond and the Sinn Feiners in the Force has gradually become wider." He even correctly identified Redmond's followers as taking the name "the National Volunteers" and reported that the "Sinn Fein section adhere to the original title of 'Irish Volunteers.' " Chamberlain also stated that the police had received intelligence from the United States that revolutionary organizations in that country were becoming more active, and that it was "probable" that an attempt would be made "to send an expedition from America and perhaps arms and officers from Germany for the purpose of stirring up insurrection in Ireland." Despite all this, however, he pronounced Ireland to be "quiet" during that month and stated that the "people generally appear to be loyal to the Empire."[73]

From this point forward, and until May 1915, the Inspector General provided the same analysis of the situation in Ireland each month. In the context of the continuing war on the continent, Chamberlain was concerned only with the Irish attitude towards Germany, not with any potentially threatening anti-English sentiment. The possibility of an armed insurrection within Ireland independent of German support was not, it seems, contemplated. In December, for example, he noted (with some relief) that "the minority of Sinn Feiners and other extremists who aspire to National independence and separation from England are probably more anti-English than pro-German."[74] When he reported on a Sinn Fein meeting at which the speaker announced that the Irish Volunteers might "soon have an opportunity to strike a blow for the freedom of Ireland" and that they should "use their weapons rather than surrender," he noted only that the speaker "did not advocate the cause of Germany." He did not comment on the insurrectionary content of the speech.[75] Quoting the Tyrone county inspector in January, Chamberlain claimed that "[a]t no time in living memory has there been such good feeling between Catholics and Protestants." He did acknowledge that the I.R.B. had told its members that the war offered them a unique opportunity to seek Irish freedom and that "when the time arrived" arms and ammunition would be provided, but he dismissed it as "improbable" that "these proposals were either made or accepted seriously."[76]

The reports submitted to the Crimes Special Branch told a different story, however. In January, in County Dublin, weekly shooting practices had taken place at the Shankhill and Rathfarnham branches of the Irish Volunteers, and skirmishing maneuvers had been practiced on two different occasions, the first with 56 volunteers, the second with 250. In County Cork, 200 Irish Volunteers had met for drill and rifle practice, and in County Kerry, 104 volunteers had each been supplied with a Martini-Enfield rifle. In Limerick, the Irish Volunteers had carried out three route marches, followed on each occasion with a "sham battle." At the first, 121 volunteers had participated, 99 of whom were armed with rifles. This number had risen to 130 (100 armed) at the second march, and 123 (116 armed) at the third. Chamberlain was not concerned about this intelligence, however, because from the outbreak of the war until January 15, 37,026 Irish recruits had joined the British Army, including 15,461 Roman Catholics. This proved to him beyond question, he asserted, that the Irish Volunteers were a minority within Irish society and thus posed no threat to the state.[77]

Chamberlain continued to hold that the physical size of an organization, combined with its relative sympathy towards Germany, indicated the level of threat to the British state. He stated in February that the "Sinn Fein or extreme section, which comprises the Sinn Fein Party, the Ancient Order of Hibernians (Irish American Alliance), and the Irish Republican Brotherhood" was "insignificant in point of numbers" when compared to the "constitutional societies" under the leadership of John Redmond.[78] He added that public sympathy was "overwhelmingly on the side of Great Britain," a point evidenced by the fact that "recruiting for the Army reached a higher figure in February than in the preceding month."[79] In March, he again proclaimed that the people of Ireland were "everywhere loyal to the Empire in the war" and that "the extremists," the Irish Volunteers, were "but a small party with no men of influence as leaders."[80]

Once again, however, the reports submitted by the police to the Crimes Special Branch contradicted Chamberlain's confidence. Throughout the country, they stated, the I.R.B. had established 21 centers with 560 members.[81]

The Irish Volunteers too had increased their numbers and were steadily arming. In County Kerry, rifles had been issued to 104 Irish Volunteers in February, who had proceeded to drill and carry out armed route marches throughout the month. In Limerick, three armed marches had been held, followed by skirmishing practice on each occasion. These practices were attended by 96, 140, and 126 volunteers respectively. In County Dublin, skirmishing and "sham battles" had been carried out on three separate days with 180, 33, and 56 volunteers in each case. In the first instance, these volunteers were "under command of Professor P.H. Pearse."[82] This was the first time that Patrick Pearse had been mentioned in the police intelligence reports. It was his name that would soon come to haunt the British government.

Only in April did Chamberlain begin to acknowledge the Crimes Special Branch reports, noting that the "Sinn Fein section is apparently better organized and is making more progress in the direction of efficiency than the Redmonites." Nevertheless, he stressed that it was "not progressing in numbers" and that the "vast majority of Irishmen" had "no sympathy with Germany."[83] Upon reading this report, the new under secretary, Matthew Nathan, who had replaced James Dougherty in October 1914, following the latter man's election to Parliament as a Liberal Home Ruler, cautioned Birrell that "the Extremists movement" seemed to be "improving their organization and spreading their views."[84] Birrell, however, dismissed the warning, casually commenting that "[t]his is what was most likely to happen," and stating that although the movement had "a genuine core," it was only "a small one."[85] Loyalty to the British state was still determined by events on the continent, not by any internal independence movement or philosophy of insurgency. If a group was not actively seeking to aid the German war effort, it was not considered a threat.

As May 1915 approached, then, the British government believed that the political situation in Ireland had calmed since the tumultuous years of 1912–1914. Recruiting for the army was going well, and the Irish people appeared to be rallying behind the flag. That a small movement of anti-war Irish republicans was using the war as an opportunity to seek Irish independence was not considered a problem. So long as a German invasion of Ireland was not imminent, the British government and Irish police were certain that Ireland would remain quiet.

The Storm Clouds Gather

When Patrick Pearse led his 180 Irish Volunteers in a sham battle in County Dublin, gaining his first mention in the intelligence reports of the R.I.C., he was not participating in his first act of defiance towards British rule in Ireland. Indeed, Pearse had worked against the British government for almost as long as I.R.B. Supreme Council member Bulmer Hobson. Born in 1879, Pearse had come of age during the revivals of Irish language, culture, and literature in the 1890s and 1900s. Caught up in these movements, he began to study the Irish language in 1893, at the age of 14, and 3 years later, in October 1896, he joined the newly formed Gaelic League. It was there that he first met Eoin MacNeill, the league's cofounder and at that time its president. In 1898, after only two years' membership, Pearse was brought onto the Coiste Gnotha, the executive committee of the league, where he worked side by side with MacNeill.

Although intimately involved with the Gaelic League, Pearse chose not to join the pro-independence Sinn Fein Party at its founding in November 1905. Instead, he concentrated his efforts on Irish cultural movements. In 1903, he became editor of *An Claidheamh Soluis*, the news magazine of the Gaelic League, a position he held until 1909. Throughout these years, he became increasingly concerned about the state of Irish education, believing it to be nothing more than English propaganda. In 1908, therefore, whilst still editor of *An Claidheamh Soluis*, he opened an Irish-speaking school in Dublin called St. Enda's, which initially enrolled 80 boys. By 1909, this number had doubled, and for the next two years, Pearse devoted himself to their education.[86]

Throughout this time, however, Pearse could not help but engage in politics. Indeed, the very act of establishing an Irish-language school sent an explicit message about the British presence in Ireland: English should not be the primary language of the Irish people, as Ireland was not an English land.[87] In 1910, Pearse began to study the life and philosophy of Robert Emmet, an Irish nationalist who had led a doomed revolution in 1803, only to be hanged by the British. For the next two years, from 1910 to 1912, Pearse became obsessed with the concept of revolutionary martyrdom for Ireland, and his writings became increasingly violent. In December 1910, he announced that the primary purpose of Irish-language instruction was to "harden individuals for the inevitable struggle ahead," a reason he had never proclaimed before.[88]

In 1910, as his writings became more extreme, Pearse came to the attention of some I.R.B. members, particularly Patrick McCartan, an Irish-language enthusiast who admired Pearse's academic work, and Tom Clarke, an ex-Fenian who had served 15 years in a British prison for a dynamite plot. In March 1911, the I.R.B. invited Pearse to speak at the annual commemoration of Robert Emmet's execution. By the summer of 1912, he regularly attended Sinn Fein and I.R.B meetings.[89] Clarke proclaimed that in Pearse, the I.R.B. had found "the future spokesman for the I.R.B.'s cause," and he increasingly advocated for Pearse's further participation in the I.R.B.[90] In November 1913, Clarke's wish was granted: Pearse became a member of Eoin MacNeill's Irish Volunteers. He also officially joined the Sinn Fein Party, and was invited to become a member of the I.R.B.[91]

By February 1915, when the R.I.C. first noticed Pearse, he had risen to the leadership of both the Irish Volunteers and the I.R.B., sitting on the provisional committee of the former and the Supreme Council of the latter. In the first half of 1914, he had also accompanied Bulmer Hobson on a tour of the United States, preaching to Irish-American audiences the necessity of violent insurrection within Ireland to free the Irish people from the chains of British oppression. When he returned to Ireland in June 1914, Pearse continued to proclaim his message, making repeated calls for a rebellion against the British.[92]

Despite this growing dissention, the R.I.C. continued to view Ireland only through the lens of the war against Germany. In May 1915, Chamberlain reported that throughout Ireland, "the people generally are loyal to the British side of the War." From April 15 to May 15, he explained, the number of recruits who had joined the Army had risen to 5,377, "which exceeds all previous returns." He added that "Unionists and Nationalists joined in promoting Recruiting meetings at several places, and some strongly anti-German speeches were delivered by the R.C. Clergymen."[93] He did admit that the Irish Volunteers were "unusually active of late" and that there was even reason to believe that "as the result of this activity, a spirit of disloyalty and pro-Germanism, which hitherto was confined to a small number, is spreading."[94] No mention, however, was made of any push for Irish independence, despite armed drills taking place in counties Cork, Dublin, Kerry, and Limerick, the largest of which numbered 1,100 men, 800 of whom carried rifles.[95]

This same flaw in intelligence analysis and interpretation continued throughout the summer months. In June, Chamberlain reported that the Irish Volunteers had been "active in all provinces," with certain leaders traveling throughout the country to organize rifle drill, and with all volunteers "bitterly disloyal" to Britain and the British Empire. Rather than inferring from this that there was a possible threat to British security in Ireland, however, he continued to view the intelligence in the context of the European war, stating that although the Irish Volunteers "would probably rejoice to see England beaten and humiliated," very few were actually "anxious to see German troops in Ireland."[96] Without an actual German invasion, Chamberlain believed, there was very little damage the Irish Volunteers could do. Just as the Ulster Volunteer Force had been left alone in the years 1912–1914, so would the Irish Volunteers be in 1915.

Despite the Inspector General's inability to look beyond the larger conflict on the continent, the Crimes Special Branch continued to report on the Irish Volunteers' ongoing training for possible action in the cause of Irish independence. In County Dublin, in July, 1,000 volunteers, 900 of whom carried arms, had conducted a route march, followed two days later by military maneuvers by 160 armed volunteers. In Cork, 103 volunteers had engaged in target practice, and 130 had led an armed parade through the streets of Cork City on the anniversary of the Howth gunrunning (July 26). Similar scenes occurred in County Kerry, where two "sham battles" were carried out by armed volunteers, and in County Limerick, where three route marches took place, with 50, 65, and 140 armed volunteers respectively.[97]

In his monthly report for that month, the Inspector General admitted that within the Irish Volunteers, "insurrectionary action was [being] urged by some members." Nevertheless, he assured the Chief Secretary that there was "no reason to believe that there is any general enthusiasm for insurrection among the Sinn Feiners." Indeed, Chamberlain confidently wrote, many of the volunteers had "very little interest in the Sinn Fein movement, beyond its opposition to recruiting for the Army."[98] The men within the Irish Volunteers were not actually seeking Irish independence, as their leaders claimed, nor were they willing to take up arms against the British government, as they threatened to do. They were merely shirking their duty of serving in France, acting not as patriots, but as cowards. That was the analysis of the Royal Irish Constabulary, anyway, an analysis that was not challenged by Chief Secretary Birrell.

The new Irish under secretary, Matthew Nathan, was not so sure. In August, the Crimes Special Branch had again reported increased activity within the Irish Volunteers. Patrick Pearse, by now identified by the police as a "suspect" (a designation of political suspicion rather than criminality), had led an inspection of 150 volunteers in Cork City Hall, 110 of whom were armed, before addressing a friendly crowd of 500. In County Dublin, 200 armed volunteers had carried out military maneuvers, and in Kerry, two armed parades had been conducted, the first with 146 volunteers, the second with 134.[99] On reading these reports, Nathan wrote to Birrell, telling him that there could now be "little doubt that the Parliamentary Party are gradually losing and the physical force party are slowly gaining strength in Ireland."[100]

In contrast to his previous faith in James Dougherty, however, Birrell chose not to listen to his new under secretary, instead deferring to Inspector General Chamberlain, who again assured him that "many, if not the majority of the new members since the outbreak of War, joined this Volunteer Force in order to shirk military services rather than from a desire to 'fight for Ireland.' " It was true, Chamberlain wrote, that "the Irish Volunteers apparently aim at the establishment of National Independence," but there had been nothing observed by the police "which would indicate preparation to afford material assistance to the Germans by insurrection in Ireland."[101] The idea that the Irish Volunteers might attempt an insurrection regardless of the Germans does not seem to have occurred to Chamberlain.

At the dawn of autumn, there was little change. Chamberlain stated in September that the Irish Volunteers were "numerically insignificant" and were "making little progress." Furthermore, he said, "the Sinn Fein leaders do not command either followers or equipment sufficient for insurrection, and the vast majority of Irishmen are looking forward to the victory of the Allies."[102] The following month, however, the Irish Volunteers made significant gains in recruitment and for the first time since the war began, the Inspector General reported that the condition of Ireland could no longer be regarded "satisfactory." These gains were in large part due to an unfounded rumor that compulsory military service might be extended from the British mainland to Ireland. Whilst the vast majority of Irishmen were "loyal to the British Empire in the present crisis," Chamberlain stated, there could be little doubt that during the month of October, a "great fear" of conscription had gripped the people, with the result that many had "gone over to the Sinn Feiners." Consequently, the National Volunteers had "ceased to be an active Force." Chamberlain further reported that "the Sinn Feiners have already planned a rising in the event of Conscription, and as this is perhaps the one project in which they would find many Redmondites in agreement with them, they might give a serious amount of trouble." During this conscription scare, the Irish Volunteers increased their numbers from 3,657 in August to 3,911 by the end of October.[103]

Two weeks after Chamberlain submitted his report, Under Secretary Nathan wrote again to Birrell, telling him, "The increase in strength in the Irish Volunteers movement referred to in this Report has gone on rapidly in the fortnight that has elapsed since its date."[104] In his November report, the Inspector General confirmed this growth. The force, he wrote, had gained 1,300 new members in a single month, bringing their strength up to 5,019. There were also 5,192 National Volunteers who were opposed to John Redmond and supported Irish independence. These "Sinn Feiners" were "saturated with disloyalty" and were having a "very undesirable effect" on the Irish population as a whole. The force was "well organized and very active," and was supported by I.R.B. circles that held meetings "here and there."[105] Significantly, the Inspector General made no mention of Germany in his November report, yet still characterized the Irish Volunteers as a threat. After 12 months of openly preaching sedition, Chamberlain was finally discerning the extent to which violent insurrection was being advocated in Ireland.

This recognition marked an important transition in the attitude of the Royal Irish Constabulary towards the Irish Volunteers. The Inspector General was now aware of the problem and, in contrast to previous months, began to actively seek out a solution. Once Chamberlain had acknowledged the desires and aims of the Irish Volunteers, the question for him became how, when, and where an insurrection might take place. For this, he would need the sort of precise intelligence that had been submitted to him on the Ulster Volunteer Force in the years 1912–1914. Such intelligence, however, was not forthcoming.

In early January 1916, Chamberlain reported to the Chief Secretary that the strength of the Irish Volunteers was 6,355, their having added 1,336 new members in December, and that "seditious literature" was being circulated by the volunteers advocating insurrection.[106] Throughout the month, such growth continued, and by January 31, their strength had reached 7,187 men. Whilst this still paled in comparison to the much larger National Volunteers, Chamberlain warned that the smaller force was "well organized, governed by a thoroughly disloyal directorate, and in the way of injuring recruiting and spreading sedition, does a great deal of harm."[107] In Ireland, the threat of insurrection was now very real, independent of Germany or the war in France. Chamberlain did not, however, have any additional intelligence to suggest when and where an insurrection might occur.

In addition to the increased talk of insurrection, those within the Irish Volunteers were becoming more physically active during January. One volunteer in County Sligo was arrested "with forty-two gelignite cartridges and some fuse in his possession which he had purchased under a false name."[108] A "large quantity of high explosives" had also been stolen from a colliery magazine in Glasgow, Scotland, the explosives thought now to be in Dublin. Explosives had likewise been stolen from a colliery magazine at Carlingford and from several railway cars in transit. In County Kildare, 60 pounds of explosives and nine bombs with the fuse attached were found hidden in a culvert.[109] There was, however, no indication of what the planned use for these explosives would be, nor when such use might occur.

In February, the Inspector General's suspicions of an uprising increased. He wrote to Birrell, telling him,

If the speeches of Irish Volunteer leaders and articles in Sinn Fein journals have any meaning at all it must be that the force is being organized with a view to insurrection, and in the event of the enemy being able to effect a landing in Ireland, the Volunteers could no doubt delay the dispatch of troops to the scene by blowing up railway bridges.

In light of such intelligence, and "having regard to the gravity of the situation," Chamberlain believed it was "now time to seriously consider whether the organizers of the Irish Volunteers can be allowed with safety to continue their mischievous work, and whether this Force so hostile to British interests can be permitted to increase its strength and remain any longer in possession of arms without grave danger to the State."[110] Chamberlain was beginning to doubt the wisdom of repealing the royal proclamations and, as he had during the period of overt militancy, now believed that the police should be given legal power to act against the volunteers and prevent them from organizing further.

Meanwhile, the Dublin Metropolitan Police recruited two new informants, codenamed "Chalk" and "Granite" respectively, who had access to the leadership of the Irish Volunteers. On February 24, Granite issued his first report, stating that rifles and ammunition were being held at the homes of Michael O'Hanrahan, Eamon de Valera, and B. O'Connor. He provided the addresses for each of these men.[111] Granite reported again in March, as did Chalk. On March 16, Chalk reported that "the young men of the Irish Volunteers are very anxious to start 'business' at once." He stated that James Connolly's Citizen Army was now working hand in hand with the Irish Volunteers, and that "things look as if they [are] coming to a crisis, as each man has been served out with the package of link and Surgical dressing, etc., and a tin of food similar to that issued to Soldiers." He also revealed that boxes of ammunition had been hidden in Father Matthew Park in the Fairview suburb of Dublin, and that "the Sinn Feiners have enough Ammunition to keep them going for six months, and the amount of .303 cartridges is estimated at 300,000 rounds."[112]

Chalk provided further information 11 days later, on March 27. He explained that an Irish Volunteer meeting had been held on March 22 at Father Matthew Park. Thomas McDonagh was the main speaker, and he had told the volunteers, "[W]hen you joined the Irish Volunteers you were made aware that you would have to make sacrifices, and to carry out your instructions, and any man who is not prepared to do so we would be better without him. . . . When we go out, whether it be on the day appointed or some other day some of us may never come back."[113] Granite also submitted a report on March 27. He said that whilst there was "at present no fear of any rising by the Volunteers," there was an effort made by the leaders to "store as much explosives as they can discreetly procure," and that this "is where the real danger comes in."[114]

In light of this information, Chamberlain reasserted his belief in the gravity of the situation, telling Birrell that "the movement is holding its ground firmly, and [is] steadily improving its organization." He reported that the force had increased to 8,179 men, "to which may be added 4,572 members of the National Volunteers (Redmondite) who are reputed Sinn Feiners." He reminded the Chief Secretary that "last month I referred to the seditious and insurrectionary aims of the Irish Volunteers," and declared that "I may now state that even in the remote places their attitude is becoming more defiant and aggressive." As evidence of this, he cited an incident that had occurred on March 20, when a party of Irish Volunteers had discharged their revolvers at a hostile crowd through an open window in Tullamore. When the police attempted to arrest the volunteers and seize their weapons, they were fired upon, and their sergeant was seriously wounded. The provisional committee of the Irish Volunteers had then issued a statement, declaring that the volunteers would not allow themselves to be disarmed, and that "the raiding for arms and attempted disarming of men, therefore, in the natural course of things can only be met by resistance and bloodshed."[115]

Despite this, however, and despite the increased intelligence attesting to the desire of the Irish Volunteers for insurrection, it still seemed unlikely to Chamberlain that such a rising could occur without aid from Germany. Although he now acknowledged the extent of dissatisfaction within the Irish Volunteers, and had moved his focus from Irish opinion on the war effort to the very real possibility of an uprising by Irish separatists, it was still too difficult for him to comprehend that the Irish Volunteers might have the capacity to carry out a rebellion without foreign assistance. He also had no information as to when exactly such an aided insurrection might occur. He told the Chief Secretary, therefore, that there was "no doubt that the Irish Volunteer leaders are a pack of rebels who would revolt and proclaim their independence, in the event of any favorable opportunity." Such a favorable opportunity, however, could only come in the form of a German invasion. Without such an invasion, and "with their present resources," he found it "difficult to imagine that they could make even a brief stand against a small body of troops."[116] Any insurrection would have to be one supported by Germany. At the beginning of April 1916, such an insurrection seemed unlikely. Certainly, there was no intelligence to suggest that one was forthcoming.

An Easter Rising and Its Aftermath

In the early morning hours of Good Friday, April 21, 1916, an Irish peasant was taking a walk along the sea coast in County Kerry, close to the fishing village of Fenit, when he discovered a small collapsible boat. Three fresh sets of footprints led from the boat to the sand dunes. The peasant, no doubt aware that Fenit was only eight miles west of Tralee, the county seat, and perhaps with a heightened sense of imperial duty in time of war, immediately reported his finding to the local police. A constable sent to investigate found some buried revolvers, together with ammunition, in some recently disturbed sand not far from the boat. On further investigation, he noticed that a "tall man" was loitering close to the beach in some ruins. He immediately covered the man with his rifle, who at once raised his hands, surrendered, and gave an English name and address. The constable took him to the Tralee police barracks to be interviewed about the buried arms. When the man was brought into the holding cell, however, the custody sergeant noticed that he bore a striking resemblance to one of the more prominent faces displayed on Ireland's Most Wanted list. The man captured on the beach looked remarkably like Sir Roger Casement.[117]

That Casement should have turned up on this Irish beach, together with arms and ammunition and using a false name, was not remarkable. Since the gunrunning escapade of July 26, 1914, he had become ever more disloyal towards the British state. Whilst Hobson and the I.R.B. had unloaded their guns in Howth, Casement had traveled to New York to work with Clan na Gael, an Irish-American revolutionary organization committed to establishing an Irish republic by force. He was met there on July 20 by John Devoy, the leader of Clan na Gael, and for the following four weeks he undertook a speaking tour of the United States, glorifying the events of July 26 and collecting funds for further gunrunning operations to aid the Irish Volunteers.[118] With the outbreak of hostilities between Germany and Great Britain, Casement became convinced that the war could be used as an opportunity to free Ireland from British control. It did not require much persuasion to convince Devoy of this fact.[119]

On August 24, therefore, Devoy led a delegation from Clan na Gael to meet with the German ambassador in Washington, D.C. Their purpose, he stated, was "to use the opportunity of the European war to overthrow British rule in Ireland." He requested that the Germans "supply the arms and a sufficient number of capable officers to make a good start."[120] The following day, on August 25, the organization sent a declaration to the Kaiser himself, written by Casement, which stated, "We . . . draw Your Majesty's attention to the part that Ireland necessarily . . . must play in this conflict . . . The British claim to control the seas of the world rests chiefly on an unnamed factor. That factor is Ireland. . . . Ireland must be freed from British control."[121] If the German Army freed Ireland from Britain, Casement argued, its action would not only serve the Irish people but would also aid the German war effort by depriving the British of Irish ports.[122]

Casement remained in the United States following his speaking tour and on October 5, he made public his decision to remove his loyalty from the

British Empire. On that date, he published a letter in the *Irish Independent*, claiming that "Ireland has suffered at the hands of British administrators a more prolonged series of evils, deliberately inflicted, than any other community of civilized men. . . . [N]o Irishman fit to bear arms in the cause of his country's freedom can join the allied millions now attacking Germany."[123] Following this letter, Casement proposed to Devoy that he travel to Germany to further their plan. Devoy agreed, and, on October 15, Casement boarded the ocean liner *Oskar II* under the assumed name James E. Landy. Sixteen days later, on October 31, he arrived in Berlin, ready to transfer his allegiances from British imperial service to the imperial service of Germany.[124]

Casement remained in Germany until his ill-fated return to Ireland in April 1916. During his 18 months there, the German Foreign Office allowed him access to Irish prisoners of war, whom he attempted to form into an Irish Brigade that could assist in the planned invasion of Ireland. On November 20, 1914, the German under secretary of state, Arthur Zimmermann, announced to the German public (and to British intelligence[125]) that Casement had come to Germany to work with the Imperial Chancellor, Bethmann Hollweg. Their aim was to together defeat the British in Ireland. Following this pronouncement, Zimmermann issued the following declaration:

> If in the course of this war, which Germany did not seek, the fortunes of war should lead German troops to the shores of Ireland, they would land there not as a force of invaders . . . but as armed forces of a government, driven by good will towards a country and a people which Germany wished only national welfare and national liberty.

A month later, on December 23, Casement and the German Foreign Office signed a treaty that officially granted him unrestricted access to the Irish prisoners of war.[126]

Casement's progress in forming his Irish Brigade was disappointing, however, as he found many Irish prisoners less than enthusiastic about invading Ireland. Most, he discovered, remained loyal to the British Empire. By the late spring of 1915, Casement had "practically given up on the idea of an Irish Brigade," and by September 1915, the Germans had likewise "all but abandoned any plan of a military invasion of Ireland." In December of that year, the Germans, seeking another role for Casement, suggested that he use his small Irish Brigade of 56 men to invade Egypt and defeat the British there. Only 38 of his men volunteered for such a foolhardy mission, however. Of these, 24 later retracted their offer, leaving an invasion force of only 14. The idea was consequently abandoned.[127]

In early 1916, however, prospects for German aid to the Irish republicans began to brighten. On February 17, Count Johann Heinrich von Bernstorff, the German ambassador to the United States, sent a telegram to the German Foreign Office, which read, "Irish leader John Devoy informs me that revolution shall begin [on] Easter Sunday [in] Ireland. Requests arms between Good Friday and Easter Sunday [in County] Limerick. . . . Longer waiting impossible, request wire reply whether I may promise help from Germany." A second telegram to the Foreign Office, sent from Devoy himself and requesting the same, arrived later that day. The German government, after some consideration, decided to return Casement to Ireland to assist this promised revolution, together with 20,000 rifles, 10 machine guns, and ammunition and explosives. The plan was that Casement would first come ashore in County Kerry to secure the area, after which the arms would be landed from three fishing trawlers at Fenit Pier, sometime between April 20 and 23. No other German aid would be given, and once Casement landed, the Irish would be on their own.[128] Thus, Casement arrived on a beach in County Kerry on April 21, only to have his boat discovered by an Irish peasant and himself arrested by a police constable.

Following Casement's arrest, the R.I.C. staged an ambush in the sand dunes close to his collapsible boat. When his two accomplices returned in a motor car from Tralee, where they had been meeting with the local Irish Volunteer leaders, the police immediately pounced upon them. One made his escape, but the other was arrested and taken for interrogation, where he gave his name as Mulchahy. Casement, who still refused to identify himself, was sent from Tralee to the Dublin Detention Barracks on April 22. From there, he was transported directly to London.[129]

That day, April 22, the police informant Chalk reported one final time, informing the D.M.P.'s detective department that on the following day, April 23, the Irish Volunteers planned to march, with each man "to carry three days rations, rifle, ammunition, etc." Thomas McDonagh had given this order the previous Wednesday, April 19, telling his men, "Boys, some of us may never come back—Mobilization orders to be issued in due course." Chalk further informed the police that an additional 700 Martini rifles had been landed in County Wexford and had been brought to the quartermaster of the Irish Volunteers, together with 200 military bayonets. Chalk had personally seen these bayonets, and commented that they had been "recently sharpened."[130] This information was given to Birrell, but as no march took place on Sunday, it was thought to be erroneous. No action was therefore taken by the Chief Secretary's Office to prepare for an Irish Volunteers' mobilization.

In Tralee, meanwhile, Mulchahy finally made a "voluntary statement" in the late evening hours of Easter Sunday, April 23, after two days and nights of continuous interrogation. He confirmed that the prisoner taken to Dublin was indeed Sir Roger Casement, identified the third escaped man as Robert Monteith, and confessed that his own name was not Mulchahy but rather

Daniel Julian Bailey. He explained that he had served as a private in the Royal Irish Rifles but had been taken prisoner by the German Army early in the war. Whilst imprisoned, he had been visited by Casement, who had persuaded him to join the Irish Brigade. He, Casement, and Monteith had left Wilhemshaven the previous week in a German submarine, together with a ship laden with German arms and ammunition bound for the Kerry coast to give support to the Irish Volunteers. He then revealed that there was going to be an armed rebellion, and that an attack would be made on Dublin Castle, the seat of British power in Ireland.[131]

This alarming piece of intelligence was immediately telegraphed in cipher to Inspector General Chamberlain in Dublin. By 6:00 a.m. on Easter Monday morning, April 24, he had forwarded the reports to the under secretary, the headquarters of the British Army's Irish Command, and the Chief Commissioner of the Dublin Metropolitan Police. Chamberlain also issued orders to all R.I.C. barracks throughout Ireland to be on extra alert and to watch carefully the movements of the Irish Volunteers. The Chief Secretary's Office, however, believed that it was "unlikely that the intended rising could take place," as Casement was now in custody and the German ship laden with arms had been sunk by the Royal Navy. No steps to prepare for an imminent rising were taken, therefore.[132] This was the only solid piece of intelligence the British government received about the Easter Rising prior to its beginning. Believing the threat to be nullified, it was ignored.

The government was not alone in its complacency towards rebellion in Ireland. On the evening of April 22, Eoin MacNeill, hearing of Casement's arrest, issued orders calling off the planned Easter parades that were to begin the insurrection and to which Chalk had referred in his report. These orders MacNeill published in the *Sunday Independent*, telling the volunteers,

> Owing to the very critical situation, all orders given to the Irish Volunteers for tomorrow Easter Sunday are hereby rescinded and no parades, marches or other movements of Irish Volunteers will take place. Each individual Volunteer will obey this order strictly in every particular.

MacNeill believed that with the thwarting of Casement and the failure of the arms landing, any volunteer rising would be foolish martyrdom, and would do nothing to advance the cause of Irish independence. He therefore preferred to postpone armed insurrection, perhaps indefinitely.[133]

The Military Council of the I.R.B. had other ideas, however. They were furious at MacNeill's order countermanding the parades, and felt that he had betrayed Ireland. Eighteen months of planning might now be for naught. Consequently, they met at Liberty Hall in Dublin at 9:00 a.m. on Easter

Sunday morning. At this meeting, there was unanimous agreement that the rising should go ahead as planned, with or without the support of MacNeill. Due to his intervention, however, it would now be impossible to stage that Sunday. Instead, they decided to launch the insurrection the following day, on Easter Monday.

Without MacNeill in command, however, the I.R.B now had to take charge. The I.R.B's Military Council proposed that the headquarters be based at the General Post Office in Lower Sackville Street, an easily defended position, and that the rising begin with the reading of a proclamation declaring an Irish republic, read by the president of the provisional government of this Irish republic. The only problem with this plan was that there was no president. He would have to be appointed from within the Military Council. The post was first offered to Tom Clarke, but after he shunned it Patrick Pearse volunteered and was duly appointed. The Military Council then voted to amalgamate the Irish Volunteers, James Connelly's Citizen Army, the women's Cumann na mBan auxiliary force, and the boy scout Fianna organization to form the Army of the Irish Republic, to which Pearse was also appointed commandant general. With these appointments, the Irish Republic was formed, and a proclamation declaring such was written. At 8:00 p.m. that evening, Pearse sent dispatches with couriers to the Irish Volunteer leaders throughout the country, telling them, "We start operations at noon today, Monday, Carry out your instructions. P.H. Pearse."[134]

When Easter Monday dawned on Dublin, the city was quieter than usual, due to the religious holiday. The shops were shuttered, and the docks lay still. But then, quite suddenly, "the storm burst in Dublin," and the R.I.C. Inspector General reported to the Chief Secretary that "for the following six days the City and the suburbs were the scene of grave loss of life and destruction of property."[135] Pearse, as the appointed commandant general of the army and president of the provisional government, had gathered together his forces early that morning at Liberty Hall. At 11:45 a.m., the first contingent moved out to take Dublin Castle, City Hall, and the *Evening Mail* offices. A second group headed to St. Stephen's Green and the Royal College of Surgeons, a third to Boland's flour mills at the Grand Canal docks, and a fourth to the General Post Office on Lower Sackville Street.[136] The rising had begun.

Immediately, volunteers commandeered all buildings surrounding the post office, and I.R.B. snipers took up posts on the corner houses at the north end of Lower Sackville Street, below Parnell Square. Volunteers also took over the ammunition shop at the corner of Bachelor's Walk and the jewelry shop at the corner of Eden's quay on the River Liffey, and snipers positioned themselves appropriately. They similarly garrisoned the four corners of Abbey

Street, just to the south of the post office. Anyone who resisted these takeovers was immediately shot. Finally, the volunteers erected barricades throughout the area, and cut the telegraph wires. The north side of Dublin was now completed isolated from the rest of the country.[137]

Elsewhere in the city, volunteers erected similar fortifications. In St. Stephen's Green, they closed the gates and posted armed guards. Contingents from the Citizen Army seized notable buildings covering the approaches to the Green, including the Royal College of Surgeons at the corner of York Street and a public house at the corner of Cuffe Street. Snipers took up positions on the rooftops of each of these buildings. The contingent of volunteers that had gone to take control of Dublin Castle made it as far as the entrance to the Upper Castle Yard, where they shot dead a police constable. Soldiers stationed within the castle prevented the volunteers from gaining any further ground, however. The volunteers thus retreated and took control of several houses surrounding the castle. The volunteers also took the offices of the *Daily Express* and the *Evening Mail*, as well as City Hall, the Prisons Boards, and other central Dublin government offices. These building were all barricaded, with snipers placed on the rooftops. Further west along the river, the volunteers seized the Four Courts judicial building, together with the adjacent Four Courts Hotel. South of the Liffey, volunteers occupied Boland's Mill and seized various private houses along Northumberland Road, Pembroke Road, and Lansdowne Road; each of these roads was a main thoroughfare that would have to be used by any British reinforcements arriving at Kingstown port to the south of Dublin.

At each of these places, the volunteers promptly shot any police constable or other official who attempted to prevent them from seizing the buildings. Upon hearing the news that several of his men had been killed in this way, the Chief Commissioner of the D.M.P. ordered an immediate withdrawal from the streets of all his uniformed force. As a result, within two hours of the rising's start, the city had descended into anarchy, and looting became widespread. By evening time, criminal behavior had overrun much of central Dublin.[138] Yet the Inspector General had greater problems to deal with: the volunteers were now hunkered down in various buildings across the city. As the situation rapidly deteriorated, he sought help from higher powers.[139]

At the commencement of the rising, the Lord Lieutenant of Ireland, Ivor Churchill, Baron Wimborne, had issued a proclamation cautioning his subjects that "the sternest measures are being, and will be, taken for the prompt suppression of the existing disturbances," and further warning them "of the danger of unnecessarily frequenting the streets or public places, or of assembling in crowds."[140] It was to this man that Chamberlain turned on Monday evening, requesting his assistance in restoring order to Dublin. Consequently, the following day, April 25, Wimborne proclaimed martial law in the City and County of Dublin for one month. On April 29, the following Saturday, he expanded martial law throughout all Ireland for one month.[141] When the allotted month expired, on May 26, Wimborne extended the continuation of martial law "until further orders by the Lords Justices."[142]

On April 27, the Thursday of Easter week, Prime Minister Asquith wrote to King George V to explain Wimborne's actions. He informed him that as "the latest telegrams present some disquieting features, especially in indicating the spread of the rebellion movement outside Dublin," the cabinet had decided to proclaim martial law over the whole of Ireland. To administer this martial law, the cabinet ordered General Sir John Maxwell to leave for Ireland at once, and Asquith informed George V that "the Irish Executives are to place themselves at his [Maxwell's] disposal to carry out his instructions."[143]

Maxwell arrived in Dublin on the morning of Friday, April 28, at 2:00 a.m. Describing the scene in a letter to his wife, he wrote, "From the sea, it looked as if the entire city of Dublin was in flames, but when we got to [the] North Wall it was not quite so bad as that, yet a great deal of the part north of the Liffey was burning. Bullets were flying about, the crackle of musketry and machine-gun fire breaking out every other minute."[144] Upon arrival, Maxwell determined to treat the volunteers with the sternest measures, and he made it clear to the soldiers under his command that "all surrenders must be absolutely unconditional." Those who refused to surrender would be shot without mercy.[145]

In response to the Lord Lieutenant's proclamations of martial law, British troops began to arrive in Dublin from the Curragh barracks on the evening of Easter Monday, and large reinforcements from England were landed at Kingstown, just south of Dublin, the following day.[146] On Tuesday, April 26, the soldiers took several houses overlooking St. Stephen's Green, and for the remainder of the week they sprayed the Green with machine gun fire at regular intervals and sniped at any volunteer who showed himself. A contingent of soldiers also stormed the offices of the *Daily Express*, and although they took heavy casualties upon entering the building, they took it from the volunteers by nightfall. On Wednesday morning, the Royal Navy ship *Helga* sailed up the Liffey, from where it bombarded Liberty Hall. Later that afternoon, under cover from the naval bombardment, troops moved closer to Lower Sackville Street and took the buildings on the corner of Bachelor's Walk, just south of the General Post Office.[147]

At this point, on Wednesday afternoon, the British Army brought field artillery into the city. On Wednesday evening, they bombarded much of D'Olier Street, completely destroying Kelly's shop, on the corner of Bachelor's Walk. The following day, the bombardment continued and destroyed the

Hotel Metropole on Lower Sackville Street, together with much of Middle Abbey Street, including the offices of the *Freeman's Journal* and the *Evening Telegraph*. Finally, on Friday, April 28, the bombardment moved to the General Post Office itself. By the following morning, much of Lower Sackville Street had been laid bare. On the west side, flames engulfed the post office and many of the surrounding buildings as far north as Henry Street. On the east side, all buildings from the River Liffey north to Cathedral Street had been burned, and the fire extended east from Sackville Street, destroying all the houses between Eden Quay and Lower Abbey Street.[148]

On the afternoon of Saturday, April 29, with much of north Dublin in flames, Patrick Pearse finally surrendered his army. Whilst he was willing to sacrifice himself upon Ireland's altar, his conscience would not allow him to do the same to unwitting civilians. In order to prevent further destruction in the city and the continued loss of civilian life, he issued a declaration of unconditional surrender.[149] James Connolly and Thomas McDonagh, second and third in command respectively, issued similar declarations.[150] At 4:00 p.m., General Maxwell ordered a ceasefire. The remaining volunteers then surrendered their positions.[151]

Beyond Dublin City, the rising was carried out in a more limited fashion, although casualties still occurred.[152] On the night of Sunday, April 23, telegraph wires were cut in County Longford, a portion of the railway line was destroyed in Queen's County, and in County Dublin three men broke into the Selby Quarry magazine and stole some gelignite explosives, which they took to the headquarters of the Irish Citizen Army in Dublin. The following day, Easter Monday, a party of Irish Volunteers at Lurgan Green, County Louth, was informed by an Irish Volunteers' dispatch rider that the Irish Republic had been proclaimed in Dublin and that no British authority was to be recognized. They immediately arrested two R.I.C. constables and began commandeering passing motor cars in the name of the Irish Republic. In one such commandeered car, they drove with their R.I.C. prisoners to the village of Castlebellingham, where they stopped another passing car. Upon finding its occupant to be an army lieutenant in the Grenadier Guards, they forced him against some iron railings, together with one of their captured police constables, and shot them both, the constable falling mortally wounded. They then released their other prisoner and went in the lieutenant's car to Drogheda, leaving the constable's body where it lay.

That same day, the volunteers cut telegraph wires in County Kildare and a party of 14 Irish Volunteers surrounded a police patrol, threatening to shoot them if they intervened in the rising. They then marched to Dublin. In the East Riding of County Galway, Irish Volunteers took over the Athenry Town Hall, which they quickly converted to a bomb-making factory.

In County Waterford, the volunteers derailed a military train carrying ammunition to Dublin, and in County Dublin itself, they rigged the bridge of the Great Northern Line with explosives, although they failed to detonate.

On April 25, Easter Tuesday, the Irish Volunteers destroyed the railway line between Galway and Oranmore, as well as the bridge in Oranmore, and cut telegraph wires in the town. Five police constables were taken prisoner whilst attempting to stop this sabotage. The volunteers then mounted an armed assault on the police barracks at Clarenbridge. When they failed to gain entry, they withdrew from Clarenbridge back to Oranmore, where they were joined by other Irish Volunteers. Together, this band of 200 volunteers attacked the police barracks; the assault continued throughout the day until a police relief party arrived from Galway that evening and forced the volunteers to leave.

Also that evening, the volunteers who had taken over Athenry Town Hall moved from the town to the Department of Agriculture's farm just beyond the town. In the early hours of April 26, a party of 23 R.I.C. constables under the command of the Galway City district inspector, together with 10 soldiers, left Galway to reconnoiter the situation at the agricultural farm. At 4:15 a.m., they encountered a band of 80 Irish Volunteers at Carnmore cross roads. A firefight developed between the two, resulting in the death of one police constable. Following this, the R.I.C. retreated to protect Galway City against any potential attack. The volunteers at the farm then moved to Moyode Castle, near Athenry. On April 27, they were joined by a contingent of volunteers from Galway's West Riding, together with five police prisoners. They stayed at the castle until April 29, when a large force of police and military arrived at Loughres, only a few miles away. By now aware that the rising had no hope of success, the volunteers dispersed, leaving the prisoners bound and gagged, where the R.I.C. found them later that day.

Meanwhile, the volunteers attacked the R.I.C. barracks at both Swords and Donabate in County Dublin on April 26. Following the death of one R.I.C. constable, both barracks surrendered and the remaining police personnel were taken prisoner, later to be released. The volunteers moved on from Swords and Donabate and raided the R.I.C. barracks at Garristown on April 27, forcing the police to withdraw. They then marched to Howth, hoping to cut the English cable there, but seeing that it was protected by a contingent of 20 soldiers and 8 police officers, they turned west. On April 28, they attacked the police barracks at Ashbourne in County Meath.

By this time, this Irish Volunteer contingent numbered 400 men. The Meath county inspector, together with his district inspector and 54 other R.I.C. sergeants and constables, left the county seat at Navan in motor cars to engage these volunteers. A vicious fire fight ensued, lasting just over five hours, before the police were forced to surrender, having expended all their ammunition. At the end of the battle, one sergeant and six constables had been killed and the county inspector and fourteen more constables had been severely injured. Upon surrender, the surviving men were disarmed and released. The volunteers remained in County Meath for two more days before dispersing throughout the countryside. On April 30, a military force arrived and surrounded the 32 volunteers who remained, forcing them to surrender.

Similar actions took place elsewhere in the country. In County Louth, 12 miles from the county seat at Dundalk, the Irish Volunteers took command of a small village on April 28, but disbanded on April 30. At Ballindadee in West Cork, the volunteers kidnapped an R.I.C. sergeant on April 30. They subsequently released him, but threatened that he would be shot if he was ever seen in the county again. Finally, at Enniscorthy in County Wexford, the volunteers took over the town on April 27, cutting the telegraph lines and besieging the police barracks and post office. In contrast to County Dublin, the volunteers were unable to take the Enniscorthy barracks, and after five days the constables within its walls were relieved by the military. At that time, on May 1, the Enniscorthy volunteers surrendered, becoming the last in the country to do so. With their surrender, the rebellion officially came to an end.

In all, the Easter Rising cost the lives of 116 British Army soldiers and officers, 13 members of the R.I.C., and 3 members of the D.M.P. A further 368 soldiers, 22 R.I.C., and 7 D.M.P. were severely wounded. The Irish Volunteers also suffered casualties, and a combination of 318 insurgents and civilians were killed and 2,217 injured (the government when compiling these statistics did not differentiate between those who were actively rebelling and those who were innocent bystanders).[153] It had been a disastrous week for the British security forces.

The immediate aftermath of the rising was a frightful sight. In addition to the loss of life throughout the country, property in Dublin City had been severely damaged, much of the city center smashed by the artillery bombardment. The Chief of the Dublin Fire Brigade reported that over 200 buildings had been destroyed during the rising, and estimated the value of all that had been destroyed to be in the region of £2,500,000.[154] The *Irish Times* reported that when residents of the city emerged from hiding, they appeared "as if spellbound" when viewing "the wreck of their once fine city":

> Here and there a cloud of smoke rose from a smoldering ruin. Only a few blackened walls remained of the whole range of business houses on one side of the street between Nelson's Pillar and O'Connell Bridge. On the other side of the street only the walls of the General Post Office remained, and the Hotel Metropole was gone.[155]

Most in Dublin at first placed the blame for this damage at the feet of the Irish Volunteers; as those arrested were escorted through the city they were spat upon and heckled. Many of those who jeered had sons, brothers, or husbands in France serving in the British Army, and they waved Union Jacks at the passing volunteers and encouraged the soldiers guarding them to carry out summary justice.[156] One British officer in charge, so concerned about the safety of the prisoners, ordered pickets to be set up with bayonets fixed to keep back the crowds, and one Irish Volunteer believed that "if military protection had been withdrawn there would have been no need for the subsequent courts-martial." Another, who had fought at the General Post Office, later recalled, "Dublin's worst was let loose, the women being the worst. They looked like a few who were around during the French Revolution. . . . The women were allowed to follow the men to the barracks shouting to the soldiers, 'Use your rifles on the German so and sos.' " For one volunteer, it was the first time in his life that he "ever appreciated British troops as they undoubtedly saved us from being manhandled that evening."[157]

Despite this initial burst of revulsion, however, the security measures enacted in the days and weeks following the rising soon came to be seen by Dubliners and those elsewhere in Ireland as unnecessarily repressive. Consequently, the tide of public opinion slowly turned away from the government in favor of the Irish Volunteers. Beginning on April 30, the British Army, R.I.C., and D.M.P. conducted a systematic house-to-house search of Dublin, clearing out the remaining Irish Volunteers. Then, on May 2, General Maxwell ordered those who had been involved in the rebellion outside Dublin to surrender their arms before May 6.[158] When the order was not obeyed, mobile columns of troops searched for arms throughout the country, each column composed of two companies of infantry, a squadron of cavalry, one 18-pounder gun, and an armored car.[159] In all, 1,244 rifles, 1,262 shot guns, and 307 revolvers were found and seized.[160]

In both Dublin and the countryside, "dangerous Sinn Feiners and men who were known to have taken an active part in the rising" were arrested. In all, 3,420 men and 79 women were captured; of these, however, 1,424 men and 73 women were later released, found to be innocent after further inquiries.[161] For those who remained, courts-martial began immediately. One hundred and sixty-nine men and 1 woman were convicted of a crime, 11 men were acquitted, and the remainder of the prisoners, 1,836 men and 5 women, were deported to England to be interned without trial. Of the 170 convicted, 90 were sentenced to death by firing squad.[162] In explaining these measures to Asquith, Maxwell wrote,

In view of the gravity of the Rebellion and its connection with German intrigue and propaganda and in view of the great loss of life and destruction of property resulting therefrom, the General Officer Commanding in Chief Irish Command, has found it imperative to inflict the most severe sentences on the organizers of this detestable Rising and on the Commanders who took an actual part in the actual fighting which occurred. It is hoped that these examples will be sufficient to act as a deterrent to intriguers and to bring home to them that the murder of His Majesty's subjects or other acts calculated to imperil the safety of the realm will not be tolerated.[163]

The executions began on May 3, with Patrick Pearse, Tom Clarke, and Thomas McDonagh all shot by firing squad. These men were followed by Joseph Plunkett, Edward Daly, William Pearse, and Michael O'Hanrahan on May 4, and John MacBride on May 5.[164] The following day, Asquith summoned Maxwell to London and brought him before the cabinet, where he was ordered not to execute any women, as public opinion would not stand for it. The general agreed, and the only woman so sentenced, Countess Constance Markievicz, had her sentence commuted to life imprisonment.[165] On May 8, the executions of men continued with the shooting of Eamonn Kent, Michael Mallin, Con Colbert, and Sean Heuston. On May 9, Thomas Kent was shot (in Cork rather than Dublin), and on May 12, Sean MacDermott and James Connolly were shot.[166] That evening, Asquith, concerned that further killing would only serve to worsen public opinion, traveled to Dublin to meet with the remaining prisoners and discuss their fate with Maxwell.[167] Following their conversation, the remaining 75 men due to die had their sentences commuted to various terms of penal servitude. Amongst these men was Eamon de Valera, who was scheduled to be shot sometime after Connolly.[168]

Despite these reprieves, the Irish public developed an increasingly negative view of the British government. In a secret report sent to the Chief Secretary's Office on June 15, R.I.C. Inspector General Chamberlain stated that although during Easter Week the National Volunteers had "showed no sympathy with the rising and were relieved and gratified when it was known that the rebels had surrendered," as time passed and security measures were enacted "a reaction of feeling became noticeable." In particular, "[r]esentment was aroused by the number of persons punished by Courts Martial and by the great number of those arrested and deported." As a result, "many Nationalists who at first condemned the rising and those who took part in it have changed their attitude towards the latter and now consider that unnecessary severity is being used."[169]

Chamberlain cautioned that although a further rising seemed "improbable" in the immediate future unless supported by German arms, the volunteers were "by no means cowed." Indeed, in his opinion, the "feeling worked up in America over the executions," together with the "sympathy aroused in Ireland," was "likely to keep the movement together." He closed his report with an ominous warning:

> The Irish Volunteers have shown what terrible destruction of life and property can be caused by three or four thousand half-trained men with firearms, and I once more urgently invite [the] Government to seriously consider the question of the continued existence of these armed Volunteer Forces in Ireland. Until they are disarmed, or placed under War Office control, there will be no security or peace, and it will always be necessary to retain large bodies of military in the country.[170]

As during the period of overt militancy, however, the government chose to ignore the Inspector General's warnings. Chamberlain reported once more, on July 15, stating clearly that Ireland was in "an unsettled condition" and that since the executions and internments, "a wave of resentment [has] sprung up and spread rapidly through the Nationalist population. . . . Public sympathy has been stimulated by the sale of photographs of the rebel leaders, and letters written by some of them on the eve of execution, together with mourning badges of green and black ribbon." He warned the government, once again, that the "very large number of arms still at the disposal of these Volunteer Forces in the present unsettled state of Ireland constitutes a grave danger to which I have again to invite the serious attention of Government."[171]

His words fell on deaf ears. Upon reading his report, the assistant under secretary, Edward O'Farrell, noted to the under secretary that the situation in Ireland was "not unsatisfactory." He admitted that although there was "much unrest," it was "not more than is to be expected following the Rebellion," and he made the by now ridiculous claim that without a German landing there was "no probability of any open attempt at insurrection." Finally, he suggested that in time, "ordinary political parties will form themselves and it is to be hoped give healthy outlets for the people's feelings."[172] The government apparently agreed with O'Farrell, and no new provisions were enacted to confiscate the volunteers' arms or to prevent them from further drill.

Following such disregard for his advice, and after four years of sound guidance ignored by the British government, Inspector General Chamberlain resigned. His successor, General Joseph Byrne, submitted his first report on August 14. In it, the new Inspector General informed the government that Ireland was still "restless" and that "owing to the very unsettled condition of the country it would, I submit, be unsafe either to relax military control which has a salutary effect without inconveniencing any law abiding citizen, or to withdraw any troops."[173] Like his predecessor, however, his advice was ignored. Within a few months, martial law had been revoked, all internees had been released and returned to Ireland, and, in the words of historian Eunan O'Halpin, "the old system of Irish government was restored in all its imperfection."[174] Despite the grave failures that had occurred during both the period of overt militancy and the period of clandestine organization, the British government had learned very little. It continued to operate as before.

A Failure of Imagination

Following the rising, Birrell resigned immediately. In a letter to his private secretary, Andrew Magill, he remarked, "It has been a melancholy ending of a once cheerful song, and though personally I am out of the bog on to the dull high road, I wonder that I endured the quagmire and insincerity of the whole position."[175] On the day of his resignation, May 1, he telegraphed Under Secretary Nathan from London, telling him, "P.M. thinks you must share my fate." Nathan followed his master's will, and resigned on May 3.[176] In his letter to Magill, Birrell noted that his only regret was for his entourage, "that they should have fallen with me and retired without letters after their name."[177]

General Maxwell was pleased to see the two men go. In a letter to his wife on May 4, he wrote, "It is the government as a whole that are to blame. Ever since they winked at Ulster breaking the law they have been in difficulties and have hoped and hoped that something would turn up. . . . Wait and see. Well, we waited and now see the result, viz rebellion and loss of life."[178] During the period of overt militancy, from 1912 to 1914, it was Birrell and his under secretary who had pursued this "wait and see" policy. Once the war on the European continent erupted, they continued to wait, but for the wrong thing; they waited for a German invasion that would never come. In so doing, they failed to see the insurgency that was developing within.

Despite Birrell's resignation and Maxwell's judgment, the blame for the rising cannot be laid solely at the feet of the British government. In contrast to the government's actions during the Ulster crisis of two years before, its behavior during the Easter Rising was dictated not by negligence but by ignorance. What is striking about the period of clandestine organization is not the inadequacy of the government but rather the lack of police intelligence. Compared with the intimately detailed files that were collated about the Ulster Volunteer Force, very little was sent to the Chief Secretary's Office concerning the Irish Volunteers and, in particular, the I.R.B. When the rising began on Easter Monday, therefore, Birrell did not have the knowledge necessary to adequately deal with the threat. As a result, Dublin was catapulted into a state of anarchy and, ultimately, martial law, from which it would never fully recover.

As with the period of overt militancy, the British government suffered a failure of intelligence during the period of clandestine organization. In the latter case, however, it was not a failure of government to act on the intelligence received but rather a failure of imagination by those tasked with collecting the intelligence and assessing the security situation in Ireland. The police were, quite frankly, not expecting an assault on the state from the I.R.B. They did not, therefore, look for any evidence that one was forthcoming. Instead, they focused their efforts on assessing Irish opinion towards the British war effort. They did so with a compulsion that size and strength mattered more than intent; thus they tended to view the larger National Volunteers as loyal and representative of the Irish nation as a whole, and the smaller Irish Volunteers as disloyal but insignificant.

Had the British government taken the Irish Volunteer leaders at their word and prevented the movement from conducting armed drilling and military practice, the rising might have been prevented. As it happened, however, nothing was done to forestall an insurrection and thus, when it came, repressive measures had to be enacted to stop it from spreading and to punish those involved. Such measures quickly added to the numbers who supported the rebelling volunteers. Just as the growth of the Ulster Volunteer Force had led directly to the founding of the Irish Volunteers in 1913 and the eventual Easter Rising in 1916, so would the response to that rising lead to a strengthening of the insurgents. The period of clandestine organization had come to an end with the advent of martial law in April 1916, but the British government was not out of harm's way. The period of guerilla war was soon to begin, and with it, the threat posed by the Irish nationalists only increased.

PART III

The Period of Guerrilla War, 1916–1921

Business as Usual

On July 31, 1916, Henry Edward Duke was named Chief Secretary of Ireland. His appointment came after a three-month period of martial law, during which there had been neither Chief Secretary nor Lord Lieutenant; General John Maxwell had acted as a military governor of sorts, installing himself in Dublin Castle at the head of the Irish administration.[1] Duke was not Asquith's first choice for Chief Secretary. Indeed, the Prime Minister had consulted with a number of other men before finally settling on Duke. He first asked E.S. Montagu, who refused to take the position because of "his own Jewish race, his lack of physical courage, and [his lack of] interest in the Irish race." Next the post was offered to John Allsebrook Simon, followed by the prominent unionists F.E. Smith, George Cave (serving at that time as Home Secretary), and Walter Long. They too refused, so Asquith asked David Lloyd George, but he declined also. The Prime Minister therefore turned to his seventh choice and offered him the position, an appointment the latter readily accepted.[2]

For Duke, the office of Chief Secretary was a distinct step forward in his otherwise lackluster political career.[3] A 61-year-old barrister, he had been a Conservative Member of Parliament since 1900, but had never held a ministerial post nor had he ever been a member of the cabinet. This was, therefore, his first foray into government. Irish Nationalist M.P.s immediately objected to his appointment, citing his political affiliations to unionism. On August 9, therefore, Asquith reinstated the resigned Lord Wimborne as Lord Lieutenant, a man who had publicly stated his commitment to Irish Home Rule.[4]

Shortly after Wimborne's reappointment, Sir William Byrne was named under secretary.[5] A 57-year-old Englishman, Byrne had been an assistant under secretary at the Home Office and was considered a compromise choice between unionists and nationalists.[6] He was a Catholic, but had never publicly advocated Irish Home Rule. Furthermore, he had worked in various aspects of administering the law in Britain for over 40 years, and he was considered a competent bureaucrat who would not be swayed one way or the other by the political passions in Ireland.[7]

The Inspector General of the Royal Irish Constabulary (R.I.C.), too, was new. Following Chamberlain's resignation in July, General Joseph Byrne had been appointed to the position (no relation to the under secretary, William Byrne). Joseph Byrne had served on General Maxwell's staff during the Easter Rising and thus had a reputation amongst unionists for being tough on political rebellion. He was also an Irish-born Roman Catholic, however, and thus acceptable to nationalists.[8] All three men, Duke, William Byrne, and Joseph Byrne, had been absent from Irish administration during both the period of overt militancy and the period of clandestine organization (General Byrne had seen the latter as a soldier only, not a civil servant). They had not, therefore, received the detailed police intelligence reports concerning the Ulster Volunteer Force, nor were they aware of the growing support for Sinn Fein and the I.R.B. that had been documented by Chamberlain for Birrell throughout 1915 and the early part of 1916. Consequently, as an administration they were unaware of how grave the situation in Ireland had become.

Upon accepting the post, Duke was faced with an unenviable task. R.I.C. Deputy Inspector General O'Connell, writing on behalf of Byrne, reported in September that the "bitter hostility towards England stirred up in Nationalist circles since the rebellion shows little if any sign of abatement." He also stated that a "discontented and rebellious spirit" had become widespread and that there was a general feeling "that one week of physical force did more for the cause of Ireland than a quarter of a century of Constitutional agitation." O'Connell concluded by warning that there were rumors of another "imminent" rising, and that although the police had "not observed any active preparations for an immediate outbreak," the possibility was still great, as "the rebels in the provinces have had no experience of the horrors of Easter Week in Dublin to deter them."[9]

The following month, in October, O'Connell told the Chief Secretary that "political unrest is probably more extensive in Ireland at present than at the time of the rebellion." He believed that the executions, imprisonments, and internments that had followed the rising had evoked within more moderate nationalists considerable sympathy for the separatist cause, and he suggested that many supporters of John Redmond had seen their confidence shaken, now becoming doubtful that Home Rule would come into operation at the close of the war as promised by legislation.[10] In December, Inspector General Byrne himself informed Duke that although the country was "outwardly calm," there was nevertheless a "widespread spirit of political unrest in a more or less suppressed state which affects all classes." On the whole, he concluded, there was "no marked improvement in the restless condition of the provinces" compared to how they had been prior to the uprising in April.[11]

Despite the Inspector General's warnings, Duke was reticent to crack down on the separatists. He was well aware that he had to consider the political ramifications when choosing which policy to adopt, and although the police would have preferred a hard-line stance against those who would spurn British rule, the moderate Irish nationalists, who still held a majority in Ireland (both in terms of parliamentary seats and population), were staunchly opposed to such a position. Furthermore, there were still over a thousand Irish internees held without charge in England's jails, and although this was perfectly legal under the martial law proclaimed by Lord Wimborne in April, it only served to further lower the standing of the British government in the eyes of the Catholic population. To help alleviate this situation, therefore, Duke established a review process under Justice John Sankey to consider each individual internee's case. By October, over half had been released after careful examination proved their innocence. In November, the political will to continue in-depth review of the remaining 600 prisoners dissipated, and the process for release was accelerated. Investigations were shortened, and internees were returned to Ireland following far less scrutiny than had originally been called for by Duke.[12]

Whilst this was happening, David Lloyd George succeeded Asquith as Prime Minister. Born in 1863, Lloyd George had entered Parliament as a Conservative in 1890, winning his seat by only 18 votes but holding it until 1945. He had risen through the parliamentary ranks rapidly, becoming President of the Board of Trade in 1905, Chancellor of the Exchequer in 1908, Minister of Munitions in 1915, and Secretary of State for War on July 6, 1916.[13] Under his guidance as Prime Minister, in December the cabinet decided to revoke martial law and release all internees by Christmas of that year "as an act of grace and reconciliation."[14] The guilty were freed along with the innocent, and the Sinn Fein and I.R.B. members who had been interned were returned to Dublin to continue agitating for an independent Irish republic. Those who had been sentenced, convicted, and imprisoned for life were freed the following June.[15]

This government complacency towards any threat of internal Irish insurgency was mirrored by the military, despite the very real peril that had emerged during Easter week and was shown to continue in the police reports. In November 1916, Major Ivor Price, the police intelligence liaison officer, submitted to both the Chief Secretary and the R.I.C. Inspector General copies of reports compiled by the military intelligence officers in the northern, midland, and southern districts of Ireland. Price had been an R.I.C. district inspector in the prewar period, but at the outbreak of hostilities with Germany he had been attached to the staff of the army commander in Ireland and had been given the rank of major. His job was to consolidate all intelligence reports received from the R.I.C., D.M.P. (Dublin Metropolitan Police), and postal service and to coordinate this intelligence in the event of a German invasion. In practice, he had become something more than a mere collator of intelligence and, in time, assumed the role of intelligence advisor to the Chief Secretary. He continued in this position until the end of the war, at which time he returned to his regular duties in the R.I.C.[16] In September 1916, after two years as the principle intelligence officer for the Irish police forces, he had requested that summaries be prepared by each of the relevant military intelligence officers to appraise the security situation in Ireland. These he submitted to the Chief Secretary in early November.

Captain G. Whitfield, intelligence officer for the northern district, stated that whilst there was "undoubtedly a feeling of bitter hostility to the British Government," a sentiment that "appears to be widespread," a "good deal" of this feeling was "due to a kind of sentimental tradition." In time, he suspected, it would "probably wither away, if treated carefully and firmly." Illegal military drilling had been conducted in County Tyrone, but this was "probably done for bravado more than anything else." In the north of the country, there were no signs to suggest that another uprising was imminent.[17] Similar confidence was displayed by Major F.C. Burke, intelligence officer for the midland district and Connaught. There was "no real discontent" in his region; unless, of course, he was to include "political" discontent. In that case, there was great unrest, the reason being "that Home Rule is not in operation, that the country is not governed by Irishmen, and that it should be thought necessary to keep Martial Law in existence." That, however, did not seem reason enough to suggest cause for an insurgency. All things considered, Burke concluded, the "presence of the military and rapid dispersal of all armed bodies in the past rebellion have put an end to all hope of success by armed opposition in the future and the extremists recognize this."[18] Captain T.W. Dickie of the southern district concurred with his two colleagues, stating that his area was "very quiet and no disturbance is anticipated."[19]

Upon reading these reports, on December 7, Under Secretary Byrne scribbled a memorandum to his assistant, saying, "I understand that the reports of military intelligence officers are received occasionally only and not systematically, and that consequently they are not circulated among the Civil Executive and recorded and filed. They seem to me to be a useful supplement to the Monthly reports of the C[ounty] I[nspector]'s, and worthy of our perusal."[20] The assistant under secretary, Edward O'Farrell, agreed, and on December 11, he forwarded a note to Byrne that read, "This matter has been arranged."[21] From that month forth, and until August 1918, summaries from the military intelligence officers were sent to the Chief Secretary alongside the Inspector General's reports, providing for the government an overview of the situation in Ireland from the perspective of both the military and the civil authorities.

At the end of 1916, these military reports, in stark contrast to those of the Inspector General, suggested that the situation in Ireland was improving. Captain Dickie in his December summary wrote that his part of the country was "quieter than it has been for some time past,"[22] and Captain Whitfield stated that his area was "peaceful."[23] Major Burke reported that whilst "public feeling cannot be said to be loyal" to the British war effort and the people were interested solely in "making money, amusing themselves at football, coursing and race meetings," there had been "no serious acts of disloyalty or sedition." As in the other two districts, he reported no signs of any large-scale discontent, nor any indication that a rising such as had occurred at Easter would take place again.[24] The military intelligence officers thus provided a quite different analysis from the police assertion that "political unrest is probably more extensive in Ireland at present than at the time of the rebellion."

As the tumultuous year of 1916 closed, then, there was a split of opinion within the intelligence community. The military, which had not been present in Ireland in large numbers prior to the Easter Rising and thus had not followed in detail the events leading up to that rising, believed that the country was calm, and would remain so in the future. The police, in contrast, were concerned at a continuation of the discontent that had been present before April 1916, and they feared that the Irish separatists' desire for an independent Irish republic, established by force, had been merely postponed, not eradicated. Faced with these two analyses, the British government, hoping against hope for peace in Ireland, chose to pursue the course of least resistance and accept as true the military reports, believing that by appeasing those who had rebelled, they would be able to prevent another uprising in the future. Thus the Chief Secretary was content to view Irish separatists not as a potential threat to the peace and security of Ireland, but rather as a merely political force that was engaging in constitutional activities.

Such refusal by the government to see anything other than calm in Ireland is troubling, although not unexplainable. In the summer, autumn, and winter months of 1916 the situation in France was worsening. Although the British had won the naval battle at Jutland on May 31, on July 1 the offensive at the Somme began, with 57,000 British casualties on the first day alone—the most losses suffered on a single day by any army during the entire war, and the bloodiest day in British military history.[25] On September 15, the British launched a renewed offensive on the Somme, which lasted until mid-November. By the end of this campaign, coming just weeks before Lloyd George's assent to the premiership, British casualties had reached 420,000.[26] The 132 soldiers and policemen killed in Dublin during the Easter Rising six months earlier paled in comparison. In the face of the Somme, all other problems confronting the British government seemed trivial.

What the government did not realize, however, was that the 600 Irish internees who Lloyd George released in December and the 125 convicted prisoners who would be released the following June had used their time behind bars to foment a political strategy for defeating the British in Ireland, coming in time to refer to their prisons as "nurseries" and "universities" of revolution.[27] The guards at these prisons, "relieved to be dealing with decent rebels instead of common criminals," allowed the internees and convicted prisoners to associate with each other openly, to receive unlimited amounts of uncensored reading material from Ireland, to establish Irish-language and history classes, and to play Irish sports. Within this setting, a "revolutionary elite" developed, who devised a new philosophy of rebellion. Upon release, these Irish separatists planned not only to use violence to achieve their aims of a fully independent Irish republic, but also to work from within the British system of government, where they hoped to create a moral high ground from which to defeat the British.[28] When these men returned to Ireland, therefore, just before Christmas 1916, the brief period of tranquility that the military claimed had followed the rising was soon to be shattered.

A New Kind of Politics

The year 1917 proved to be a watershed for the British position in Ireland. That year, in parliamentary elections across the country, Sinn Fein candidates stood for office and won, becoming the first Irish separatist Members of Parliament in British constitutional history. The first of these elections occurred in early February, in County Roscommon. Count George Noble Plunkett, father of Joseph Plunkett (one of the 16 executed in the aftermath of the Easter Rising), won a byelection caused by the sudden death of the sitting member.[29] In so doing, he defeated the Nationalist candidate and favorite to win, T.J. Devine. County Roscommon had long been in the hands of the Nationalist Party and its predecessor the Irish Home Rule Party, the latter first taking the seat from the Irish Liberals in the 1870s. Thus, the defeat of Devine by an outspoken and avowedly republican candidate was all the more startling.[30]

Plunkett had himself been arrested after the Easter Rising and deported to England for internment, largely on account of the role played by his sons in the rebellion. In addition to the executed Joseph, his two other sons had been tried by courts-martial and were at that time serving life sentences in English prisons. Although his own involvement in the rising had been limited, Plunkett had been ostracized from mainstream Irish society upon internment, forced to resign both his presidency of the National Museum and his membership of the Royal Dublin Society. He was released only following Lloyd George's Christmas pardon, and upon announcement of the byelection in County Roscommon, he immediately put his name forward as an independent candidate.[31]

Despite his internment and ostracism from middle-class Ireland, Plunkett was able to generate great support amongst the Roman Catholic clergy, as the Pope had previously conferred upon him the title Count of the Holy Roman Empire. In the rural constituency of North Roscommon, such support was more important than the blessing of Nationalist politicians in Dublin. Thus, Plunkett was also able to gain the backing of the large Catholic peasantry.[32] Due to the prominent role of his sons in the rising, Plunkett had the approval of Sinn Fein too. Even though he was not officially their candidate, they did not nominate anyone from their party to stand against him. As such, he gained the unanimous support of Irish separatists throughout the county.[33] With this combination of Catholic, peasant, and separatist backing, Plunkett was able to overcome the traditionally moderate sentiment of the county and defeat the Nationalist candidate by a large margin, 3,022 votes to 1,702.[34] Upon winning the election, however, he refused to take up his seat at Westminster, claiming not to recognize the authority of the British government over Ireland.[35] The Sinn Fein Party, which Plunkett soon joined, adopted this policy of abstention as its own.

Following the election, Inspector General Byrne wrote to the Chief Secretary, warning him that although nationalists in general seemed to continue their support for Redmond's Irish Nationalist Party, County Roscommon was "not a Sinn Fein stronghold." This showed, Byrne believed, that "in the political unrest affecting the community at present, much reliance cannot be placed on their allegiance to Mr. Redmond." He warned Duke that the Catholic clergy, ever influential in Irish society, "to a regrettable extent show sympathy with Sinn Fein," and expressed his belief that many of the younger clergymen "cannot be regarded otherwise than as Sinn Feiners." Because of these clergymen's "immense influence over the youth in their parishes," Byrne feared that "disaffection will be dangerously spread." The only relief he felt was that those sentenced to death (who had their sentences commuted) and those sentenced to penal servitude for life were still imprisoned in England and had not been released following the Prime Minister's pardon. They could thus not bring to bear their influence in combination with the clergy. If these prisoners were released, Byrne cautioned, the spread of separatist sentiment would be hard to contain. Of course, his warnings were ignored in June, when these very prisoners were released and their crimes forgiven.[36]

The military intelligence officers, too, were alarmed at the February election. Casting aside his previous optimism, Captain Dickie of the southern district (which included County Roscommon) reported that the election of Count Plunkett was popular throughout the district and provided "striking evidence of the strength of the Extremist movement." The nationalist population all through the county, he claimed, now identified itself "with the Sinn Fein policy as opposed to the constitutional movement."[37] Captain Whitfield also reported that Plunkett's victory had led to "an increase in Sinn Feinism," and he warned that there had been "a large number of cases of carrying arms, generally guns, without a permit."[38] Major Burke provided perhaps the starkest report, expressing his belief that "were a General Election to take place, the Sinn Fein candidates would be returned in most constituencies in Connaught, and candidates would be seen in practically all the Counties in this district." These candidates, he stated, would all be "anti-recruiting, anti-military service, [and] anti-British."[39] Sinn Fein, it seemed, was succeeding in its strategy of political agitation.

No more elections were held until May, so Burke's predictions of further Sinn Fein electoral success could not be proven. The Sinn Fein Party, however, continued to gather strength throughout the late winter months. In a report written at the end of February, Byrne stated that political unrest continued "to spread and menace the public peace," and that the Irish Volunteers and Sinn Fein Party "still cherish[ed] the belief that they will be able to effect a fresh rising and overthrow British Government in Ireland." He reported that although "the released rebel prisoners were generally quiet," they had given "no indication of a more loyal spirit; on the contrary they are suspected to be secretly promoting sedition, and it is known that several of them who had been Volunteer organizers before internment, resumed their seditious practices directly [when] they were released."[40] In March and April, the political situation remained tense, with "no indication of an improved spirit" in Sinn Fein. Those involved in the Irish Volunteers, Byrne reported, were still "bitterly disloyal and hostile to British rule," and there was "no abatement of political discontent."[41] This was confirmed by the military intelligence officers, who reported that the Irish Volunteers continued in their "organizing and propaganda work" and met in small groups where "instruction is often given in musketry [and the] use of explosives."[42]

At the end of April, the increased strength of Sinn Fein was put to the test when the Nationalist Member of Parliament for South Longford unexpectedly passed away, forcing a byelection to be held in May. With the announcement of the byelection, the police reported that the county was "flood[ed] . . . with Sinn Feiners and other extremists from all parts of Ireland." This, Byrne claimed, had the desired effect, and he reported that the people of the county, "hitherto quiet and law-abiding, became Sinn Feiners, and more or less disloyal."[43]

The Irish Nationalist Party was confident of victory. Their candidate, Patrick McKenna, was a local businessman, well known to the voters in the county. He was supported by the parliamentary establishment in Dublin and London, with John Redmond and 18 other Members of Parliament campaigning throughout the county on his behalf.[44] In contrast, the Sinn Fein candidate, Joseph McGuiness, had been sentenced by court-martial following the Easter Rising and was, whilst the election was being held, still imprisoned in England. He was thus unknown to the voters and could not be seen by the public.[45] Furthermore, the constituency was one of the Nationalist Party's safest seats, in their hands since the 1870s.[46]

Nevertheless, McGuiness had campaigning on his behalf the recently elected Count Plunkett, winner of another Nationalist safe seat, who in the two months since his victory had established himself as a prominent voice in the movement for Irish independence. In March, he had called for a National Convention to be held on April 19 in Dublin's Mansion House, where 70 local authorities across the country were invited to send representatives. His premise in calling such a meeting was that the British government had no right to hold elections in Ireland as they were foreign occupiers, and that the Irish should themselves establish a government independent of Westminster.[47] The convention met as planned on April 19, and on that date Plunkett and his fellow separatists formed the Sinn Fein National Council, which "denied the right of any foreign parliament to make laws for Ireland."[48] When the South Longford constituency came vacant several days later, the newly formed National Council decided to continue Plunkett's stance of abstention, nominating the imprisoned McGuiness as their candidate but pledging that he would not take up his seat if elected.

Plunkett traveled to Longford shortly thereafter, and on April 29, he declared to a crowd,

I did not come here specially to speak on behalf of Joe McGuiness, but on behalf of the cause which Joe McGuiness represents. My son was shot in

Dublin, and my other sons are now in Lewes prison with Joe McGuiness, because of their fight for Ireland in Easter Week. I myself was arrested, and my house robbed of a thousand pounds worth of property by the military. I was taken to England and thrown into an English prison with Joe McGuiness, until the men of Roscommon, by electing me as their representative opened the prison doors [sic]. The followers of Mr. Redmond claim to be Constitutionalists, but what Constitution do they serve? The British Constitution. The Constitution we serve is the Irish Constitution.[49]

Plunkett repeated his claims throughout the campaign, telling voters that the Irish Nationalist Party stood for "the Union Jack, Foreign Tyranny, and Irish oppression," while Sinn Fein stood for "Ireland and Irish freedom."[50] It was a message that apparently convinced the voters of South Longford. When the electoral results were declared on May 10, McGuiness won by 37 votes.[51]

Following his victory, Plunkett spoke on McGuiness' behalf: "The first blow for separation was struck in Easter week last year; the second in North Roscommon, a few months ago, and the third in Longford today. This is a nation's victory—the victory of the Irish nation over her one enemy nation—England. . . . We stand to-day for Sovereign Independence and complete separation, and that we must have."[52] Fearful of the attention Plunkett's rhetoric was generating, and aware that McGuiness' imprisonment was granting him a status beyond other elected candidates, the British government decided to grant him clemency. Upon his release from prison, McGuiness refused to take up his seat at Westminster as promised. The police stated that across Ireland, people responded to McGuiness' release with public displays of the Sinn Fein flag in city streets and private residences, and they reported that in the counties of Cork, Kerry, Limerick, Meath, Queen's, Sligo, Tipperary, and Wexford, there were "seditious and turbulent demonstrations" in which "the Police were attacked."[53]

On June 7, almost a month after this victory, John Redmond's brother, Major William Redmond, the sitting Member of Parliament for East Clare, was killed at the Battle of Messines in France, necessitating the third byelection of the year.[54] Seven days later, on June 14, the British government granted amnesty to the remaining prisoners convicted after the 1916 rising, and restrictions placed on the travel of certain Sinn Fein suspects within Ireland were removed.[55] This was done in part because of a "slight mutiny" that had taken place amongst the Irish prisoners at Lewes Prison, a mutiny that the government did not wish to evolve into a place of moral high ground from which the Irish separatists could work, and in part to prevent Sinn Fein from nominating another imprisoned candidate in the upcoming byelection.[56]

Such reasoning was strange; after all, mutinies are seldom rewarded with concessions, particularly when such concessions include the release of convicted murderers and insurgents. Besides, many political observers believed that replacing William Redmond with another Irish Nationalist Party candidate would be a simple affair, and thus the government did not have to worry about any Sinn Fein candidate. William Redmond was, after all, the brother of the party leader and a war hero, who had joined the Irish Brigade in the first months of the war, stating, "I can't stand asking fellows to go and not offering myself."[57] He had died in characteristic fashion, leading his men in the first wave although he had been ordered to participate in the third, and being shot twice before finally falling.[58] Ironically, after he was hit, it was the men of the Ulster Division who carried him from the battlefield.[59] The Irish Nationalist Party selected Patrick Lynch as his replacement. Lynch was a respected civil servant, a native of East Clare, and was fully expected to become the next Member of Parliament for that constituency.[60] The Irish Nationalist Party did not count, however, on Sinn Fein selecting as their candidate Eamon de Valera.

De Valera had been born in Brooklyn, New York, in 1882 to a Spanish father and an Irish mother. When he was just two years old, his father left his mother and she sent the young Eamon back to Ireland to live with her relatives. As a young mathematics teacher, de Valera joined the Gaelic League in 1908, where he first became acquainted with Patrick Pearse. Together, they joined the Irish Volunteers in 1913, and in 1914 de Valera stood with Pearse and MacNeill against John Redmond when the Irish Volunteers split into the National Volunteers and the Irish Volunteers. The following year, he became a member of the I.R.B. and in the 1916 Easter Rising, he acted as commandant in charge of the volunteers at Boland's Mill. He was one of only three commandants to escape execution, and although sentenced to life in prison following the commuting of his death sentence, he was released along with the other prisoners in June. Shortly thereafter, he became the Sinn Fein parliamentary candidate for East Clare.[61]

The contrast between de Valera and Patrick Lynch could not have been more pronounced. Lynch came from a prominent County Clare family, and had been a Crown Prosecutor before joining the civil service. De Valera was the son of a Spanish immigrant, an American-born citizen who was coming to the election not from the corridors of governmental power but from prison, where he had been held on charges of insurrection and murder. Lynch campaigned on the patriotism, life, and accomplishments of William Redmond, arguing for a continuation of Irish support for Great Britain in the present war and an eventual Irish Home Rule dominion within the British Empire. De Valera campaigned for an Irish seat at the expected Peace

Conference, where Ireland could declare independence from Great Britain and the British Empire and establish an Irish republic free of British influence.[62]

The R.I.C. reported that during the campaign, "violent, disloyal, and inflammatory speeches were delivered on behalf of the Sinn Fein candidate."[63] For the first time since the Easter Rising, uniformed Irish Volunteers paraded in public,[64] and the police informed the Chief Secretary that "the turmoil increased with the approach of election day, intimidation was freely practiced, and there was a growing disregard for law and order." This lawlessness was, in part, due to de Valera's message that if the Irish people united, "they would make the English law impossible, and that English law had no moral or legal sanction in Ireland." As a result, simple laws were broken in deliberate acts of defiance, and the police were spurned in their attempts to enforce order.[65]

With the breakdown of regular police control, those campaigning for de Valera became increasingly violent and brazen in their language of separation. Edward Mackey, for example, told a crowd that "[a]ny Irishman who goes out to fight for England deserves to be shot," and Thomas McDonagh proclaimed that "anyone who joins the English Army is a traitor to Ireland." He then encouraged those listening to "[b]e prepared to fight against England, your oppressor, England your enemy." Eoin MacNeill told voters to "keep your powder dry and be prepared to fight for independence," and J.J. Walsh proclaimed that "[n]othing can be got from England but by the spilling of blood." De Valera himself encouraged his followers to "[a]rm yourselves when you get the opportunity. Although we fought once and lost, it is only a lesson for the second time. . . . It is my wish that the British Empire will be blown into ruins."[66] The Crimes Special Branch recorded in full each of these speeches, and sent them in typed reports to the Inspector General. He in turn forwarded them to the Chief Secretary. There could be no doubt that Sinn Fein had moved beyond the boundaries of a mere parliamentary party, with constitutional and peaceful aims. Sinn Fein was pledging armed insurgency, and the British government knew it as early as July 1917.

When polling day arrived on July 11, de Valera defeated Lynch by 5,010 votes to 2,035.[67] His first action as Member of Parliament for East Clare was to denounce the legitimacy of a British election in Ireland and to refuse his seat at Westminster.[68] Following the election, John Dillon, a prominent member of the Nationalist Party, who would succeed Redmond as party leader following the latter's death in March 1918, ominously warned party members that "at this moment they [Sinn Fein] could sweep the greater part of the three Southern Provinces."[69] His warning was shared by the British intelligence community. The R.I.C. reported that de Valera's "sweeping success gave a great impetus to Sinn Fein not only in Clare, but throughout the entire country."[70] On July 19, just eight days after de Valera's election,

Countess Markievicz, the only woman sentenced to execution following the Easter Rising, was presented with the freedom of Kilkenny City, just as Count Plunkett had been six months earlier.[71]

Later that month, the sitting Member of Parliament for Kilkenny, Paddy O'Brien, the Nationalist Party's Chief Whip, passed away and a fourth byelection was called. W.T. Cosgrave, a released prisoner who had been interned following the Easter Rising, stood as the Sinn Fein candidate against John Magennis, the ex-mayor of the city and a prominent nationalist. There followed a bruising campaign in which "Sinn Fein leaders delivered a number of violent speeches in support of Cosgrave."[72] Stephen O'Meara, for example, announced, "We will drive every Englishman out of Ireland. England is toppling. Have your forces ready to fight"; and David Kent proclaimed, "We have only one enemy in the world, and that is England. We must get rid of her." The newly elected Eamon de Valera went further, explicitly stating Sinn Fein's policy: "We fight England for freedom with votes, and then if we fail, with rifles. . . . If we don't win freedom we will win it by force of the rifle. . . . Our policy is to resist British rule and British laws."[73] Again, the Crimes Special Branch, and in turn the Inspector General and Chief Secretary, received copies of each of these speeches. On August 14, when the votes were tallied, Cosgrave beat the Nationalist candidate by 772 votes to 392.[74]

These elections had a significant impact on the country. Following his election in July, de Valera was named to both the Sinn Fein National Council and the Provisional Executive of the Irish Volunteers. Here, in the leadership of both bodies, he proposed uniting the two, claiming that Sinn Fein was the political wing and the Irish Volunteers the military wing of a unified Irish separatist movement. On October 27, Sinn Fein held its tenth annual convention, where its members ratified a new constitution confirming that Sinn Fein was the political arm of the separatist movement. At the convention, de Valera was unanimously elected president of Sinn Fein. The following day, October 28, the Irish Volunteers held their own convention, where they confirmed that they were the military wing of the movement, and once again, de Valera was elected president.[75] Sinn Fein and the Irish Volunteers were now officially linked, with de Valera leading both. The intelligence community in Ireland, however, was unaware of this development. Not until late 1918 did they acknowledge that Sinn Fein and the Irish Volunteers were under unified control.[76]

Whilst this was occurring at the national level, at the grassroots level workers began to organize Sinn Fein clubs, the purpose of which were to gather support for Sinn Fein candidates in the upcoming 1918 General Election and to project an image of strength amongst the Irish population. These clubs were formed throughout the country, increasingly so after the

October Sinn Fein convention. Again and again in 1917, the police reports spoke of the emergence of Sinn Fein as a prevalent force in Irish politics. In the counties of Leinster Province, Sinn Fein began to slowly chip away at the majority of John Redmond's Irish Nationalist Party. In County Carlow, the party was said to have made "considerable headway," whilst in Dublin it had made "considerable strides."[77] In King's County, Sinn Fein "opinions and influence began to spread, and the mass of the young people of both sexes attached themselves to that party," whilst in County Kilkenny, the police reported an "undercurrent of unrest and disaffection, especially amongst the younger section of the people, due to . . . the growing strength of, and sympathy with, Sinn Fein views as opposed to those of the Irish Parliamentary Party."[78] The same was said in County Louth, where "sympathy with the [Sinn Fein] movement on the part of men of moderate opinions is said to be on the increase," and in County Westmeath, where "the number of persons who sympathized with the movement was large."[79] In all, 214 Sinn Fein clubs were formed in Leinster Province in 1917, with an active membership of 13, 133 men and women.[80]

The southern and western provinces of Munster and Connaught saw even greater advances for Sinn Fein. In County Clare, "disaffection lurked under the surface ready to break out on a very small provocation," and by the October convention, the condition of peace and law and order in the county had become "bad owing to the growth of Sinn Fein and revolutionary ideas." The police painted a poor picture of the situation: "Drilling was extensively carried on, numerous Sinn Fein clubs were formed, and a strong spirit of disloyalty prevailed. Police action was resented, the law openly defied, and everything seemed to point to a time in the near future when the land would be set aside for the laws made up by the Sinn Fein Convention." In certain places in the county, police property was destroyed, and "persons who were not Sinn Feiners" had to "show sympathy with the movement if they wished to live in peace with their neighbors." In summing up the political dynamics of the county, the police reported that, "Sinn Fein held the field and was practically master of the situation."[81]

In County Cork, the situation was no better. Although the year had started off peaceably, over time "the growing strength of the Sinn Fein movement led to a certain amount of unrest and was accountable for the marked seditious and disloyal feeling which existed amongst a considerable section of the people."[82] On July 8, for example, a contingent of female munitions workers was mobbed and beaten by Sinn Fein members, and later in the month, two rifle shots were fired through the window of Glountane R.I.C. barracks. In September, several American sailors on leave were attacked, and the police were stoned by rioters, who did not disperse until set upon by baton charges.[83]

Elsewhere, the police were regularly stoned by members of the Sinn Fein Party whilst carrying out patrols, and on one occasion in County Kerry rioters attacked the police barracks at Bullybunion, breaking the windows and firing rifle shots inside. The barracks was only saved when the police returned fire, killing one of the rioters. The county inspector, summing up the situation in November, reported that Sinn Fein was "doing all they could to defy the law and make government impossible; that the attitude of Sinn Feiners in the northern part of the county was very hostile towards the police; that in Listowel the police were partially boycotted; that in many places even the well-disposed people were afraid to be seen talking to a policeman."[84]

Such intimidation was present in other counties. In Limerick, the sitting Irish Nationalist Member of Parliament was attacked and seriously assaulted on January 21, 1917. Several members of the Sinn Fein Party were later arrested and convicted for the assault. On March 22, Sinn Fein members attacked the police whilst they were transporting three Sinn Fein prisoners, forcing them to retreat into the nearby police barracks. Similar attacks occurred in May and June.[85] The police were also attacked and stoned in County Tipperary, County Waterford, County Galway, and County Sligo. Gun shots were fired in the first three of these places.[86] In all, in the two provinces of Munster and Connaught, 564 Sinn Fein clubs were formed, with a membership of at least 36,989.[87]

Even in the traditionally unionist stronghold of Ulster, Sinn Fein seemed to be gaining ground. In Antrim and Down, the two most loyal of Ulster's counties, 17 Sinn Fein clubs were formed, with a combined membership of 474.[88] In County Armagh, the R.I.C. reported that Sinn Fein had "made considerable headway, having 14 clubs with a membership of 786," and in County Donegal, Sinn Fein closed the year with 34 clubs and 1,634 members, all of whom had been "very active" in "propaganda work."[89] The same was true in County Tyrone, where Sinn Fein established 36 clubs and recruited 2,135 members, and in County Cavan, where 53 clubs were founded with 2,623 members.[90] In County Fermanagh, the police reported that "[n]ationalists who were altogether opposed to Sinn Feinism began to look with favor on the extreme movement in the belief that the constitutional movement had failed, with the result that the Sinn Fein movement made considerable progress."[91] In County Monaghan, Sinn Fein "gained strength in all parts of the country," and there were "displays of Sinn Fein flags in the principal towns and throughout the county generally."[92]

Throughout 1917, Sinn Fein had increased its strength on the national level, winning all four byelections held that year, and had formed more than 1,000 Sinn Fein clubs with a membership of more than 66,000 men.[93] From July onwards, the Irish Volunteers had begun to parade openly again, conducting uniformed and armed route marches and sham battles, in a manner similar to those carried out before the rising in April 1916. Eamon de Valera had taken control of both Sinn Fein and the Irish Volunteers, and in October he had united them into a single separatist movement with a political and military wing, its sole purpose being to achieve Irish independence. He and his followers had made no attempt to hide their disdain for the British political system, nor their willingness to use violence to overthrow British rule if they were not successful at the polls.

Despite this, however, the military intelligence officers did not share the concern of the police, instead reverting to their previous skepticism on the threat that Sinn Fein presented to the British state. In December 1917, Captain Whitfield of the northern district opined that the Sinn Fein party was "declining in influence and power."[94] Captain Maunsell reported that there was "a distinct improvement in the state of the area," and wrote, "I am of the opinion that there is a slackening of support to the Sinn Fein movement."[95] Major R.C. Holmes, replacing Major Burke as the intelligence officer for the midland and Connaught district, reported that his area had been "peaceful," and that the "state of feeling as a whole cannot be described as strongly anti-British." In many places, he claimed, Sinn Fein seemed to be "developing on more constitutional lines."[96]

As had been the case in December 1916, the British government chose to follow the analysis of the military intelligence officers over the police. Under Secretary Byrne, in echoes of an earlier under secretary, wrote a memorandum for the Chief Secretary on December 11, examining the rise of Irish Volunteer drilling in 1917. He admitted that "[i]t may be causing increased contempt of police authority," but doubted that it was "bringing about scenes of disorder or serious action against the police." As measures to stop this harmless drilling would, by necessity, be severe, he suggested that the drilling could "be winked at for the present without serious danger to the State: and the grave inconvenience can be avoided of having scores of candidates for imprisonment which cannot be enforced."[97] The year 1917, therefore, finished much as 1916 had, with a split of opinion within the intelligence community despite a demonstrated threat, and a government that was more than willing to give those who called for its overthrow a platform upon which to speak, with the police helpless to do anything to prevent it.

Ireland's Fateful Year

The new year began for the British government with a report from Captain Maunsell that the Chief Secretary no doubt wished had not been written. "The District is considerably more disturbed since my last report," he began, "owing to the numerous raids for arms made at the houses of soldiers on leave from France, and of civilians."[98] This raiding for arms had also taken place in counties Galway, Leitrim, and Meath in the midland and Connaught district, and, the military intelligence officers suspected, was "likely to spread to other localities."[99] No longer did Ireland seem peaceful to them.

The Inspector General of the R.I.C. had no more cheery news for the Chief Secretary. He reported that in January, an additional 80 Sinn Fein clubs had been formed, bringing an extra 3,000 members into the fold, and 188 branches of the Irish Volunteers had engaged in 386 cases of illegal drilling, up from 293 in December. The Inspector General stated that Sinn Fein had been, from the beginning, a "movement of organized defiance of the law," whose leaders made "grossly seditious speeches and even incitements to violence with comparative impunity." Furthermore, drilling was carried on and uniforms worn openly by both Sinn Fein and the Irish Volunteers, in complete defiance of the law. This had resulted, he said, in a "spirit of lawlessness and turbulence which is daily becoming more embarrassing to the Police in their efforts to maintain order." Finally, in a rare instance of insubordination to his political superior, he laid the blame for this situation at the feet of the British government:

> It is of course nearly impossible to preserve order when there is no means of enforcing authority. In cases of organized illegality the law breaker is able to defeat the law by hunger-strike, and the constitutional methods of prosecution and imprisonment no longer have any deterrent effect. I submit that this is a serious situation.[100]

The hunger strikes to which Byrne referred had first taken place in September 1917. Approximately 40 prisoners were held in Dublin's Mountjoy Prison, all convicted not under the ordinary criminal code but under the Defence of the Realm Act (D.O.R.A). D.O.R.A had passed the House of Commons unanimously on August 8, 1914 and was published in the Dublin *Gazette* on December 2, 1914, bringing it into force in Ireland.[101] Its purpose was to allow for the suppression of any criticism of government policy in time of war, to allow for imprisonment without trial of those posing a threat to the British state, and to allow the British government to commandeer any economic resources needed for the war effort. It was enforced throughout the United Kingdom and was aimed at aiding the fight against Germany, not at suppressing Irish insurgency.

Augustine Birrell had held true to its original intent, opposed in general to what he saw as its draconian measures. Thus, he did his best to ensure that it was not used in Ireland except under the gravest of circumstances; no one was arrested under D.O.R.A until Easter week, 1916.[102] Under the leadership of General Maxwell and the statutes of martial law, however, D.O.R.A was used more extensively from April to July 1916. Upon his appointment, Duke continued to employ the act when necessary, although not to the same extent as Maxwell.[103]

Those held in Mountjoy Prison had been arrested under D.O.R.A for a number of crimes, ranging from delivering seditious speeches to participating in illegal armed drill. One of those held, Thomas Ashe, was president of the Supreme Council of the I.R.B. In September 1917, he suggested to his fellow prisoners that they had been prosecuted for their political actions, not for any crime, and thus should be afforded special treatment as political prisoners. He took his case to the prison authorities, but they refused to see his position in a similar light. Following his failure to acquire special status by force of reason, Ashe instead tried physical force and organized a prison riot. As punishment for this destruction, the prison authorities removed the boots, beds, and bedding of those who had been involved. On September 18, Ashe organized the prisoners in a hunger strike, demanding separate facilities and special treatment for those convicted in Ireland under D.O.R.A. After five days of striking, the authorities introduced forcible feeding. Two days later, on September 25, Ashe died from heart failure during a bungled forced feeding.[104]

The response to Ashe's death by the nationalist population in Ireland was vast and immediate. Michael Collins, a fellow I.R.B Supreme Council member and veteran of the Easter Rising, donated an Irish Volunteer uniform to be worn by Ashe, and his body was dressed in it as it lay in Dublin's Mater Hospital. Hospital authorities estimated that 30,000 people filed past his body in a show of respect as it lay awaiting burial.[105] His funeral was equally well attended, bringing Dublin to a standstill as his coffin was paraded through the city streets, followed by a stage-managed procession of I.R.B. men, armed and uniformed Irish Volunteers, Catholic priests, and 20,000 mourners.[106] Following a series of rifle volleys over the grave, Collins delivered the funeral oration, telling the crowd, "Nothing remains to be said. That volley which we have just heard is the only speech which it is proper to make above the grave of a dead Fenian."[107]

Duke was alarmed by this turn of events but, unable to come up with a solution to the problem of D.O.R.A. prisoners, he did nothing. A second hunger strike followed, at which the Chief Secretary, fearing another funeral procession, transferred the prisoners from Mountjoy Prison to Dundalk Jail, in part acceding to their demand for separation from common criminals.[108] He was not content with this accession though, and on October 23 suggested to the cabinet that they might consider banning Sinn Fein's National Convention, which was scheduled for October 25 and 26. He was told by his colleagues, however, that "it might be undesirable to pay too much attention to it [the convention]" as there was no "real grievance at the back of the Sinn Fein movement."[109]

Despite their refusal to ban the convention, the cabinet did grant Duke the authority to arrest Eamon de Valera, whose speeches, they judged from police reports, had ceased to be "mere provocation and wild talk" and had become "actual incitements to seditious and rebellious acts." The Chief Secretary resolved to make use of this new power, but by the following morning he had lost his nerve, fearful, as Birrell had been before him, that an arrest might provoke more unrest than it would prevent.[110] De Valera, therefore, was not arrested, despite the cabinet granting such authority to Duke. It was two days later that he was unanimously elected president of both Sinn Fein and the Irish Volunteers, uniting the two.

The election and soaring popularity of de Valera again unnerved Duke, and because of his increasing uncertainty about whether it was wise to imprison Irish subversives under D.O.R.A, he unconditionally released all Sinn Fein prisoners on November 17, most having served only a fraction of their sentences.[111] Henceforth, those arrested and convicted under D.O.R.A were promptly released rather than imprisoned, essentially negating the utility of the act. It was about this policy that the Inspector General complained in his January report, and about Duke's cowardice in the face of unconventional politics that he suggested there had now arisen a "serious situation" in Ireland.[112]

From September to November 1917, the government had sought at all costs to avoid provoking Sinn Fein. Despite intelligence reports revealing that Sinn Fein was gaining strength, the government had acceded to the demands of the hunger strikers, eventually releasing them, and had failed to move against the leader of the Irish Volunteers and Sinn Fein, even though they acknowledged that he was stirring up sedition. This raises an important question: why would the government be so hesitant to move against Sinn Fein and the Irish Volunteers? Although there are no cabinet memoranda to be found on this topic, and no cabinet member laid down the reasoning of the government on this issue in a letter or diary, the answer to the government's inaction in the autumn of 1917 can be speculated upon, again in the context of the larger European war.

From July to November, British forces were engaged in the Third Battle of Ypres, followed immediately in November by the Battle of Cambrai.[113] They were also engaged in the Third Battle of Gaza in October and November, and the capture of Jerusalem in December.[114] In total, the British suffered more than 350,000 casualties in these battles. Whilst this destruction was by no means on the same scale as the Somme, it was still considerably greater than any deaths that could feasibly be imagined in an Irish insurgency. When compared to the gravity of the situation in Europe and the Middle East, therefore, Ireland could only have been seen by Lloyd George to be a less important problem, the solution of which could be postponed until the war in Europe had been won. Thus, although insurrection was being threatened within the borders of the United Kingdom, the government chose to appease rather than confront the Irish militants.

The political climate in Ireland did not improve in 1918. Byrne informed the Chief Secretary that during February, "lawlessness and turbulence, the outcome of the Sinn Fein revolutionary movement, grew rapidly in the Western provinces." He reiterated his belief that the success of the hunger strikes in gaining prisoners clemency had "given rise to contempt for the law and to the belief that it could be disregarded with impunity," and stated that this had become evidenced by a new wave of attacks on the police. On February 20, two constables in County Clare had been knocked down, beaten, and kicked by a crowd that stole their weapons. Four days later in that same county, two constables were shot by a party of masked men and again had their weapons stolen. Another group of constables was forced to fire on a hostile crowd, wounding five men, one of whom later died.[115]

By the end of the month, the situation had become so grave that the Inspector General, under the authority granted to him by D.O.R.A and in defiance of the Chief Secretary's general wishes, declared County Clare a Special Military Area and relinquished his control in that county to the military commander in Ireland. This latter man placed the area under a commandant and drafted in a large number of troops to restore order. Troop detachments were also sent to counties Sligo, Mayo, Roscommon, Galway, and Tipperary, although in these areas the counties remained under police control. Circumventing the necessity of arrests under D.O.R.A, the police arrested many Irish Volunteers under the 1887 Crimes Act, which prevented illegal militias. They then kept them imprisoned in local jails, fearful that if they were sent to a prison in Dublin they would be released rapidly following hunger strike. The Inspector General argued that only if the government adopted a "firm attitude" towards hunger strikers, and allowed the continuation of Special Military Areas such as had been established in County Clare, would there be a "tranquilizing effect" in Ireland.[116]

The military intelligence officers concurred with Byrne. Captain Maunsell, the officer responsible for the southern district into which County Clare fell, reported the following:

> As a result of the successful use of the hunger strike in securing the early release of persons committed to prison either by civil or military courts, and seemingly to orders issued by the Sinn Fein or Irish Volunteer executives to do everything, short of actual rebellion, to subvert all authority and civilized order, large portions of the area have deteriorated into a state of anarchy.

He reported that he had visited the disturbed areas and was shocked to discover that the police were being attacked by armed gangs, and that in one town—Thurles, in County Tipperary—the Irish Volunteers had "conducted elaborate maneuvers," occupying the railway station and patrolling the town in place of the police.

Maunsell recommended that the Irish Volunteers be proclaimed an illegal organization, and all drills by this force (armed or otherwise) be dispersed by the military. The force was, he said, "at the back of all the trouble in Co. Clare and elsewhere, is governed by what can only be described as a secret society, and has become a terror to every loyal inhabitant in Ireland." Finally, in a scathing indictment of government policy, Maunsell concluded that the "feeling of the loyal inhabitants" was "one of disgust with and resentment against the Civil Government," a feeling held "in fact by everyone in Ireland who has anything to lose." He warned that the "open and unmitigated Blackguardism permitted daily, sometimes in the presence of the police, by the dregs of the population, directed and organized by adventurers paid from unknown sources, is giving rise to a feeling of despair," and suggested that had the military not intervened in County Clare, "no man's life would have been safe there."[117] Major Holmes of the midland and Connaught district supported Maunsell's conclusions, adding, "The general situation throughout the District is one of general unrest, and a tendency to disturbance exists, which is likely to become more general if the tactics of the more violent in the affected areas succeed."[118]

Duke was dismayed by what he read and was angered by the reproving tone displayed by Maunsell and Holmes. He immediately scribbled a note to Under Secretary Byrne, saying, "I should be glad of some information as to the probable competence of these I[ntelligence] O[fficer]'s in the Southern and Midland Commands to read lectures on Irish policies to the Civil Executive."[119] Byrne reported back three days later, on March 6, informing the Chief Secretary: "I am told that Capt. Maunsell is a barrister and has seen service since he entered the Army. He is said to do his work very well. . . . Major Holmes is a [former] D[istrict] I[nspector] in the R.I.C. and I am told he is an excellent officer who has done good work in difficult districts."[120] Duke had attempted to lay blame for the bad news he received at the feet of the messengers, but his endeavor had failed. The messengers were found to be sound, and the Chief Secretary would finally have to face up to the deteriorating situation in Ireland.

Duke was not alone in deciding an Irish policy with which to confront the gathering unrest. On March 2, just one day before the Chief Secretary questioned the competence of his military intelligence officers, his staff had sent to the under secretary a report written on December 11, 1882, at the height of the nineteenth-century Land Wars, by Colonel Sir John Ross, the Irish Military Secretary, to the Chief Secretary, Lord Spencer. The report evaluated the legality of employing military troops in support of the civil power in Ireland.[121] Byrne forwarded the report to the Chief Secretary, the military commander, and the Inspector General on March 3, noting, "This is an interesting Report, and of present value."[122]

According to the 1882 memorandum, troops could be stationed in Ireland, at the request of the Irish government, for one of three reasons: first, "to give confidence to the well disposed, and to exert a moral effect in the District"; second, "to be ready to act on emergencies, should sudden riots or disturbances arise"; and third, "to patrol the neighborhood." The memo stated that the military detachments should number 50 men under two officers, and should be strictly used in disturbed districts. Those within the Irish government who had the authority to request such detachments included the sheriff (a defunct position by 1918), local justices of the peace, R.I.C. county inspectors, and the Inspector General himself. Significantly, and no doubt much to his chagrin, the Chief Secretary was not listed as one permitted to request troops, the reason being that he was not in a position to directly scrutinize the security situation on the ground and thus could not make the best judgment of where troops were most needed.

Once the troop detachments were deployed, the memorandum continued, patrols should be carried out on a joint basis between the police and the military. These patrols were to be as small as possible and were to include at least one constable. Although the route of patrol could be determined by the military officer commanding, prior approval of that route had to be obtained from the R.I.C. county inspector. The purpose of these patrols, the memorandum stressed, was not to give the military the authority to carry out operations within the borders of the United Kingdom, but rather to allow a greater number of police patrols to take place with greater protection for the individual constables. Thus, soldiers were to be employed for protection purposes alone, and only members of the R.I.C. were permitted to "perform those duties which belonged exclusively to the Constabulary," such as making arrests and detaining suspects.

In addition to military protection for regular police patrols, the memorandum allowed for soldiers to be placed on "special service," where they would be able to "more directly relieve the Police of some of their duties." In these cases, soldiers were enrolled temporarily as Auxiliary Policemen, and were assigned to personal protection duty of certain endangered people, such as magistrates and judges, and to protect government property, functions usually assigned to constables. This relieved those constables usually tasked with these jobs, and thus provided more manpower for police patrols. In "very disturbed districts," these auxiliary policemen could take on duties beyond personal and property protection and "act as escort to a small number of the Constabulary in all their duties," including arrest of suspects.

The 1882 memorandum thus laid out two roles that military troops could play in assisting the civil authority in Ireland: they could operate joint patrols with the police, and they could take on some of the protection duties usually assigned to constables. They could not arrest or detain suspects, and they could not patrol independently of the police. Finally, whilst the memo stated that "the plan of employing Soldiers on Special Service has proved a success [in 1882], in that an efficient Force was at hand to aid the Police very materially during a great emergency," it also warned that in future, such power should be used circumspectly, as there were "many objections to it both from a civil and a Military point of view." These objections largely centered on there being no clear chain of command, with soldiers' loyalty split between their military and police commanders, and on the problems raised by conducting military operations on what was considered British soil, constitutionally no different than the soil of England, Wales, or Scotland.

If it was found necessary to once again employ soldiers in the support of the police in Ireland, the memo concluded, four guidelines should be followed. First, the local authorities (sheriff, justices of the peace, and county inspectors) should apply for assistance to the government (the Chief Secretary), via the Inspector General, rather than directly to the military commander, as had happened in 1882. Second, soldiers should be rotated through police duties on a more regular basis, with shorter service in Ireland. Third, the local authorities should submit to the Inspector General and the Chief Secretary monthly reports detailing how many soldiers were deployed, and which duties they were undertaking. Finally, if more than one local authority had requested assistance in a single district, only one such authority should be tasked as liaison between the police and the military to avoid confusion of command.[123] Overall, the message presented by the 1882 memorandum was that if soldiers were to be deployed in Ireland, they must be there solely as a support for the Royal Irish Constabulary, they must not be engaged in any policing activity themselves, and they must be under a single command. The military, in other words, did not wish to become the lead security agency in Ireland. That was a job best left to the police.

Duke received this memorandum from his under secretary on March 3, just one day after receiving the reports from the military intelligence officers suggesting that the time had now come to consider more aggressive military intervention in Ireland and 12 days before he read the Inspector General's words on the establishment of a Special Military Area in County Clare.[124] In Clare, the procedure that had been followed was somewhat different to the recommendations laid out in the memo. The Inspector General, on the advice of his county inspector, had directly requested troops from the military commander in Ireland, bypassing the Chief Secretary's Office altogether. The dispatched soldiers had carried out joint patrols with the police, but they had been under the command of a military officer, not the county inspector. Furthermore, upon the declaration of a Special Military Area, a designation not used in 1882, police power had been supplanted by the military, and arrests had been made and suspects taken into custody by soldiers, albeit with police constables present. The military, therefore, was assuming more authority in Ireland than the statesmen of 1882 thought wise.

Duke, however, had neither the personal inclination nor the political acumen to act on the 1882 recommendations and implement a structured security policy. Instead, he issued no new directives, allowing the Inspector General to continue his ad hoc system of directly requesting military assistance when required, and allowing the military to establish Special Military Areas where civilian control was relinquished within the borders of the United Kingdom.[125]

Throughout March, Duke continued to adopt a hands-off approach to the deteriorating situation in Ireland, regularly reading the increasingly pessimistic reports of the Inspector General and the military intelligence officers but refusing to consider any policy changes or to pursue a more aggressive approach to Sinn Fein and the Irish Volunteers. The cabinet increasingly lost patience with the Chief Secretary, one member commenting, "Duke is hopeless and has lost his nerve if he ever had any: Birrell was a tyrant compared to him."[126] On March 1, Walter Long wrote to the Prime Minister, telling him that it was time to "change the Irish government from top to bottom," and suggesting that the country be run not by a single Chief Secretary but by a triumvirate of hard-nosed politicians and military officers.[127] Duke, sensing change in the air, suggested to Lloyd George that any cabinet reshuffle take place before the end of the month.

In response, the Prime Minister asked not for Duke's resignation, but instead informed him on March 25 that he had decided to extend conscription to Ireland, making all four countries of the United Kingdom equally eligible for national military service. There were 150,000 men of appropriate age for immediate conscription in Ireland, men who were sorely needed in France, and the expediencies of the continental war were placed above domestic security in Ireland. The measure was announced to the public on April 9. Duke, fearful of the violent outbreak that would surely accompany conscription and having no stomach to organize its suppression, resigned his position on April 16. When he did so, he warned the Prime Minister that conscription would "produce a disaster."[128]

With Duke's resignation, Lloyd George was afforded the opportunity to consider Walter Long's suggestion for full-scale reform of Irish governmental administration. He did not proceed as far as Long had proposed, and abolish entirely the post of Chief Secretary, but he did shift the base of power away from the Chief Secretary and onto the Lord Lieutenant, under whom three councils were established: one to coordinate Irish business and economic affairs, one to determine security policy in Ireland, and one to develop Irish social policy.[129] This was an important transition of power. Since the

1801 Act of Union, Irish administration had been based on the British system of constitutional monarchy with the Chief Secretary playing the role of Prime Minister and the Lord Lieutenant the role of figurehead king.[130] Now, under Lloyd George's reforms, real authority was once again placed in the person of the Lord Lieutenant, transforming him from a symbolic being above the partisan fray to a direct participant in the day-to-day running of Ireland.

Lord Wimborne, the Prime Minister believed, was clearly unsuited to such power. He had, after all, been appointed under the old system, and his background reflected that selection. He had succeeded his father as Baron Wimborne in 1914, and prior to his appointment as Lord Lieutenant, he had served as Lord in Waiting on King George V. He had sat as a Member of Parliament from 1900 to 1910, but in that time he had held no ministerial post. On April 28, therefore, 12 days after Duke's resignation, Lloyd George's Chief Whip (and the brother of Wimborne) informed the Lord Lieutenant that the Prime Minister would find it "helpful" if he resigned. He immediately did so and was rewarded with an aristocratic promotion to Viscount Wimborne. He lived the rest of his days in patrician splendor in England.[131]

Lloyd George selected as his replacement Field Marshal Lord French. There could not have been a more pronounced contrast between the two men. French had been born in 1852, the only son of a naval captain. Following an education at Harrow, he entered Eastman's Naval Academy in early 1866, at just 13 years of age. Later that year, he passed the entrance exam to the Royal Naval Academy at Dartmouth, and, two years later, emerged as a newly commissioned midshipman. Naval life did not appeal to French, though, particularly as he could not indulge his passion for riding, and in November 1870, he resigned his commission, hoping to join the army.

His ultimate goal was to enter a cavalry regiment, but in the privileged and hierarchical world of the nineteenth-century British Army, without the proper pedigree such a move was impossible. Thus, French began his army career in the Suffolk Artillery Militia, before finally securing a commission in the 19th Hussars in 1874. His new regiment took him to Ireland, where he remained until 1881. During that time, he rose from lieutenant to captain and took part in suppressing the agrarian unrest that has become known to history as the Irish Land Wars. In 1881, he was seconded to the Northumberland Hussars as adjutant, where he remained until October 1884. Whilst there, his regiment, the 19th Hussars, was sent to Egypt. Their mission was to restore the authority of the Khedival dynasty following a nationalist coup in 1882 and to protect the British government's interests in the Suez Canal.[132]

French, newly promoted to major, rejoined his regiment in Cairo in late 1884, but by the time he arrived most of the fighting was over, the Khedival dynasty was restored, and the Suez Canal was safely in British hands. This lack of active service was soon remedied, however, as his regiment moved in December to Wadi Halfa, where they took part in the relief of pro-British Egyptian troops in Khartoum, who had become trapped after Sudan claimed independence from Egypt. French's first experience of battle occurred on January 16, 1885. Following a month-long campaign in which the 19th Hussars provided a rearguard protection to the escaping British and Egyptian forces, French was promoted to lieutenant colonel and made second-in-command of the regiment.[133] Four years later, in 1889, he became full colonel and commander of the 19th Hussars. His regiment traveled to India in 1891, where it remained until 1893.[134] Upon his return to England, his term as commander of the 19th Hussars ended, and he accepted a staff position at the War Office, working for General Sir George Luck, who had been given the task of reorganizing the British cavalry. During his brief time at the War Office, French composed a new edition of the *Cavalry Drill Book*, and then, in 1896, was appointed assistant adjutant general of the Horse Guards.[135]

French's young appointment as assistant adjutant general (he was just 44 years old) rapidly advanced his career. In 1897, he left London to command the Second Cavalry Brigade at Canterbury; in 1898, he was promoted to the rank of major general and given command of the First Cavalry Brigade at Aldershot. A year later, in September 1899, French boarded the steamer *Norman* and set sail for South Africa to command the British cavalry in Natal, where the president of the Transvaal, Paul Kruger, had demanded British withdrawal from the colony, a demand the British government was unwilling to grant.[136] French made his reputation in South Africa, leading his cavalry brigades in the early battles of Elandslaagte and Ladysmith, playing a crucial role in the relief of Kimberley and the subsequent battle of Paardeberg, and being instrumental in the surrenders of Bloemfontein and Johannesburg. He finished the war not only commanding the cavalry brigades, but also in supreme command of the entire Johannesburg district and in charge of all mobile columns in the Cape Colony. As a reward for his success, he was knighted and given the Aldershot Command, the premier command in the British Army, which included two infantry divisions and a cavalry brigade.[137]

With the Aldershot Command, French's career continued to thrive. In 1907, he was promoted to the rank of full general and made Inspector General of the forces. Five years later, in March 1912, he became Chief of the Imperial General Staff.[138] He was soon thereafter promoted to field marshal, but in March 1914, he became embroiled in the Curragh affair, in which cavalry officers in Ireland mutinied over the possibility of acting against the Ulster Volunteer Force. French, as head of the British Army, resigned over the incident, and at the age of 61 retired from the army.[139] The general thus had two experiences in Ireland, as a young subaltern during the Land Wars of the early 1880s and as head of the army during the Ulster crisis of 1914. Neither experience had been particularly positive. He had been relieved to leave Ireland in 1881, and in 1914 he had lost his job because of the disputes within the country. Thus French seemed he have achieved far more success robustly combating colonial populations in Egypt, Sudan, India, and South Africa than he had attained at home in Ireland.

He was not long out of employment, however. As a field marshal, he had remained on the active service list, and on July 30, 1914, he was summoned by his replacement as Chief of the Imperial General Staff and was told that if there was a war with Germany, as surely there seemed there would be, he was to be recalled into service and to take command of the British Expeditionary Force. When war was declared six days later, French took up his post. He arrived in France on August 14, and within a matter of weeks obtained the title Commander-in-Chief in France.[140]

The war, which all but War Secretary Lord Kitchener had expected to be over by Christmas, did not go as well as hoped. French, as commander of those forces tasked with halting the German advance, took much of the blame. In the army's first engagement at Mons, he was forced to retreat, and following a brief advance at the Marne and the Aisne in September, he was faced with deadlock. Following the British defeat at Loos in 1915, he was forced to resign as commander.[141] On December 15, therefore, he took the demotion to Commander-in-Chief of the Home Forces and planned to ease slowly into full retirement. But then, militant separatists in Ireland took over Dublin during Easter week, 1916, and the home front suddenly seemed under great threat.

As Commander-in-Chief of the Home Forces, French was ultimately responsible for the army in Ireland, the superior officer to the General Officer Commanding Ireland. During Easter week, he remained in London, believing General Maxwell more than capable to deal with the rising. In its aftermath, however, he began to take an increasing interest in the country, visiting on a number of occasions. He became convinced of the rightness of an Irish home rule parliament within the British Empire, and believed that the wishes of the peaceful majority for home rule were being silenced by a violent minority insistent on complete independence. For French, to deal ruthlessly with Sinn Fein and the Irish Volunteers was the most appropriate course to follow to quickly grant the desires of the Irish people. Once the separatist violence was suppressed, he believed, a home rule parliament could be safely established.[142]

With the resignation of Chief Secretary Duke in April 1918, Lloyd George approached French and offered him the greatly empowered position of Lord Lieutenant. French accepted on May 5, telling the Prime Minister that "in ordinary circumstances or in peace time such a position would be impossible for me," but "on the understanding that I was to go to Ireland for the purpose of military order and combating German intrigue; as a Military Viceroy at the head of a Quasi-Military Government I would consider it my duty to obey what I regard as a distinct order or direction to me by H[is] M[ajesty's] govt."[143] French believed that his primary task in Ireland was to suppress Sinn Fein and the Irish Volunteers so that a home rule government could take effect, and he argued that "all modern scientific means of warfare" should be used in such suppression, including seaplanes and airships. Air attacks, he wrote to the cabinet shortly after being appointed, "ought to put the fear of God into these playful young Sinn Feiners."[144] The man ruling Ireland from May 1918, could not have been more different than Birrell or Duke, and Lloyd George was pleased with his selection.

French took control of Ireland at a more precarious time than had either Birrell or Duke. Just three weeks before his appointment, the government had announced conscription for the island, and Duke's parting words predicting disaster when such conscription was enforced were far from exaggerated. In the first intelligence report French received from the R.I.C., Inspector General Byrne reported that upon Lloyd George's announcement, "Constitutional Nationalists and Sinn Feiners at once joined hands to resist any attempt to enforce it," and the Irish Volunteers raided houses for arms and stole explosives from quarries to shore up their armory.

Perhaps more alarming to Byrne, the ever powerful Catholic Church in Ireland announced, by way of proclamations by its bishops, that "England had no right to conscript the Irish people against their will and that resistance would be justifiable." On Sunday, April 21, the Catholic clergy posted announcements in each Catholic Church declaring that a covenant would be produced in which signatories would pledge to resist conscription. The Inspector General reported that "strong efforts" were being made by the clergy to "induce the younger members of the R.I.C. to resign rather than take part in the enforcement of Conscription." Byrne warned that although the constabulary was a "great and loyal Force," it was a "new experience for its members to be assailed through their consciences by members of their Church."[145]

French had other problems. On April 12, the R.I.C. had detained a man stranded on a small island off the coast of County Clare, following a warning from naval intelligence that a German emissary was being sent to Ireland to foment another rising. The man was sent to London, where under interrogation he admitted to being Corporal Joseph Dowling, an Irish prisoner of war in Germany who had joined Roger Casement's Irish Brigade. He had been put ashore from a German U-boat to make contact with the Irish separatist movement to see if a German landing was possible. He was, however, distinctly uninformed about affairs in Ireland, and told those who interrogated him that his plan was to liaise with John Redmond, who had passed away the month earlier and was not a separatist in any case. Based on his ignorance, the police did not consider Dowling a threat, nor did they believe a German invasion was imminent. He seemed to be working alone.[146]

Nevertheless, Dowling's capture and his story justified more aggressive action against Sinn Fein. On April 24, Inspector General Byrne recommended to the British government the arrest of all Sinn Fein and Irish Volunteer leaders, a recommendation French supported when appointed as Lord Lieutenant on May 5. Consequently, on the night of May 17–18, a wave of arrests took place across Ireland, the first major sweep since the Easter Rising two years earlier. Seventy-three leaders of Sinn Fein and the Irish Volunteers, including Eamon de Valera, were arrested and sent for immediate internment in England. The morning following the arrests, French issued a proclamation to the Irish people, explaining the reasons for the arrests (involvement in a German plot) and postponing the implementation of conscription until September. If Ireland had provided 50,000 new volunteer recruits for the army by that time, French announced, conscription would be postponed indefinitely.[147]

This action, unthinkable under Birrell or Duke, was greeted with immediate praise by the police. The Inspector General reported that it had come as a "severe shock to the extremists who really thought that the Government would not dare to arrest their leaders." He now believed that Sinn Fein had finally realized that "open illegality cannot be continued in defiance of the manifest determination of Government to suppress it." Furthermore, he stated that such suppression had "certainly lowered the prestige of the Sinn Fein organization," and the police had been privately informed by many moderate nationalists that they were "pleased, though afraid to say so openly." He warned, however, that although Sinn Fein had become "far less aggressive and defiant" since the internments, they were still "bitterly disloyal, and hostile to any form of British rule." The threat had been deflected but not eliminated.[148]

Following receipt of this advice, on June 15, French used powers granted to him under the Coercion Act of 1885 to make the cities of Cork and Limerick and the counties of Clare, Cork, Galway, Kerry, King's, Longford, Mayo, Queen's, Sligo, Tipperary, and Westmeath "proclaimed" areas. This gave the police additional powers of arrest and detention. On June 18, counties Limerick and Tipperary were declared Special Military Areas, as County Clare already was, and on July 3, French declared Sinn Fein and the Irish Volunteers to be "dangerous" organizations. Under section 6 of the

Coercion Act, anyone seen associating with them could be arrested. The following day, using section 9 AA of the 1914 Defence of the Realm Act, he prohibited all "meetings, processions, and assemblies throughout Ireland" unless special written permission was first acquired from the Inspector General of the R.I.C.[149] Unlike previous administrators in Ireland, French would not allow his tenure in the country to be a passive affair.

The benefits of the arrests, internments, proclaimed counties, and Special Military Areas were short-lived, however. Michael Collins had not been arrested during the sweep, and in the absence of other Sinn Fein and Irish Volunteer leaders, he was able to grow in prominence within the separatist movement and steer it in a more aggressive direction. Unlike de Valera, Collins had not been involved with the Irish Volunteers movement from its origins. Although born and educated in West Cork, he had immigrated to England in 1906, where he worked for ten years in various places of employment ranging from the post office to a stockbroking firm. He did join the I.R.B. whilst overseas, however, and by 1914 he had become treasurer of the London and South England district. He returned to Ireland shortly before the Easter rising, and joined the volunteers as a junior staff captain. He was arrested in the immediate aftermath and imprisoned in England, but was released as part of Lloyd George's Christmas pardon. By May 1918, when de Valera and the other volunteer leaders were arrested, he had risen to become Adjutant General and Director of Organization for the Irish Volunteers. He was, therefore, in a natural position to fill the void created by French's arrests.[150]

Collins' philosophy of Irish independence was more militant than de Valera's. Whilst de Valera's background was in academia and his first encounters with Irish nationalism had been through the cultural and linguistic movements of the early twentieth century, Collins was schooled in business and had his introduction to the concept of Irish nationalism through the I.R.B. He was, therefore, less patient with the political process and more ready to engage the British directly with violence, using a more secretive organization than the Irish Volunteers. Nevertheless, he was astute enough to realize that with many of the leaders now imprisoned, reorganization was necessary before any military action could take place.

Beginning in June, and corresponding with French's crackdown, Collins steered the Irish Volunteers underground, whilst encouraging Sinn Fein to become more active publicly. With the August announcement that a General Election would be held throughout the United Kingdom in December, Collins decided upon his strategy. If in those elections Sinn Fein could secure enough seats to claim a moral mandate to rule Ireland, he would have his justification to wage war against the British beginning in January 1919.

He had, therefore, just a few months with which to turn the Irish Volunteers into a guerilla fighting organization.[151]

The intelligence community in Ireland was completely unaware of the reorganization taking place under the command of Michael Collins. Whilst in the years 1912–1914 they had developed an accurate picture of both the Ulster Volunteer Force and the Irish Volunteers, and in the years 1914–1916 they had slowly become aware that the Irish Volunteers intended a rebellion against the British government (although they were not certain when it would occur), in 1918 the government in Ireland was completely ignorant of the developing threat. The military intelligence officers spoke only vaguely of "Sinn Fein work" and "Sinn Fein organizing," whilst suggesting that the Irish Volunteers had become "quieter" and drilling had "very largely ceased."[152] The R.I.C. Inspector General spoke of "numerous" Sinn Fein meetings, but reported that the Irish Volunteers had "displayed no open activity."[153] In August, he stated that "the prospect of armed insurrection is remote."[154]

With apparent stability having finally come to Ireland, and with the Irish separatist movement seemingly turned political in nature, the threat that had been so pronounced in April and May appeared to have abated by August. In keeping with this belief, that month the British government informed the military commander in Ireland that it was no longer necessary for him to forward copies of the military intelligence reports to the Chief Secretary and Lord Lieutenant. From September onwards, the government would once again rely on the police reports alone.[155]

Despite this lack of detailed intelligence on Michael Collins' reorganization of the Irish Volunteers, and despite the government's decision to no longer collate intelligence reports from the military officers, the R.I.C. Inspector General grew concerned about the separatist movement in the autumn of 1918. In his October report, he wrote that a "dangerous state of disaffection" was spreading in the country, which required the "continuance of firm measures and the maintenance of a strong Military force."[156] Following the November armistice that brought an end to the war in France, together with an end to the necessity of conscription, Byrne pleaded with the government not to reduce troop levels in Ireland. He warned that the Irish Volunteers continued to be "sufficiently organized with the weapons at their disposal, and supported in every direction by numbers of turbulent young men who if not actually in their ranks are in close sympathy with them, to be unmanageable and to make government impossible in the event of the Military Force in the country being reduced." With the upcoming General Election, Byrne argued, it was crucial not to allow the Irish Volunteers to reenergize with military displays in support of Sinn Fein.[157]

Byrne had reason to worry about the future of British rule in Ireland, particularly if Sinn Fein, supported by a paramilitary arm, succeeded in gaining ground in the election. The party's election manifesto was simple: it demanded the establishment of a completely independent Irish republic, a withdrawal of all Irish representatives from the parliament at Westminster, and the immediate founding of an Irish parliament, housed in Dublin.[158] There was no room for compromise, no mention of a Home Rule parliament within the British Empire or of a conferred dominion status. Sinn Fein wanted complete independence for Ireland, and if the British government would not grant it, it would be taken by force.[159]

When December 14 and the General Election dawned, it was a day marked by widespread violence and intimidation. For the first time since June when Michael Collins had taken command, detachments of the Irish Volunteers marched in military formation, parading close to polling stations in contested districts. Pickets were also staged by the Irish Volunteers in front of places where constituents had to vote.[160] Such intimidation was hardly a surprise. In the months leading up to the election, the Inspector General had reported that the Sinn Fein Party "dominates public bodies and terrorizes society in at least three provinces."[161] Indeed, throughout 1918, the police had laid down in confidential reports evidence of extensive political intimidation carried out by the Sinn Fein Party against more moderate Irish nationalists. In County Clare, for example, the police reported,

> Intimidation was, and is, rampant in the County. It is done secretly and takes the form of threatening letters, attacks on houses, firing shots, sometimes with effect. It has reached such a pitch that the people are afraid of incurring the displeasure of their neighbors or the Sinn Fein leaders in their locality.[162]

The police in County Kerry likewise stated that in 1918,

> [i]ntimidation by the parading and marching of young men was rampant. Respectable farmers and shopkeepers were compelled to subscribe to Sinn Fein funds and to pretend to be followers of Sinn Fein. No information would be given to the police, and in many cases *men were threatened and assaulted for the offense of having been seen speaking to a policeman.* The Magistrates and Jurors failed to do their duties mainly through fear.[163]

In County Tipperary, the police stated that a "reign of terror" existed, owing to the "influence and impudence of the Sinn Fein organization in all its forms."[164] Such a characterization was shared by police in other counties.[165]

As a consequence of this campaign of intimidation, Sinn Fein candidates stood completely unopposed in the counties of Cavan, Cork (with the exception of Cork City), Kerry, and King's. In the province of Munster, there were no candidates from other parties in 17 of 24 constituencies. In a total of 77 constituencies contested by Sinn Fein throughout Ireland, the Irish Nationalist Party could find candidates willing to stand for election in only 37. In 40 constituencies, no candidate would dare put his name forward, even in areas that typically offered strong support for political moderates.[166]

When the votes were finally tallied, it came as no surprise that Sinn Fein had won 73 of the 105 Irish seats, 40 of which were without opposition. The Irish Nationalist Party came away with only 6, and the Ulster Unionists won the remaining 26 seats, all of which were in Protestant districts in the north of Ireland.[167] Of those elected for Sinn Fein, 28 were in internment, 6 in prison, and 3 exiled in the United States.[168] Despite these absences, Michael Collins had the result he wanted. He was now in a position to demand immediate British withdrawal from Ireland. Anything less, he believed, would constitute a justification for war.

What seems remarkable about this period of intimidation leading up to the General Election is the lack of response by the British government to the increasingly pessimistic and alarming police reports. It was clear to all who read Byrne's assessments, as both the Lord Lieutenant and the Chief Secretary did, that by August, when the General Election was announced, the chances of a fair campaign in Ireland were low. Entire areas of the country had descended into a state of anarchy, and reports of violent coercion and forced support for Sinn Fein were in no short supply.

Indeed, such violence had become so serious that counties Clare, Limerick, Tipperary, and Cork had been designated Special Military Areas and the police in counties Galway, Kerry, King's, Longford, Mayo, Queen's, Sligo, and Westmeath had been given additional powers when these became "proclaimed" areas. Nevertheless, throughout 1918 not a single additional company, battalion, or regiment was dispatched to Ireland, and troop levels on election day were the same as they had been for the previous 12 months. No security plan was debated or set in place to ensure a fair election, and at many polling stations, contingents of Irish Volunteers greatly outnumbered the few police who were on patrol. The British government, it seems, simply wished to get the election over and done with, and the fact that Sinn Fein candidates, dedicated to overthrowing British rule by force, stood unopposed by moderate nationalists in the majority of constituencies does not appear to have raised much concern.

When the results were announced, the Sinn Fein candidates immediately pledged not to take up their seats at Westminster. Instead, they declared that they would establish an Irish National Assembly, the Dáil Éireann, which would "take over the functions of Government" and demand that the Irish people "obey its orders," regardless of whether or not they lived in a constituency that had returned a Sinn Fein candidate.[169] To accomplish this goal, the 26 Sinn Fein representatives who were not interned, imprisoned, or exiled met on January 7, 1919, at the Mansion House in Dublin. Their purpose was to draw up a constitution for the government of Ireland and to plan for the public opening of the Dáil, which they scheduled for two weeks hence.[170]

The police were well informed of these events, and the Inspector General provided a detailed report for the government. The Dáil Éireann held its inaugural meeting as planned at 3:30 p.m. on January 21, again in Dublin's Mansion House. Twenty-nine of the newly elected Members of Parliament were present. On arrival they all took an oath that read,

> I hereby pledge myself to work for the establishment of an independent Irish Republic; that I will accept nothing less than complete separation from England in settlement of Ireland's claims; and that I will abstain from attending the English Parliament.

The chair of the meeting opened the session by reading a declaration of Irish independence and a document titled "Message to the Free Nations of the World" that sought to detail the morality of Irish separation from the United Kingdom. He then announced that the Irish Republic proclaimed on Easter Monday 1916 had come to pass, before reading the new Irish constitution, which gave Dáil Éireann the sole power to legislate for Ireland and placed full executive power with the ministry, which consisted of a Prime Minister, and ministers of Finance, Home Affairs, Foreign Affairs, and Defence.[171] Eamon de Valera was promptly elected Prime Minister by those present, with Arthur Griffith Minister for Foreign Affairs and Cathal Brugha Defense Minister. The meeting was then called to a close.[172]

Inspector General Byrne did not seem overly impressed with the proceedings. He told the government that the Dáil was "not taken seriously" by a "majority of people," and suggested that it was "improbable that armed rebellion will be attempted."[173] The Lord Lieutenant agreed with Byrne's analysis, commenting that the Dáil was a "ludicrous farce."[174] What both Byrne and French were unaware of, however, was that during that first day, Michael Collins had met with the other leaders of the Irish Volunteers and disbanded that organization, converting it instead into what he called the Irish Republican Army (I.R.A).[175] With the Dáil's declaration of independence, those in Sinn Fein believed that the I.R.A. had become the sole and only legitimate army of Ireland.[176] Consequently, all other forces present in the country, including the British Army and the R.I.C., were foreign occupiers engaged in an act of war. At its first meeting, the Dáil had thus asserted that the newly proclaimed Irish Republic and the British state were at war. Relations between the two, it proposed, should reflect that situation. The British government, however, regarded the Dáil as nothing more than a political stunt and fully expected the Sinn Fein members to take their seats at the Westminster Parliament when it reconvened in February—the government was ignorant of the reality on the ground.[177]

An Unacknowledged Insurgency

Whilst the declaration of independence was read in the Dáil, proclaiming Great Britain to be a foreign occupier and hence the enemy of Ireland, the I.R.A. carried out its first action against the Crown forces. At the beginning of January, the Irish Volunteers had received information that explosives were often delivered to the Soloheadbeg Quarry in County Tipperary in a horse cart guarded by armed R.I.C. constables. With the Irish Republic freshly proclaimed on January 21, the I.R.A. units in County Tipperary pledged to commence their war with an ambush on the explosives shipment. Those involved in planning the attack agreed that they would "not merely capture the gelignite" but would also "shoot down the escort."[178]

On the day the Dáil convened, the horse cart appeared as expected, with two R.I.C. constables following closely behind. When the police came upon a point in the road where the I.R.A. men were hiding, those lying in ambush jumped upon them and demanded they raise their hands. When they refused, they were shot dead. The I.R.A. stole the horse and explosives, leaving the cart driver and the county council employee in charge of the explosives alone with the dead policemen.[179]

The attack at Soloheadbeg served three purposes for the I.R.A. First, it gained for them explosives with which to carry out further attacks. As such, it could be argued by those involved that they had attacked a military target and thus the killings were justifiable, not merely murder. Second, the cart and its guards were an easy and unsuspecting target, and the mission was therefore likely to succeed. As the opening action of the I.R.A.'s campaign, a victory was essential for purposes of morale and propaganda. Finally, and most importantly, the attack identified the R.I.C. as the I.R.A.'s chief adversary. That the majority of those employed within this force were Irish Catholics was not a deterrent against their being targeted. Indeed, the fact that the constables were Irish was, in a sense, their chief crime, for they were viewed by the I.R.A. not merely as occupiers but, worse, as traitors. As the commander of the

Soloheadbeg ambush said in justification of those he killed, "What were they but a pack of deserters, spies and hirelings?"[180]

The R.I.C. Inspector General reported the attack to the British government, but he did not identify it as the opening salvo of a guerrilla campaign or war, nor did he associate what happened in Tipperary with the declaration of independence in Dublin. In his report, he listed it not as political activity but as ordinary crime, preceding it with the following sentence: "[T]he country was comparatively free from ordinary crime." He said blandly,

> 2 Constables were shot while escorting 160 lbs of gelignite to the County Council Quarry. Both Constables were fully armed, but the attack was so sudden that they were killed before they had time to defend themselves. The assailants took the police rifles and ammunition and mounting the cart containing the gelignite drove off with it.[181]

The "assailants" were given no label and were presumed to be mere Irish brigands.[182] In response to this apparent banditry, French proclaimed South Tipperary a Special Military Area under the provisions of D.O.R.A, but no further action was taken. No investigation was conducted, and no suspects were arrested.[183]

Byrne cannot be entirely faulted for his inability to connect the attack with the establishment of the Dáil. Throughout the previous year, attacks on the police had been growing in number and intensity, both by the Irish Volunteers and by others unconnected to the Irish separatist movement. As Ireland had fallen deeper into a state of anarchy and the police had found it increasingly difficult to keep order, those who would under other circumstances be deterred from participating in crime had used the unstable political situation to their advantage. As a result, so-called ordinary crime had increased exponentially throughout 1918. In that 12-month period alone, the Inspector General had listed for the British government 41 separate occasions when civilians had been shot or attacked, 21 times that cattle had been stolen, 8 instances of landowners being attacked, 16 occasions when weapons had been stolen from the homes of civilians, 2 post offices that had been robbed, 2 quarry magazines raided for explosives, 6 R.I.C. barracks attacked with homemade bombs, 8 instances of police weapons being stolen, 14 times that R.I.C. patrols had been attacked and constables beaten, and 13 instances of police being shot and wounded, but not killed. This was a far greater level of crime than in previous years.[184]

Most of these actions were judged by the Inspector General to be unrelated to the separatist movement, and no historical evidence has been produced to contradict this finding.[185] The unprecedented deaths of the constables at

Soloheadbeg seemed merely to indicate an abnormal outcome from a normal pattern of crime that had been occurring at a high rate for the past year. There was nothing to indicate that it was the beginning of a planned campaign by the Irish separatist movement against the British presence in Ireland.

Following the Soloheadbeg ambush, attacks on the police by the I.R.A. became more common. In more moderate counties, such as Longford, Tyrone, Monaghan, and Galway, attacks came relatively infrequently. In April, for example, two off-duty constables were shot but not killed in County Longford.[186] On August 15, in County Tyrone, a district inspector and police sergeant were knocked down and stoned, surviving but with severe wounds.[187] Also that day, shots were fired into Tubber R.I.C. barracks in the West Riding of County Galway, although no one inside was hit.[188] On August 28, a constable was badly assaulted in Castleblayney, County Monaghan, and the following day a second attack was launched against another constable.[189] On December 7, in County Galway's West Riding, a raid was made on the R.I.C. barracks at Maam.[190] On December 26, whilst the police were celebrating Boxing Day, a bomb was placed on the window sill of Menlough R.I.C. barracks in the East Riding of that county, injuring several constables when it exploded.[191]

Other areas of Ireland experienced more extreme levels of violence. In the East Riding of County Cork, police constables were shot and wounded on March 30, July 19, and September 28. Araglen R.I.C. barracks was attacked on April 24, with the barracks orderly bound and gagged, and all police weapons and ammunition taken. Soldiers were also targeted in the East Riding. On September 7, five soldiers were shot, one fatally. Another shooting followed on September 25, although no one was killed that day, and on both October 12 and December 14, soldiers were captured and disarmed.[192] The West Riding of County Cork experienced even more attacks. In all, 144 "outrages" were recorded by the police, including attacks against R.I.C. patrols on March 17, April 8, April 27, May 26, June 19, July 7, October 20, and November 16. On December 14, the violence in County Cork came to a bloody climax when an off-duty R.I.C. constable was shot dead whilst returning to his barracks for tea.[193]

In County Limerick, a police party was attacked whilst guarding a hunger striker in Limerick Workhouse Hospital on April 6; one constable died, another four were injured.[194] On May 13, a police patrol from the North Riding of County Tipperary was ambushed whilst escorting a prisoner by rail at Knocklong station; two policemen were killed. A month later, on June 23, a district inspector was shot dead whilst attending the Thurles races in County Tipperary; a constable was also killed in that county in an ambush on September 2.[195] In some counties, attacks were too numerous for the police to list individually. County Clare, for example, reported only that "political crimes were committed frequently. They were inaugurated by armed attacks with rifles, guns, revolvers, and in one case bombs, on Police Huts and Barracks." Police patrols were also "fired on by masked parties," and two police constables were killed during the course of the year. Three police huts and one barracks were burned to the ground, and one barracks was blown up with explosives.[196]

Overall, the police reports showed a marked increase in violence in 1919. From the end of the Easter Rising in May 1916, until the General Election in December 1918, no police constable had been killed by the separatist movement. In contrast, from the declaration of independence on January 21, 1919, until the end of that year, 21 policemen were killed. Attacks on police patrols occurred monthly, and R.I.C. barracks were attacked with bombs.[197] Whilst Byrne could have been mistaken about the motive and the responsibility for the Soloheadbeg ambush in January, intelligence reports in the months that followed left no doubt that the Irish separatists were waging a concerted insurgent campaign against the R.I.C.

Throughout this time, however, no attempt was made to ascertain the identity of the attackers or to track and capture those who had been involved in the attacks. This lack of persistence on the part of the R.I.C. had deadly consequences. Many of the attacks were carried out by the same members of the I.R.A. The principal leaders of the Soloheadbeg ambush, for example, were Sean Treacy and Dan Breen. Both were also involved in the May 13 ambush at Knocklong railway station in County Limerick, where a police party from County Tipperary was escorting an I.R.A. prisoner. A sergeant and constable were killed that day.[198] Breen would later be involved in an ambush on the Lord Lieutenant in December 1919 (see below).[199] Had a proper investigation been carried out after Soloheadbeg and the suspects found and arrested, future attacks could have been prevented.

Despite this, and although no intelligence was forthcoming on the identity of the attackers, the Inspector General did receive intelligence other than just this litany of physical attacks against the police. In February 1919, for the first time he informed the Chief Secretary and Lord Lieutenant that the Irish Volunteers were now being referred to as "the Republican Army."[200] In March, he reported that the police had found documents in the houses of suspects "relating to insurrectionary plans and attacks on police and military." These plans, he explained, showed that the I.R.A. was now "well organized on military lines" and considered the R.I.C. to be its primary enemy. Such sentiment was backed up by speeches given throughout the country by Sinn Fein representatives. One such speech, Byrne reported, claimed that it was the "R.I.C. that held the country for England during the last 100 years," and another proclaimed that "the English Government had always held down this country by police force and gaols."[201]

The I.R.A's ultimate strategy, as reported by "reliable informants," was to "draw Government by raids, murders, explosions, etc. in the belief that shooting once started would rapidly extend over the country, that soldiers could not be sent everywhere, and that a state of terror could thus be created which must compel attention to Ireland's claim to Independence." Taken together with the confiscated plans and the attacks on the police, this intelligence showed the Inspector General that Ireland was in a "highly inflammable condition." Unless an "overpowering military force" was dispatched, armed rebellion would soon commence. Byrne did not, however, suggest that such rebellion had already begun.[202]

Even in May, with the attack at Workhouse Hospital in Limerick and the first police deaths since the Soloheadbeg ambush, the Inspector General was more concerned with the industrial strike that it produced than with what it demonstrated about the I.R.A.'s commitment to attack the R.I.C. He noted that following the "murderous attack," the City of Limerick had been proclaimed a Special Military Area, with those employed at Cleeve's Factory outside Limerick's borders required to obtain permits in order to go to work. Because most of these workers were members of Sinn Fein, Byrne explained, they refused to apply for such permits, holding that the British government had no authority in Ireland to issue them. Consequently, these Sinn Fein workers decided to call a strike to protest their inability to work. They were supported in this endeavor by the Irish Transport and General Workers Union. For two weeks, Limerick City came to a standstill, but following the failure to have military restrictions lifted, the strike collapsed and business returned to normal. Byrne considered this strike far more serious than the attack on the police; it occupied nine sentences of print in his report, compared with only three for the hospital attack.[203]

It was not until June that the Inspector General began to fully grasp the situation in Ireland. In his report for that month, following the killing of two more police constables and one district inspector, Byrne summed up the situation. He wrote that there was a "conspiracy in furtherance of the Republican policy to terrorize the police with a view to render government impossible." The rationale behind this conspiracy, he explained, was that "the Irish Republic being at war with the British Empire the soldiers of the Irish Republican Army, i.e. Irish Volunteers, [believe they] are justified in killing the police as enemies." He stated that this rationale was "evidently accepted by many of these fanatical young men with the result that the ordinary duty of investigating crime is not only extremely difficult, but likewise dangerous."[204] Nevertheless, Byrne still regarded these killings as the crimes of a desperate and extreme minority, who would soon give way to political moderates. He even suggested that the Dáil Éireann was not in favor of the actions of the I.R.A., and, consequently, it was "not improbable that the republican movement may eventually give way to a more moderate aspiration."[205]

By August, in the face of mounting attacks on the police, Byrne was compelled to inform the government that Ireland had fallen into a "state of lawlessness." He repeated his previous assertions that these attacks were carried out by the Irish Republican Army and stated that they were regarded by this organization as "military operations against the enemy," that is, the police, who were believed by the I.R.A to be "the last obstacle in the way of the establishment of an Irish Republic." In addition to these attacks, Byrne reported, notices had been posted by the "G.O.C. Western Command, I.R.A," declaring the police to be "spies and traitors" and warning civilians that unless they wished to be treated as such, they were not to cooperate with the police or "in any way tolerate their existence."[206]

The consequences of this campaign of intimidation were widely felt. Byrne reported that "in the face of such terrorism witnesses cannot be induced to come forward and give evidence against the criminals." As a result, the police were attacked with impunity, with little hope of finding or prosecuting those involved. Under such an onslaught, the R.I.C. could not maintain regular patrols. In counties Clare, Galway, and Limerick, Byrne had been forced to "concentrate the police; some outlying barracks have been vacated and the remainder fortified for defense." The police, unable to continue in their normal duties, were digging in.[207]

The I.R.A. stepped up its campaign in the autumn months, directly intimidating and threatening those who attempted to aid the police in any way. In County Clare, for example, proclamations were posted listing crimes that constituted high treason to the Irish Republic, including associating with the police, supplying them with goods or transport, or cooperating in criminal investigations. The punishment for such treason was death.[208] Lesser crimes were punished accordingly. Women who were seen in the company of police or soldiers had their hair cut off and were publicly shamed; clergymen who did not support the Irish Republic from their pulpits were assaulted. Letters sent to businessmen and farmers who supplied the police warned them that if they did not cease their trade, they would be shot. Property belonging to the police and those who cooperated with the police was destroyed, ranging from mounds of turfs and hay bales to horse carts and agricultural machinery. Motor cars were stolen when judged to have been used in support of the British government, and warning shots were fired at houses that the police had visited.[209]

Still, Byrne continued to underestimate the I.R.A., failing to see a connection between the political wing of the separatist movement (Sinn Fein) and the military wing (the I.R.A.). In his September report, for example, he made no mention of the constable killed that month, devoting just 4 pages of a 16-page report to the attacks on the police and the military. In contrast, he wrote at length about industrial disputes, and included sections on agricultural produce, future business prospects, and the weather. His final paragraph warned not about the I.R.A. but about a threatened railway strike, which he noted with some relief was "not now imminent." His closing line stated that "a general armed insurrection is unlikely."[210]

The British government, represented by both the Chief Secretary and the Lord Lieutenant, received copies of all the reports Byrne compiled. In February, however, and for the following two months, French fell ill, so the responsibility for governmental administration in Ireland once again rested solely on the shoulders of the new Chief Secretary, Ian Macpherson. Only 39 years old, Macpherson had been a junior War Office minister since 1916, and called himself a "consistent home ruler."[211] He had been Chief Secretary only since January, following a cabinet reshuffle in which Lloyd George promoted the former Chief Secretary, Edward Shortt, to Home Secretary. Macpherson, therefore, had little knowledge or understanding of the trouble in Ireland.[212]

As a Home Ruler, Macpherson was "predisposed to a conciliatory policy." In March, under his leadership, the 36 Sinn Fein Members of Parliament who remained in internment were released in a gesture of goodwill reminiscent of Lloyd George's Christmas pardon 2 years earlier.[213] Not surprisingly, Macpherson's deed did no more to quiet the political discontent than had the Prime Minister's. Following this failure, he confessed to Lloyd George that "the state of the country was never worse than it is today." Although himself a Home Ruler, he could no longer see how the rule of law could be "surrender[ed] to the criminal forces of Sinn Fein."[214] Fortunately for Macpherson, French recovered from his illness shortly thereafter and took back control of Irish affairs.

Following the killing of the two R.I.C. constables at the Workhouse Hospital in County Limerick on May 13, French suggested to the Prime Minister that Sinn Fein should be outlawed and that the British government should forcibly prevent the Dáil from meeting. Lloyd George agreed, but the cabinet refused to approve the step, claiming that it would lead to open warfare between the separatist forces and the British Army.[215] Having failed to secure the support of the cabinet, French turned to Inspector General Byrne, demanding an explanation for the continued violence and pressing for the "Detective Service," by which he meant the Crimes Special Branch, to be reformed.[216]

In his call for reform, French was acting wisely. At this time, all intelligence was relayed in an ad hoc manner to the Crimes Special Branch in Dublin.

At each county headquarters throughout the country, there was a Crimes Special Branch sergeant, with a Crimes Special Branch constable at each district headquarters. The major cities, such as Dublin and Belfast, had additional constables attached to the Crimes Special Branch. It was the duty of these officers to collect intelligence on all political organizations within their area, to compile reports based on that intelligence, and to send these reports to the Crimes Special Branch headquarters in Dublin. These officers did not, however, coordinate their activities with the military intelligence officers, nor, generally speaking, did they associate with police constables or sergeants on regular duty. The Crimes Special Branch, therefore, operated in a vacuum, separated from regular police activities and from other intelligence-gathering organizations.

This system of intelligence collection had been in place since 1872, following the Fenian rebellion of five years earlier. It had changed very little since that time. In its first real test, during the Land Wars of the 1880s, informants were numerous and had readily given information to the police. The system had worked well, therefore. During the period of overt militancy 30 years later, Crimes Special Branch officers in Ulster had also successfully obtained thorough and accurate intelligence on the founding and growth of the Ulster Volunteer Force. Throughout these years, Crimes Special Branch officers were rewarded well for their service, given extra time off, an extensive clothing allowance, and additional pay. In early 1916, however, Chief Secretary Birrell eliminated their extra pay and time off and greatly reduced their clothing allowance, believing that the Crimes Special Branch was no longer a necessity in the Irish police force; he felt certain at that time that the threat of an Irish separatist insurgency had dissipated with the start of the First World War. These cuts in incentives discouraged some qualified constables and sergeants from continuing in what was quickly becoming one of the more dangerous jobs in the R.I.C. From 1916 to 1918, many officers who were well schooled in the craft of intelligence collection left the branch, therefore.

With the start of Sinn Fein's intimidation campaign in 1917, and with its intensification in 1918, the Crimes Special Branch system of relying on informants to approach the police with information became untenable. Informants could not be found, and those who would previously have spoken to the police ceased to do so for fear of being branded traitors and shot. By May 1919, when French encouraged Byrne to reform, the Crimes Special Branch had ceased to function as an effective unit and was in desperate need of restructuring.[217] Byrne replied, however, that the police were doing all they could but, as he had stated in his previous reports, were prevented from operating under normal conditions because of widespread intimidation that made informants difficult to find.[218] French accepted Byrne's analysis for the time being but continued to pressure the Inspector General to be more proactive in collecting intelligence, investigating not just attacks carried out by the I.R.A. but also the manning of the organization. French continued to hold the belief that police intelligence capabilities were "dangerously weak and ineffectual," and he made this known to Byrne whenever possible.[219]

After the assassination of the district inspector at Thurles in June, French again asked the cabinet to declare Sinn Fein a banned organization, but again they declined. French, therefore, took it upon himself to act against Sinn Fein. On July 4, he proclaimed Sinn Fein an illegal organization in County Tipperary under the powers invested in him through D.O.R.A. The cabinet was furious, but they did not force him to retract his proclamation.[220] However, in August, Winston Churchill, now Secretary of State for War and Air, suggested to the cabinet that "nothing would annoy the Irish more than the conviction that they were not absorbing the minds of the people of Great Britain."[221] The cabinet agreed, and for the remainder of the year they ignored the security situation across the Irish Sea.

Meanwhile, the police in Ireland continued to bear the brunt of the war waged against Sinn Fein and the I.R.A. French again took matters into his own hands, on September 10 proclaiming Sinn Fein, the Irish Volunteers, and the I.R.A. illegal organizations in 27 of the 32 Irish counties, and outlawing Dáil Éireann.[222] Without the support of the British government, however, there was little more he could do. The R.I.C. and the military were outmatched and understaffed; without an order from the cabinet, there could be no reinforcements. French would have to make do with what he had.[223]

The situation in Ireland was slowly slipping beyond the control of the British government. Sinn Fein had been elected in a majority of constituencies following a year of intimidation and violence. With this electoral mandate, they had declared independence, proclaimed the Irish Republic, and established the Irish Republican Army. Now, within that Irish Republic, there was no room for dissent. Those who chose not to acknowledge the legitimacy of Sinn Fein rule or the authority of the I.R.A., or who continued to follow the laws of the British parliament, were deemed guilty of treason, subject to execution without recourse to a trial or jury. The state that Sinn Fein claimed to have established was one of ruthless autocracy.

From his intelligence reports, Byrne was well aware of how dire the situation had become. He had read accounts of the intimidation against civilians, seen copies of the proclamations of treason, and heard in detail of attacks against the police. He acknowledged in his reports to the Chief Secretary and Lord Lieutenant that it was the policy of Sinn Fein to undermine British government in Ireland and to prevent the R.I.C. from carrying out its duties. He was also aware that the attacks against the police had been carried out by the

I.R.A., and that it was the I.R.A. that was behind much of the intimidation against civilians. Nevertheless, he refused to characterize the violence as a cohesive campaign and maintained that the best way to eliminate the influence of the I.R.A. was to seek a compromise with Sinn Fein's Dáil Éireann.

French disagreed. In a letter to the Chief Secretary on November 4, he wrote that Byrne was "showing great weakness."[224] Together, they decided to remove him from his post. On November 10, French ordered the Inspector General to take a month's leave to recover from the stress he was under. When Byrne returned to Dublin in December, his desks had been sealed and his deputy, T.J. Smith, had been installed in his place as head of the R.I.C. The Prime Minister supported this bureaucratic coup, telling French on December 30 that Byrne had "lost his nerve."[225]

Early in January 1920, French tried to force Byrne into retirement, but neither age nor health proved to be appropriate grounds.[226] Byrne therefore remained on the payroll until 1922, the ostensible Inspector General of the R.I.C., locked out of his offices. From December 1919 onwards, Smith wrote and compiled the intelligence reports for the British government. Byrne did not object and was rewarded for this passive compliance when he finally left his post, becoming Governor of the Seychelles from 1922 to 1927, of Sierra Leone from 1927 to 1931, and of Kenya from 1931 to 1937.[227]

Byrne was given his leave in hasty fashion, it seems without any single event to provoke his removal. Certainly French had been displeased with the state of police intelligence since May and had informed Byrne of this fact to no avail; despite his concern, the Inspector General had taken no steps to reform the Crimes Special Branch. Furthermore, French had been increasingly frustrated at Byrne's lack of focus on Sinn Fein and the I.R.A. in his monthly reports and at his steadfast insistence that Sinn Fein was a legitimate political party, distinct from the I.R.A. Both French and Lloyd George took this insistence as weakness rather than conviction, believing Byrne had grown timid in the face of a concerted campaign of violence. Yet General Nevil Macready, soon to be appointed General Officer Commanding Ireland, suggested another reason for Byrne's dismissal:

> The affair was shrouded in a good deal of mystery, but I have little doubt that the origin of the trouble was due to Byrne being a Roman Catholic and therefore regarded with suspicion by the Chief Secretary, Ian Macpherson, and certain other Castle officials tinged with that religious intolerance which has for so long been the curse of Ireland.[228]

Neither French nor Lloyd George admitted to such in their discussions over his removal, and Macpherson does not appear to have been directly involved in their deliberations. Nevertheless, the fact that Byrne, a Catholic, chose to see the separatist movement in a more limited and passive manner than either the Chief Secretary, Lord Lieutenant, or Prime Minister could have done nothing other than add to their decision to remove him.

Immediately upon replacing Byrne, Smith wrote a more damning report than any produced by his predecessor. He characterized the widespread violence in Ireland as a "republican conspiracy to paralyze government by a campaign of murder and outrage secretly organized and primarily against the police," who had now become dependent on the military for protection in many districts and were almost incapable of carrying out their regular duties. This "terrorism," he said, was "extensively prevalent," and although those carrying out this campaign were only a small minority, "largely through intimidation the general public will neither inform against nor denounce them." Finally, becoming the first member of the British establishment to do so, he placed on paper the words "guerrilla warfare," if only indirectly, stating, "They [the I.R.A.] have sufficient arms and explosives under their control but hidden away for committing outrages—guerilla warfare they call it—and would probably be ready to cause trouble on a larger scale if the garrison were not maintained at adequate strength." The police, he reported, were now incapable of keeping the peace in Ireland without military support.[229]

His words proved to be accurate. On December 19, French was almost killed in an ambush at Ashtown in County Dublin. A motorcade in which he was riding was attacked by small-arms fire and hand grenades as it departed the train station. The Lord Lieutenant's car was struck in four places, but remarkably he was uninjured. One of the assailants was shot and killed by French's guards, but ten others escaped and were never identified by the police.[230] Immediately following this attack, French set up a committee to "place matters in Dublin and the country on a proper footing." The committee found that there was an "organized conspiracy of murder, outrage, and intimidation," and recommended that police constables be better trained in detective work, that the R.I.C. play a greater role in intelligence collection, that there be more joint military-police patrols, and that a "secret corps" of R.I.C. men be formed who would be "young active men of courage and determination, good shots and preferably men accustomed to city life," who would shadow R.I.C. and D.M.P. detectives to kill potential assassins before they had the chance to strike.[231] In response to this report, French instructed Smith to appoint a "very capable" R.I.C. officer from Belfast to "take care of political crime." One such man was duly appointed, but after only a month's service, he was shot dead by the I.R.A.[232]

At the end of January, Smith informed French and Macpherson that the I.R.A.'s "campaign of murder and violence" had reached greater levels of brutality than ever before. In that month alone, over 600 offenses had been reported by the police, including 10 armed attacks on R.I.C. barracks, 2 cases of police patrols being ambushed by over 40 men, and 5 constables being shot and wounded (1 fatally). The civilian population also continued to be intimidated. A tailor who prepared uniforms for the police had his shop raided and all material stolen, a woman who had assisted one of the wounded constables received a letter threatening death, and a landowner who had begun proceedings against the I.R.A. for trespass had half of each of his ears cut off and his wife's hair shaven. Smith concluded that this campaign was one of "guerrilla warfare," characterized by "murder and sporadic raids on barracks." From the intelligence reports he had received, he felt certain that the I.R.A. was "determined to carry it on."[233]

Upon receiving this report, French told Macpherson, "I can best describe the situation here . . . as something in the nature of an incipient Boer War."[234] The Lord Lieutenant was no longer talking in terms of isolated crimes, attacks, and outrages, but of open hostilities. He saw the situation in Ireland for what it was. The I.R.A. was engaged in a war with the British Crown forces, and, if French had his way, the government would respond in kind.

Intelligence Reorganized

On April 4, 1920—Easter Monday—the Irish Republican Army took a dramatic step forward in its campaign against the British. On that date, its volunteers raided the tax offices in Dublin, Cork, and elsewhere, destroying the tax records for all of Ireland and burning to the ground more than 300 local government buildings, including courthouses. These attacks were so successful that from that day forth the Crown legal system ceased to function in Ireland and the British government was reduced to the collection of customs and excise for its revenue.[235]

In late 1917, Sinn Fein had established a system of "arbitration courts" as an alternative to the government's justice system. With the opening of Dáil Éireann in January 1919, Sinn Fein had proclaimed that British law no longer held any authority in Ireland, and had declared that any person using the British court system was guilty of treason. By the summer of 1919, at least one Sinn Fein court had been established in each Irish county.[236] The material destruction of the courthouses in April 1920, therefore, was merely a physical testament to the reality of the past two years, but it was one that painted that reality in stark colors.

Following these attacks, the British cabinet finally decided to intervene in Ireland, abandoning Churchill's policy that the best course of action was to ignore Ireland and deny the militants the satisfaction of occupying the minds of Britain's statesmen. Having determined that the situation in Ireland had deteriorated beyond civil control, the cabinet decided to shift the base of power away from French and the office of the Lord Lieutenant and onto the General Officer Commanding Ireland. Thus, in the space of two years, authority in Ireland had migrated from a political Chief Secretary, whose power was modeled on the British Prime Minister, to a military governor of sorts, to the military commander himself. This swift transition of power marked a distinct change in the mentality of the British government.[237]

From 1912 to 1918, the period covering the rise of the U.V.F. and the Irish Volunteers, the Easter Rising, and the first inklings of a guerilla war, the government had held to a policy of civilian control and, in a sense, blind optimism. In the early years of this time (the period of overt militancy, 1912–1914), it was their hope that the U.V.F. and Irish Volunteers would disband without intervention, despite solid intelligence suggesting otherwise. The outbreak of the First World War allowed the British government to maintain this delusion and prevented them from seeing the potentially deadly consequences of their wait-and-see policy.

In the run-up to the 1916 rising (the period of clandestine organization), the government was too preoccupied with events on the continent to worry much about Ireland, and the intelligence services there were likewise too busy looking for a German invasion to notice a domestic insurgency. When the I.R.B., Irish Volunteers, and Citizen Army did take to the streets of Dublin, they were ruthlessly suppressed but then largely forgotten. Sinn Fein, the political party that represented the separatist movement, was mistakenly thought to be peaceful in intent. Only following the tumultuous year of 1917 and the resignation of Chief Secretary Henry Edward Duke did the government decide to reform Irish administration and centralize power around the person of the Lord Lieutenant.

Even then, the attitude of the government continued to be one of hoping for the best. With the declaration of Irish independence, the establishment of the Dáil Éireann, and the beginning of the I.R.A.'s campaign of violence, there could be little doubt that all hopes of a political settlement in Ireland had been shattered, yet the British government's chief consideration continued to be to act with moderation in Ireland. They refused to support French when he called for stronger action against the separatist movement and attempted to increase the role of the military. Instead, the members of the cabinet held that if they ignored the violence, the militant elements of the separatist movement would simply wither away and the Sinn Fein representatives in the Dáil would eventually seek compromise. The attacks on the tax offices and courthouses in April 1920, finally shook the government from its stupor, and convinced it of the need for significant reform.

For the first three months of 1920, British policy had been to reduce the size of the military in Ireland and fill this void with additional police manpower. This was difficult to do, however, because increasingly large numbers of constables had been leaving the R.I.C since 1918, fearful for their own lives and the lives of their families in the face of the I.R.A's campaign of intimidation.[238] In January, therefore, Deputy Inspector General Smith authorized recruitment to take place outside of Ireland. Byrne had opposed this, claiming that it would lead to an unnecessary militarization of the R.I.C. and further isolate the men from the communities in which they served, but as soon as he was removed, his successor embraced the policy.[239]

In February and March, posters began to appear in English cities calling for recruits for the R.I.C., and recruiting offices were opened in London, Liverpool, and Manchester.[240] There was no shortage of candidates, as demobilization had recently occurred following the armistice, resulting in large numbers of unemployed and demoralized young men looking for adventure. Consequently, R.I.C. recruiting sergeants took only men trained in the use of firearms, with experience in the trench warfare of France. The first contingent of these new recruits arrived in Dublin on March 25, 1920; all were former British soldiers.[241]

Upon arrival, these ex-soldiers were duly sworn in as R.I.C. constables and given regular warrant numbers, but they had to complete only six weeks training compared with the regular R.I.C. course of six months. They were also supplied with the R.I.C's rifle-green uniform to distinguish them from the regular soldiers in the British Army and to identify them as policemen. By the end of May, over 1,500 had been recruited and had completed their short training course. Due to this large influx of manpower, R.I.C. uniforms began to run short. Consequently, the new recruits were given a strange hybrid of uniforms, a mixture of military khaki and R.I.C. green: some with R.I.C. tunics but khaki trousers, others khaki tunics with R.I.C. trousers, and still others an entire khaki uniform with R.I.C. hat. The only thing that all had in common was the standard black belt of the R.I.C. As a result of this improvised uniform, these English recruits were easily identified when on patrol, and thus were given a nickname both by those they coerced and by those they served with: the Black and Tans.[242]

In July 1920, four months after the first Black and Tans arrived in Ireland, an additional group of men was recruited to augment the police there, the Auxiliary Division. The Auxiliaries, in contrast to the Black and Tans, had all been commissioned British Army officers during the First World War, and were placed under the command of Brigadier General F.P. Crozier, never part of the R.I.C force. They were given no warrant numbers, operated out of their own independent bases, and wore a distinctive dark-blue uniform, glengarry-style cap, and an ammunition bandolier strapped across their chest. Each Auxiliary unit was placed under the command of its own officer, who coordinated operations with the R.I.C. county inspector, but otherwise worked independently.[243]

Ironically, this intervention by the cabinet, which French had been calling for since becoming Lord Lieutenant, resulted first in the erosion of his power and eventually in undermining his position altogether. On March 23, just two weeks before the raids on the tax offices, General Sir Nevil Macready succeeded General Frederick Shaw as the General Officer Commanding Ireland.[244] Macready was in the unique position of having served as a military commander in Belfast in 1914, at the height of the U.V.F.'s militancy, and then as a police commander for two years, the Commissioner of the London Metropolitan Police (Scotland Yard). When explaining his appointment to the House of Commons, the Prime Minister spoke of his "military and police experience and remarkable powers of organization with exceptional judgment and tact."[245] Like most British officials tasked with duty in Ireland, Macready had strong feelings about the country to which he was sent. When writing to Macpherson to congratulate him on being appointed Chief Secretary in January 1919, he had commented, "I cannot say I envy you for I loathe the country you are going to and its people with a depth deeper than the sea and more violent than that which I feel against the Boche."[246]

Lloyd George had at first wanted Macready to take control of both the R.I.C. and the army, but the general refused.[247] Consequently, in May, the Prime Minister appointed Major General Sir Henry Hugh Tudor as the "Police Advisor to the Viceroy on the Royal Irish Constabulary and Dublin Metropolitan Police." When Deputy Inspector General Smith later resigned from his position in December 1920, he was not replaced, and Tudor took complete control of both the R.I.C. and the D.M.P, taking the title Chief of Police.[248] Although both Macready and Tudor were technically subservient to French, Macready made known to the Prime Minister his belief that Ireland should be ruled directly by the military, without civilian control. Tudor, as head of the lead security agency (the police), outranked Macready, but Tudor had been interviewed and chosen for the post by Macready, and thus in practice he played the role of Macready's deputy, reporting not to French but to Macready. Consequently, although French was ostensibly still head of all Irish administration, following the appointments of Macready and Tudor in the spring of 1920, his authority waned considerably, and Macready became the true source of power in Ireland.[249]

The cabinet did not stop at reform with the appointment of Macready and Tudor. At the beginning of April, the Prime Minister replaced Chief Secretary Macpherson with Sir Hamar Greenwood, a Canadian-born Member of Parliament with only one year's experience as a junior minister. Macpherson had been showing signs of increasing stress and had succumbed to minor illnesses on several occasions since the previous December when French had been ambushed; although not present in the motorcade, the potential for such attacks had clearly shaken him. Lloyd George, therefore, told him that "he was ill and should take a quieter job."[250]

Following this replacement, the cabinet commissioned Sir Warren Fisher, head of the British Civil Service and Permanent Secretary at His Majesty's Treasury, to travel to Dublin and write a report on the state of the Irish administration. His report, submitted to the government in May, was damning. It concluded,

> The [Dublin] Castle administration does not administer. On the mechanical side it can never have been good and is now quite obsolete; in the infinitely more important sphere (a) of informing and advising the Irish government in relation to policy and (b) of practical capacity in the application of policy it simply has no existence.[251]

Fisher recommended that a complete reorganization of Irish administration take place to accompany the new appointment of Greenwood. The government agreed to all recommended changes. Sir John Anderson was appointed joint under secretary, to assist James MacMahon, who had held the position since May, 1918; A.W. Cope was appointed assistant under secretary; and Mark Sturgis was sent to Dublin with no title, but in time became the unofficial liaison between French, Greenwood, and Anderson.[252]

In making these appointments, the government added to Irish administration an element of disunity. Fisher had written his report not only with efficiency of governance in mind, but also with a distinct political intent. He recommended to the cabinet that just because "the Sinn Fein movement includes amongst its ideals ultimate separation from Great Britain is no argument for withholding recognition of Sinn Fein as a political party. . . . The policy I advocate is not one of 'conciliation,' but the restoration to the community at large of elementary human rights as understood by Anglo-Saxondom."[253] He was opposed to martial law, opposed to the outlawing of Sinn Fein, and opposed to tougher security measures. Those whom he recommended, all having served in London their entire careers, held these same beliefs. On the day of his appointment, Mark Sturgis wrote,

> For several days I have been more at the Treasury [with Fisher] than anywhere else talking about Ireland and trying to learn. I am told that the old "Castle gang" made the mistake of attributing the murders and

outrages of a small extreme section of Sinn Fein to the whole political party, and so alienated from our side not only the ruffians but the decent part of the party who now stand by in apathy or grim complacence of the activities of the gun men.[254]

These new appointees held the same conviction as Inspector General Byrne, namely, that Sinn Fein was a legitimate party, with only a minority engaged in or supportive of violence. They therefore broke ranks with French's policy of increased precautions, and remained skeptical of the intelligence reports produced by Tudor.

Lloyd George attempted to bridge the gap between the two. On April 30, 1920, he told Macready that the policy he wished to carry out in Ireland was "in the direction of endeavoring to bring about a better feeling between the authorities at the Castle and de Valeria's followers." At the same time, however, he made it plain to the general that "a continuance of the campaign of assassination would necessitate measures more drastic than any which had been hitherto enforced." To maintain such a balancing act proved too difficult for the government, and politics was placed above security. Consequently, Macready later noted, "[N]ever up to the time the troops finally left Ireland did the Government take the one step by which alone order could have been restored, that is to say, the declaration of martial law throughout the land."[255]

Macready was not the only official in Ireland frustrated at the government's vacillation. Mark Sturgis, although initially supportive of the policy of conciliation, quickly came to realize that such a policy was unfeasible in the lawless climate of Ireland. On July 23, commenting on a speech given that day by the Chief Secretary, he noted in his diary that the speech was "disappointing and gave no hint of compromise or conciliation *nor* alternatively of effective coercion. We must have one or the other."[256] Eight days later, he wrote that "pacifists and all sorts agree that some thing must be done by London and that quickly if the whole thing isn't to crash. It makes all one tries to do seem so futile—if only the Londoners would realize how serious it is perhaps they'd get a move on."[257] By August, he had lost all pretensions of appeasement, writing on the third of that month, "If we aren't to treat we must hit, and if we must hit then we must hit damn hard." That same day, he lamented, "Why does some hideous fate make all politicians love half measures which of all so called policies is the only surely fatal one. The Irish aren't fit to govern themselves; of course they aren't, but I'm damned if the English are either."[258]

Meanwhile, as Sturgis was despairing over politicians in London, Tudor was struggling with the security forces in Ireland. When appointed Chief of Police in May 1920, he found the police intelligence community in a state of disrepair. Very little intelligence was being produced by the Crimes Special Branch that could not be easily discovered by reading the local nationalist newspapers. In light of this, Tudor suggested to Macready that a branch of his newly formed Chief of Police's office should be made responsible for reorganizing the Irish intelligence system. Macready agreed, and on May 11, police and military intelligence was united under a single leadership, that of Brigadier General Ormonde Winter, who reported directly to Tudor.[259] Winter seemed to be the right man for the job. One of his contemporaries commented in his diary,

> "O" [Winter] is a marvel—he looks like a wicked snake and can do everything! He is an Artillery Colonel and commanded a Division of artillery in France: in India, they say, he was tried for murder for a little escapade when doing secret service work. He started a race course near Calcutta and made a pot o' money. He is clever as paint, probably entirely non-moral, a first class horseman, a card genius, knows several languages, is a super sleuth, and a most amazing original. When a soldier who knew him in India heard he was coming to Ireland he said "God help Sinn Fein, they don't know what they're up against."[260]

In late May, Winter established a centralized network of intelligence collection, in an attempt to rectify the problems inherent in the Crimes Special Branch. Both that branch and the detective's department of the D.M.P. were merged into this new service. At the heart of the network was the central bureau, located in Dublin, in which all intelligence information was received, analyzed, and disseminated to the government. Throughout Ireland, in each police district, local intelligence centers were formed, which would cooperate with regular police constables and military intelligence officers in collecting intelligence to send to the central bureau. These local intelligence centers were situated in the headquarters of the R.I.C. divisional commissioners, for convenience of intelligence sharing and for quick action.

Winter recognized that due to the unstable condition of much of Ireland, it would take time to establish these intelligence centers, but he hoped the system could be completed by the summer of 1921. These local centers, when formed, were empowered by Winter to employ any local informants or agents that they could find, and the local police were ordered to provide all information of interest directly to the police intelligence officers based there. A police intelligence officer was also posted to each Auxiliary Company, and worked closely with the intelligence officers at the local center closest to which his company was operating.[261]

In September 1920, three months after the first of these local intelligence centers opened, an intelligence center was established in London, in conjunction with Scotland Yard, to obtain intelligence information by correspondence. This was formed in recognition of the difficulties in finding informants in Ireland due to the intimidation tactics of the I.R.A., and thus information could be sent anonymously to a P.O. Box in London.[262] Three months later, in December, Winter ordered a raids bureau to be established, the sole purpose of which was to collect all documents captured by the R.I.C. and army during raids, to analyze them, and to produce précis of this information for Macready, Tudor, Greenwood, and French. The first of these précis was produced in January 1921; in time, over 1,200 précis were circulated through the British government, some more than 200 pages long.[263]

The intelligence gathered from these raids was considered by Winter "the most valuable" of all sources, in part because each captured document brought evidence of where to find others. Commenting on this, Winter wrote, "After the first important capture, which, to a great extent, was fortuitous, other searches were made from the addresses noted and names obtained, and the snowball process continued, leading to fresh searches, new arrests, and the obtaining of a more intimate knowledge of the plans, resources, and methods of the rebel organization." In Dublin City alone, between December 1920, and July 1921, 6,311 police raids were undertaken. In many cases, intelligence was produced from these raids that showed the police where to carry out the next raid.[264]

Initially, the police constables carrying out these raids were slow to utilize the intelligence system established. Those who took part in the raids were "apt to retain important documents as personal souvenirs, and relegate documents of no local interest to the waste paper basket." In time, however, this practice was eliminated, and all documents were sent to the raids bureau, regardless of how insignificant they seemed. This process revolutionized the intelligence collection system. As Winter explained,

> Prior to its inauguration it was found that, not only was a lot of valuable information missed, but that quantities of documents were either lost or discarded as valueless. Letters seized in one part of Ireland were often meaningless, but, when compared with documents in a similar handwriting, captured in another locality, either afforded valuable clues or led to the prosecution of the writer. An instance may be cited to emphasize this point. An unsigned letter, inciting to murder, was found in the North of Ireland, and by reason of the want of a signature, was retained there as being of little value. It was accidentally discovered and brought to

Headquarters, and other letters of a harmless nature, duly signed, were found in Dublin. A comparison of the letters disclosed the identity of the writer and his conviction was obtained.

As a result of such evidence, in Dublin City alone, 1,745 arrests were made between November 21, 1920, and February 21, 1921, and 310 revolvers, 34 rifles, 20 shotguns, and "a large quantity of bombs, explosives, detonators, and articles or equipment" were seized.[265]

This intelligence system, of course, was not perfect, chiefly because many who normally would have cooperated with the intelligence officers had been "rendered inarticulate by terrorism." Recruiting suitably qualified men to man the intelligence centers was also difficult, as those within the R.I.C. were frightened to take a more overtly political role in the campaign against the I.R.A. Winter reported that recruits could be found in England, but acknowledged that the Englishman operating in Ireland would be at a "serious disadvantage" and the Irishman who was resident in England and willing to serve had often "lived out of Ireland for some time, and had few facilities for gaining inside knowledge." Recruiting and training suitable officers would take time, and Winter suggested that "to build up an Intelligence organization for the investigation of political crime in a few months is, practically, an impossibility. The Criminal Investigation Department of India was in being seven years before it commenced to yield any appreciable results."[266]

Nevertheless, on July 4, 1921, the last local intelligence center was opened, and the intelligence network was finally operating at its full capacity. These local intelligence centers employed 150 specially trained officers throughout Ireland. From their founding in June 1920 to their completion in July 1921, these centers opened files on 449 political suspects across Ireland.[267] The Crown forces now had a working intelligence system in Ireland, and were finally prepared to combat the I.R.A. on an equal basis. Two weeks after the last center was opened, however, the British government sued for peace, and on July 11, a truce was called between the I.R.A. and the Crown forces. The war, never officially acknowledged by the British, was finally over.

A Failure of Action

The I.R.A's guerrilla campaign had been a bloody one. In all, it cost the lives of 405 policemen, and caused the serious wounding of another 682. Also killed were 150 soldiers, with 345 wounded. A total of 522 vacated R.I.C. barracks, 25 occupied barracks, and 88 courthouses were destroyed.

When placed against the 267 barracks that were attacked and seriously damaged but not destroyed, these numbers testify to 31 months of vicious warfare.[268] In response to these attacks, the R.I.C., Black and Tans, and Auxiliaries began a campaign of reprisals against the Irish civilian population. This commenced with the burning of public buildings, businesses, and factories in Tuam on July 20, 1920, in retaliation for the deaths of two R.I.C. constables. The police hoped that by destroying public property and punishing civilians for I.R.A. attacks, the Irish population would turn against the I.R.A. and make known the whereabouts of key I.R.A. figures to the authorities.

On July 17, three days before this first reprisal occurred, Macready had written to the Chief Secretary, providing for him an appraisal of the security situation in Ireland. He reported that Sinn Fein had "gained ground from the point of view of obtaining more adherents throughout the country, either from fear or conviction," and noted that "the state of affairs in this country has been allowed to drift into such an impasse that no amount of coercion can possibly remedy it." The country might be "cowed into quiescence" if martial law were implemented "as understood by soldiers," but it would result in a "good deal of blood" being spilt. If such a system were applied, Macready cautioned, "[A]lthough the country might be quieted, I believe the solution of the Irish question would be further off than ever." He concluded, writing,

> I am sorry if my outlook seems rather gloomy, but as the days pass, I am convinced that nothing but what might be called a bold, dramatic, political stroke will solve this matter, and I do not for one instant think that the British public would stand Martial Law, as I understand it, for a week over here, and anything less than that in the direction of coercion would be little better than what we are doing at present.[269]

Macready was convinced that the only security measure guaranteed to quiet the I.R.A. was full-scale martial law. He was equally convinced, however, that to institute such would dash any hopes of a lasting political settlement in Ireland. The British government, having adopted a policy of vacillation for the past eight years, now found itself in an impossible situation.

Three days after Macready wrote to Greenwood, on the day Tuam was torched, Sir John Anderson also sent a letter to the Chief Secretary. He related that when he had arrived in Dublin as joint under secretary on May 22, the "ordinary machinery of Civil administration in the Chief Secretary's Office at Dublin Castle" was "practically non-existent"; the police forces were in a "critical condition," with the "all important matter of intelligence and secret service . . . entirely neglected"; the prison system was "thoroughly bad"; and the military forces were "insufficient in numbers" and "for the immediate purpose of giving support to the civil authority in the ordinary task of maintaining law and order throughout the country almost unless." In the two months since he had been in Ireland, he continued, the situation had not significantly improved, despite a full-scale reform of the Irish administration. Over those two months, he reported, Sinn Fein had been "gathering strength rapidly." More alarmingly, violent crimes had "increased greatly in number," and "terrorism" was "widespread over a large part of Ireland."[270] Regardless of the changes made to governance in Ireland, Anderson asserted, the British were not winning—they were losing.

In response to this letter, Greenwood asked that Anderson prepare a memorandum for the cabinet, which he submitted five days later, on July 25. He warned its members that "the entire population in the South and West, so far as it is not actually hostile, is out of sympathy with the Government and cannot be relied upon to co-operate in the carrying out of even the most reasonable and moderate measures." Like Macready, he saw the only hope of restoring order in martial law: "If force and force alone is to be relied upon, the strongest measures must, in my judgment, be applied and with the least possible delay. . . . This means, in effect, a military dictatorship—in other words, a form of martial law—extending over the whole sphere of administration, including those services not now controlled by the Irish Executive." Like Macready, however, he believed that although such security measures would quiet the population, they would also further distance it from the government, making future political relations more difficult. He therefore felt "profound misgivings on the point."[271]

The following day, July 26, Macready prepared his own memorandum for the cabinet, which they received, distributed by War Secretary Winston Churchill, on August 6. He wrote, "In a few words, the position is this, that while our opponents are making war on us, we are acting in support of civil power, the forces of which are less reliable than they were six months ago, and, as a necessary corollary to our support, a great number of troops are engaged in purely defense of localities, buildings, &c." He concluded with the ominous statement that "the situation in Ireland to-day is far worse and more difficult to all ranks of the Army than if they were engaged in actual warfare against an acknowledged enemy."[272] Coming from a man who had spent the better part of the First World War in France, his words painted a dark picture.

Meanwhile, as Anderson and Macready sent their memoranda to the cabinet, reprisals by the security forces in Ireland continued: at Limerick, Thurles, and Upperchurch in late July; Templemore on August 16; Balbriggan on

September 20; Ennistymon, Lahinch, Malbay, and Miltown on September 22; Trim on September 27; Mallow on September 28; Boyle on October 5; Listowel, Tralee, and Tubbercurry in late October; Templemore for the second time on November 1; and Ballymote and Granard on November 4.[273] Not surprisingly, they did not have the desired effect; the civilian population became at first passive towards and then supportive of the separatist cause.

Macready, sensing this trend, wrote again to the government in late October. He noted that he had written earlier, on September 27, suggesting that the unofficial reprisals were having a detrimental effect on the morale and discipline of the troops, and carried out in such a haphazard and uncoordinated fashion, were doing little to combat the I.R.A. He had therefore recommended to the government that stronger action on an official level be approved to eliminate the necessity for unofficial reprisals. As "[n]o action so far in that direction has been approved by the Government," however, Macready was now writing to suggest to the government that a remedy was "the proclamation of Martial Law." If they were not willing to proclaim such, he impressed upon them that "some steps must be taken, and taken very shortly, to regularize reprisals for outrages committed upon troops." This was necessary both to defeat the I.R.A. and to restore discipline within the army. He offered a suggestion for how such reprisals should be carried out:

> Whenever a house or houses are burnt or destroyed by rebels, the house of a prominent member or officer of the I.R.A. in the immediate vicinity should be destroyed. Where shots are fired or bombs thrown from houses, those houses should be destroyed. Where, as is often the case, ambushes are laid for troops in the vicinity of houses where inhabitants must be well aware of the presence of the ambush, those houses should be destroyed. [These reprisals] should be undertaken, so far as the Army is concerned, only by order of officers not below the rank of Brigadier-General, except in certain selected cases where battalions are on distant detachment, and where in the opinion of the Divisional Commander the Battalion or Regimental Commander might be trusted and empowered to use his discretion. In regard to reprisals by the Police, I suggest that Divisional Commissioners and County Inspectors alone should be authorized to order reprisals.[274]

The problem with Macready's suggestion was that no intelligence was forthcoming on the individuals participating in I.R.A. attacks, and thus their houses could not be properly targeted. Besides, the cabinet refused to sanction such a clear-worded statement of intent and preferred the reprisals to continue on a more covert and unacknowledged basis. Thus the I.R.A. continued to attack the police and military, and the police and military continued to carry out reprisals on the civilian population, often indiscriminately.

This campaign of I.R.A. assassination and ambush, followed by police retaliation, was punctuated throughout the year by more daring and, in some cases, atrocious attacks on both sides. On March 20, 1920, for example, a contingent of the R.I.C., disguised in civilian clothing, broke into the house of Cork City's Lord Mayor, Tomas MacCurtain, and shot him dead for being a known I.R.A. sympathizer.[275] In retaliation, the I.R.A. assassinated R.I.C. District Inspector Oswald Swanzy, who was believed by them to have organized the death of MacCurtain.[276] On June 26, 1920, Brigadier General Cuthbert Lucas was captured by the I.R.A. whilst on a fishing trip in County Cork. Lucas, the highest-ranking British official captured, was held for a month before finally making his escape.[277] In September, in that same county, the I.R.A. kidnapped a resident magistrate and shot him in the head before dumping him on a manure heap. When the I.R.A. returned to the spot later that night, they found that the executioner had failed to kill the magistrate. Thus they took him to a beach and buried him up to his neck in sand to wait for the tide to come in. The following morning, they found him still alive, above the high-tide mark. They therefore unburied him, took him further out into the sand, and reburied him, where he eventually drowned later that day.[278]

By far the most dramatic series of attacks occurred on November 21, a day soon to become known as Bloody Sunday. Beginning at 9:00 a.m., 180 I.R.A. men in Dublin and elsewhere set about in a concerted effort to assassinate the leadership of the British security apparatus. Most of the men found were shot dead whilst still in bed, some in the presence of their wives. In all, 14 were killed by the I.R.A., operating in gangs of 20–25 in number.[279] In response, a contingent from the Black and Tans, Auxiliaries, and British Army sought out suspects in the Gaelic Athletic Association Headquarters at Croke Park in Dublin, where a Gaelic Football match was underway between Dublin and Tipperary. As they marched onto the field, a warning shot was fired by one of the spectators. The Crown forces thus turned and opened fire into the crowd. Twelve people died, including 1 player, and more than 70 were injured. Later that evening, with tensions still running high, three I.R.A. suspects were shot dead within the walls of Dublin Castle, where they were being held. Their captors claimed they were trying to escape.[280]

Following Bloody Sunday, events in Ireland quickly spiraled beyond all control. On November 28, exactly a week after the killings, 18 British Auxiliaries were ambushed and killed whilst on patrol in West Cork.[281] In response, on December 8, 1920, Macready finally proclaimed martial law in

4 Irish counties. In January 1921, he extended this to another 4 counties and increased the military force in Ireland to 51 battalions.[282] By the end of 1920, however, there was little the Crown forces could do to stop the I.R.A. insurgency. Martial law only served to anger and inconvenience the general population, and provided incalculable propaganda value to Sinn Fein and the I.R.A. in their campaign to paint the British government as foreign occupiers.[283]

From January to July 1921, despite the intelligence reorganization undertaken by Winter, the I.R.A., R.I.C., and British Army fought to a bloody stalemate without advantage to either side, a seemingly endless campaign of tit-for-tat retaliation, terror and counter-terror. When the truce was finally announced on July 11, it came as a relief to all parties. French had resigned in April, leaving Macready in complete control, yet in the three months that followed there was little the military commander could do to improve the situation. The British government had failed in Ireland in the period of guerilla war; it failed not because it was unable to beat the I.R.A. militarily, nor because it had neglected to establish a working intelligence network, but failed because it had refused to grapple with the rise of Sinn Fein and its tactics of intimidation in the years 1917 and 1918. The period of guerilla warfare was a failure of action in the face of political illegality, and the consequences of such failure were felt for years to come.

Conclusion

On January 7, 1922, Dáil Éireann divided to vote on the newly signed Anglo-Irish Treaty of December 6, 1921. Since the July truce, Sinn Fein had been engaged in extensive negotiations with the British cabinet. De Valera, as the putative president of the republic and the president of Dáil Éireann, met with Lloyd George in Downing Street four times between July 14 and July 20. The Prime Minister offered to grant qualified Dominion status to the southern 26 counties of Ireland, those with Catholic majorities, but de Valera refused the offer. On August 10, the Sinn Fein president proposed his own solution: an Irish Republic with "external association" with the British Commonwealth. It would acknowledge its historical and cultural ties to the Empire, but would not be a formal member. The cabinet recognized this as "an attempt—even though a clumsy one—to keep open the discussion," and agreed to a conference with Sinn Fein, to begin October 11.[1]

De Valera chose not to attend the conference. Instead, he sent Michael Collins as his chief negotiator, supported by Arthur Griffith, Robert Barton, E.J. Duggan, George Gavan Duffy, and Erskine Childers. Facing them on the British side were Lloyd George, Winston Churchill, Austen Chamberlain, Lord Birkenhead, Sir Hamar Greenwood, Sir Gordon Hewart, and Sir Laming Worthington-Evans. After almost two months of constant negotiation, the British delegation presented its final offer to Collins at 9:00 p.m. on December 5. He requested a few changes, waited for them to be typed, and finally, at 2:10 a.m. on December 6, he and his colleagues signed the Anglo-Irish Treaty. They had not consulted with de Valera before doing so, and when he read of the terms the following day in the *Evening Mail*, he was aghast. The Irish delegation had failed to gain external association, and had fallen far short of securing a 32-county independent Irish Republic.[2]

Under the terms of the treaty, effective immediately, Ireland was partitioned into two countries: the 6-county Northern Ireland and the 26-county Irish Free State Dominion. Northern Ireland would remain within the United Kingdom, but with a home rule parliament of its own. The Free State would no longer be part of the United Kingdom but would remain within the British Empire, with "the same constitutional status in the community of nations known as the British Empire as the Dominion of Canada, the Commonwealth of Australia, the Dominion of New Zealand, and the Union of South Africa." The unionists in Northern Ireland had accepted what they pledged they never would, a home rule parliament, and had acknowledged peacefully a treaty that would have prompted civil war seven years earlier. The Sinn Fein delegation had agreed to conditions not too far removed from the Home Rule Act of 1914, conditions that they had fought viciously against.[3]

The treaty stated that a Governor General would be appointed in the Free State, to have the same powers as the Governor General of the Dominion of Canada. All members of the newly constituted Irish Free State Parliament would take an oath of office before taking their seats, pledging true faith and allegiance to the constitution of the Irish Free State and to the king, "in virtue of the common citizenship of Ireland with Great Britain and her adherence to and membership of the British Commonwealth of Nations." Under the treaty, the British retained control of three strategic ports within the Free State—Berehavan, Queenstown, and Lough Swilly—and "in time of war or strained relations" could requisition any other port or facility that was thought necessary. Finally, the size of the Irish Free State Army was fixed at an upper limit of 700,000 men, and the British Army and Royal Navy retained the right to recruit in the Free State. Far from being an independent republic, the Irish Free State would assume the position of a loyal member of the British Empire, the fifth of the "white settler" dominions.[4]

When the votes were tallied in Dáil Éireann on January 7, 1922, those in favor of the treaty numbered 64, those against 57. De Valera, the chief opponent, immediately claimed that the republic could "only be disestablished by the Irish people" and thus ruled the vote and the treaty invalid.[5] Two days later, having failed to persuade the majority of his view, he resigned as president of the Dáil and declared it an illegitimate body. His followers staged a walk-out behind their leader, leaving only a rump parliament under the leadership of Arthur Griffith.[6] The Irish Civil War had begun. At its close, as many as 4,000 Irishmen lay dead, including Michael Collins.[7]

The civil war was not the last time that blood was shed in the name of Ireland, however. Following the victory of the pro-treaty forces (those members of the I.R.A. who followed Michael Collins) over the anti-treaty forces (those members who followed de Valera), Sinn Fein remained an active party, still supported by the I.R.A, now outlawed by the Irish Free State government. This I.R.A. launched further campaigns of violence against both the Free State government and the British government until the official, and internationally recognized, declaration of the Irish Republic in 1949.[8] Following that year, the I.R.A. turned its attention to Northern Ireland, launching an ineffective campaign from 1951 to 1962.[9] In 1966, it resurfaced in support of the Northern Ireland civil rights movement, and when some of its more extreme elements deemed it too passive, it split in 1969 into two organizations, the Official Irish Republican Army and the Provisional Irish Republican Army. The Officials slowly withered away, eventually declaring a permanent ceasefire with the British government in 1972, but the more aggressive Provisionals continued to fight until 1998. In all, the Northern Ireland Troubles cost the lives of 3,664 people. Paramilitary groups were responsible for 3,340 of those deaths; 2,269 were the result of groups associated with the I.R.A., and 1,071 were the result of groups descended from the Ulster Volunteer Force.[10] The violence did not end there, however. As the Provisionals took steps towards a peaceful settlement, those within the organization who wished to continue violence split again, and two new groups were formed, the Continuity Irish Republican Army and the Real Irish Republican Army. At time of writing (2006), both are still active, and the Real I.R.A. has claimed responsibility for one of the deadlier atrocities in recent Irish history, the 1998 Omagh bombing that killed 29 people, including 9 children.[11] With the rise of the I.R.A. and the Protestant paramilitary groups, the twentieth was one of the more bloody centuries in the annals of Irish history. It did not have to be so.

When the Ulster Unionist Council first met in December 1912 and decided to form an army to thwart Irish Home Rule, the British government knew of its decision. At that time there was no I.R.A., no Irish Volunteers, not even an Ulster Volunteer Force. There was just a handful of men, in a private residence, threatening treason. Had these men been prevented from following through on their sedition, and had the Ulster Volunteer Force been quelled when the British government first acknowledged it as an illegal organization, whilst it was still small, the R.I.C. might not have been placed in the position of facing a fully armed force. If the U.V.F. had not formed, pledging to prevent the implementation of a Home Rule Parliament, there may have been no reason for the Irish Volunteers to form, committed as they were to defending that Home Rule Parliament. If there was no early Irish Volunteers to split into the moderate Irish National Volunteers and the more extreme Irish Volunteers, the Irish Republican Brotherhood would have been forced to find another base from which to work, perhaps making it more difficult to grow. Without the I.R.B., it is unlikely that the Easter Rising could have taken place.

Even when H.E. Duke became Chief Secretary in July 1916, the dramatic rise of Sinn Fein and the I.R.A. was by no means inevitable. Whilst the moderate majority in Ireland was, quite naturally, irked by the martial law implemented by Maxwell and outraged by some of the more repressive actions undertaken by the Crown forces, the Irish people as a whole were far from committed supporters of Sinn Fein. Thousands of Irishmen were still loyally serving in France, and John Redmond's Irish Nationalist Party still held the hearts and minds of most Irish Catholics. The R.I.C., the organization chiefly responsible for gathering internees and restoring order following the Easter Rising, was manned primarily by Irish Catholics, and held the respect of most. In December 1916, when Lloyd George released all Irish internees in his Christmas pardon, Redmond's pro-war, pro-British National Volunteers still held a membership of 105,000, whilst the pro-independence, anti-British Irish Volunteers numbered less than 5,000. Upon release, had the internees been properly screened, and those guilty of a violent crime been tried, convicted, and sentenced, there would have been little protest. Without the revolutionary leadership developed in the prisons and set free by the Prime Minister, it may have been more difficult, if not impossible, for the Sinn Fein movement to develop with the strength that it did.

Nevertheless, even with its newly constituted leadership, the Sinn Fein Party was able to gain an electoral victory only through intimidation and violence. Without such a victory, Michael Collins would have had a lesser claim of British occupation, and a greatly reduced justification to launch his war against the British presence in Ireland. This war, then, when it came, was by no means a product of a growing Irish separatist movement, unreservedly supported by the Irish people, as the colony-to-nation school of historians has alleged. Nor was it the direct result of British oppression after the Easter Rising, as those within the repressive-reaction school maintain. The guerilla war that raged from 1919 to 1921 was the outcome of poor British policy in the face of a documented threat. It was the failure of the British government to act on sound intelligence that ultimately led to rebellion in Ireland, and to the rise of a tradition of paramilitary violence that still haunts the island to this day.

To understand why the British government failed so dramatically in Ireland, and why it was so unsuccessful in stamping out the scourge of militancy before it sank its roots, it is necessary to take a close look at the intelligence the government received, and to analyze the way that intelligence was used. In the period of overt militancy, from 1912 to 1914, the R.I.C. produced remarkably detailed and precise intelligence. The government, however, chose to ignore that intelligence. In the period of clandestine organization, from 1914 to 1916, the R.I.C. was less meticulous, choosing to focus on Irish public opinion towards the British war effort rather than an Irish insurgency. When the Inspector General finally did direct his attention to the situation within Ireland, his intelligence network was unable to uncover the rising that was being planned. Finally, in the period of guerilla war, from 1916 to 1921, the R.I.C. was unable to rely on the use of informants for intelligence, as was its practice, due to intimidation of these potential informants by the I.R.A. In time, however, the R.I.C. did establish a working intelligence network independent of informants and the government began to receive thorough intelligence once again. By this point, however, the intelligence proved too late, and there was little the government could do to quell the raging insurgency.

Had the government no knowledge of the rise of the Ulster Volunteer Force and the Irish Volunteers in the years 1912–1914, the edge of the precipice on which Ireland quivered in July 1914 could be considered in some ways unavoidable, an inescapable conflict erupting between two distinct cultures. Yet Chief Secretary Birrell was well aware of the growing threat. With deliberation, he chose to ignore it. In December 1916, Chief Secretary Duke had intelligence attesting to the threatening stance of a still weak Sinn Fein Party, yet he acquiesced with Lloyd George's pardon, just as the Irish Volunteers were beginning to parade openly once again. In 1917 and 1918, the British government received detailed intelligence showing Sinn Fein's practices of intimidation, and attesting to the fact that free politics was becoming polluted with terror. To prevent the escalation of violence, Duke and the British government needed to assure those who supported the moderate Irish Nationalist Party that they could continue to do so in safety, whilst making it clear to the extreme minority that violence and intimidation would not be tolerated. Instead, however, Duke accepted as true Sinn Fein's assertions of purely political intent, despite ample intelligence showing otherwise. The party was thus permitted to organize and propagandize as any other.

To avert the guerilla war of 1919–1921, the British government needed to act in 1917 and 1918, when Sinn Fein was publicly professing the desire for violent separation from Great Britain and the Irish Volunteers were beginning to attack the police with impunity, witnesses refusing to testify against them for fear of the threatened consequences. The government had intelligence to show the threat that Sinn Fein posed, just as it had held intelligence on the Ulster Volunteer Force in the years 1912–1914 and on the Irish Volunteers after 1916. The government, however, chose inaction over intrepidity, terror over triumph. In the years 1912–1921, the turning points of the Irish Revolution were clearly visible to the British government, but they were ignored. The consequences of such neglect were unforgiving.

Notes

Introduction

1. Michael Foy and Brian Barton, *The Easter Rising* (Stroud, U.K.: Sutton Publishing, 1999), 127–128.
2. That Patrick Pearse and his followers were romantic nationalists is not disputed. David Fitzpatrick explains that the I.R.B. and other Irish nationalists "drew inspiration from an idealized vision of the past, in which the nation had been free to pursue its chosen course until besieged and ravaged by alien forces of darkness. . . . The nation, including its dead and its unborn, was entitled to freedom; those claimed for the nation as its living citizens had the duty to pursue that abstract liberation" (*The Two Irelands, 1912–1939* [Oxford: Oxford University Press, 1998], 26). Pearse himself never expected to survive the rising, nor did he want to. He held the belief that before Ireland could be truly free, a blood sacrifice was necessary to purify the Irish people from their past sins of cooperating with the British government. Sean Farrell Moran writes that these "ideas about blood sacrifice, redemptive violence, chiliastic expectation, and Irish national identity constitute the ideological heart of the physical-force tradition" (*Patrick Pearse and the Politics of Redemption: The Mind of the Easter Rising, 1916* [Washington, D.C.: Catholic University of America Press, 1994], 2).
3. Charles Townshend, *Political Violence in Ireland: Government and Resistance since 1848* (Oxford: Clarendon Press, 1983), 25–27.
4. Ibid., 35.
5. Ibid., 238–239.
6. Irish nationalists had called for Irish Home Rule of some sort since the 1801 Act of Union dissolved the Irish Parliament and united Great Britain and Ireland into the United Kingdom, sharing a single parliament at Westminster. The movement picked up force in the 1870s with the rise of Charles Stuart Parnell. In 1886 the Liberal Prime Minister William Gladstone brought a Home Rule Bill before the House of Commons. This failed by a narrow margin, but in 1893 a Second Home Rule Bill was brought before the Commons and this time it succeeded. The House of Lords, however, vetoed it, as was their constitutional right, and an Irish Home Rule Parliament never became a reality. Calls for Home Rule did not

subside, however, and the Irish Home Rule Party continued to grow in size and strength. In the 1910 General Election, the results returned 274 Liberals, 272 Conservatives, and 82 Irish Home Rulers, giving the Home Rulers the balance of power. The following year, in 1911, the House of Commons passed the Parliament Act, which reduced the power of the Lords from having a complete veto to only a temporary veto for two parliamentary sessions. In other words, if a bill passed through the Commons three sessions in a row (roughly two and a half years) it would become law on the third attempt, with or without the assent of the Lords. This being the case, and with the Liberal Prime Minister dependent on the Irish Home Rule Party for his parliamentary majority, it seemed likely that a Home Rule bill would be presented before the Commons in early 1912, and that an Irish Home Rule Parliament would be a reality by 1914. The Protestant unionists, a political and religious minority in Ireland, feared that the implementation of a Home Rule Parliament would mean the loss of their position of power and ascendancy in Ireland, which they had held since the seventeenth century. It was for this reason that they were determined to prevent the implementation of Home Rule and for this reason that they were willing to form an illegal army, the Ulster Volunteer Force, to aid them in this quest.

7. The Irish Volunteers had as their sole aim the protection of the anticipated Home Rule Parliament. Although they claimed not to be formed specifically to fight the U.V.F., any protection of Home Rule would almost certainly lead to such a fight, and the leadership of the volunteers prepared for this in their training and organization.

8. A.T.Q. Stewart, speaking with the consensus of historians, writes, "At the very end of July [1914] war in Ulster seemed certain, and only the outbreak of war in Europe averted it. The fierce light which has been directed on the German war has thrown the preparations for that other war into the shadows, but they were, in fact, extraordinarily elaborate" (*The Ulster Crisis: Resistance to Home Rule, 1912–1914* [Belfast: Blackstaff Press, 1967], 231). Following the British declaration of war upon Germany, the U.V.F. wished to show their loyalty to the crown, believing that such loyalty would be rewarded with continued representation in Westminster, and thus they fully supported and participated in the First World War. Likewise, the Irish Volunteers also wished to show their loyalty, believing that such loyalty would be rewarded with a Home Rule Parliament. Hence, they too fully supported and participated in the war, thus preventing the outbreak of the much anticipated civil war in Ireland.

9. The National Volunteers had agreed in a compromise with the Ulster unionists to suspend the implementation of a Home Rule Parliament until after the hostilities ended in Europe. This compromise was unacceptable to the breakaway Irish Volunteers, who wanted to see the immediate establishment of a Home Rule Parliament.

10. Out of the original 168,000 Irish Volunteers, 156,000 supported the war effort and formed what became known as the National Volunteers. Only 12,000 split off into the new Irish Volunteers. Of these, the I.R.B. made up only a tiny

minority, although an increasingly influential one. By Easter 1916, the leadership of the Irish Volunteers and the I.R.B. had become one and the same.

11. James Connolly was the leader of the Irish Labor movement. He established the Citizen Army in November 1913 with the express purpose of protecting Irish workers from the police during strikes. Connolly soon decided that socialism could come to Ireland only by embracing Irish nationalism, however, and so he committed the Citizen Army to insurrection. In January 1916, he joined with the Irish Volunteers, and together they planned the Easter Rising.

12. Foy and Barton, *The Easter Rising*, 52–54.

13. Ibid., 54.

14. Ibid., 164.

15. Fitzpatrick, *The Two Irelands*, 61. For more on the courts-martial and executions, see Brian Barton, *From Behind a Closed Door: Secret Court Martial Records of the 1916 Easter Rising* (Belfast: Blackstaff Press, 2002).

16. The Sinn Fein Party, literally meaning "Ourselves Alone," was founded by Arthur Griffith in 1905. At first, it advocated a Dual Monarchy, which would preside over the two separate nations of Ireland and Great Britain, each with their own parliament and political autonomy. Sinn Fein initially gained little political ground in the years after its founding, with Irish nationalists preferring instead the Irish Home Rule Party. Following the Easter Rising, however, the Irish Volunteers took over the leadership of Sinn Fein and its philosophy migrated towards advocating a fully independent Irish republic.

17. Joseph Lee, *The Modernisation of Irish Society, 1848–1918* (Dublin: Gill & Macmillan, 1989), 156–159.

18. The Irish Free State was created as a British dominion, analogous to Canada, Australia, New Zealand, and South Africa. This meant that it was still within the British Empire and still had the British sovereign as its head of state, yet it also had its own parliament, civil service, and security forces.

19. The one exception to this is Joost Augusteijn's edited volume *The Irish Revolution, 1913–1923* (New York: Palgrave, 2002), which attempts to draw together scholarship on a ten-year period. Even within this volume, however, there is not a single essay that considers in its entirety the years 1912–1921, and none that considers the Ulster Crisis of 1912 to 1914 as part of this Irish Revolution.

20. Stewart, *Ulster Crisis*, 231. Stewart's work is not only well written but also extremely well researched. The main sources he uses are the Ulster Unionist Council papers, the Spender papers, the Craigavon papers, the Crawford papers, the Hall papers, the Kilmorey papers, the O'Neill papers, the Richardson papers, and miscellaneous records of the Ulster Volunteer Force held at the Public Record Office of Northern Ireland.

21. Patricia Jalland, *The Liberals and Ireland: The Ulster Question in British Politics to 1914* (New York: St. Martin's Press, 1980), 262. See also Patricia Jalland, "A Liberal Chief Secretary and the Irish Question: Augustine Birrell, 1907–1914," *The Historical Journal*, volume 19, number 2 (June 1976).

22. Eunan O'Halpin, *The Decline of the Union: British Government in Ireland, 1892–1920* (Dublin: Gill & Macmillan, 1987), 99.

23. D. George Boyce and Alan O'Day, eds., *Defenders of the Union: A Survey of British and Irish Unionism since 1801* (London: Routledge, 2001).

24. Stewart, *The Ulster Crisis*.

25. Patrick Buckland, *Irish Unionism: Two: Ulster Unionism and the Origins of Northern Ireland, 1886–1922* (Dublin: Gill & Macmillan, 1973).

26. O'Halpin, *The Decline of the Union*, 100.

27. I owe a debt of gratitude to Canadian historiography for the use of this term "colony-to-nation school," which was taken from A.R.M. Lower's text, *Colony to Nation: A History of Canada* (Toronto: Longmans, Green & Company, 1946). In Canadian historiography, it is used to describe a cluster of Canadian historians who interpret significant events within their country's past as a series of inevitable (and natural) steps on the path to eventual independent nationhood.

28. Theobald Wolfe Tone formed the United Irishmen in 1791 to agitate for parliamentary reform and equal religious rights within Ireland. Wolfe Tone soon became radicalized, however, after witnessing the French Revolution and its Great Terror. In 1795, he transformed the United Irishmen into a secret society intent on bringing revolutionary terror to Ireland, the aim of which was to create an Irish republic on the French model. In 1798, he led a rising, supported by 1,000 French troops, which was brutally suppressed by the British Army. It was this rising, and the continued fear of a revolution in Ireland, that led the British Parliament to pass the 1801 Act of Union, joining Great Britain and Ireland into a single state, the United Kingdom. See Nancy J. Curtin, *The United Irishmen: Popular Politics in Ulster and Dublin, 1791–1798* (Oxford: Oxford University Press, 1994); and Marianne Elliot, *Partners in Revolution: The United Irishmen and France* (New Haven: Yale University Press, 1982).

29. The Young Irelander movement was formed in 1842. It was at first committed to cultural nationalism and the establishment of a Gaelic-speaking "Irish Ireland" through nonviolent means. As such, it began to publish a newspaper, *The Nation*, to promote a distinctly Irish culture. Following the Great Famine of 1845–1849, however, it abandoned its pacifism for a policy of physical force. In 1848, it led a small and unsuccessful rebellion against the British. See S. Cronin, *Protest in Arms: The Young Ireland Rebellion of July–August 1848* (Dublin: Gill & Macmillan, 1984).

30. George Dangerfield, *The Damnable Question: A Study in Anglo-Irish Relations* (Boston: Little, Brown & Company, 1976), 5.

31. Ibid., ix.

32. Ibid., x. The italics are Dangerfield's.

33. Ibid., x–xi.

34. See also Leon Ó Broin's two works *Dublin Castle and the 1916 Rising* (New York: New York University Press, 1971) and *Revolutionary Underground: The Story of the Irish Republican Brotherhood, 1858–1924* (Totowa, N.J.: Rowman & Littlefield Publishers, 1976); Desmond Williams' collection of essays *The Irish Struggle, 1916–1926* (Toronto: University of Toronto Press, 1966); and F.X. Martin's edited

volume *Leaders and Men of the Easter Rising: Dublin 1916* (Ithaca, N.Y.: Cornell University Press, 1967).

35. David Cannadine explains that the most important public function of the Lord Lieutenant, or Viceroy, was "to show imperial subjects overseas that while imperial monarchs might live in London, they reigned over everyone in the empire, wherever they might be, and were to receive appropriate expressions of homage and fealty in return" (*Ornamentalism: How the British Saw Their Empire* [Oxford: Oxford University Press, 2001], 105).
36. R.B. McDowell, *The Irish Administration: 1801–1914* (London: Routledge & Kegan Paul, 1964), 52.
37. Ibid., 52.
38. O'Halpin, *The Decline of the Union*, 6.
39. Ibid., 7. See also McDowell, *The Irish Administration*, 2–3.
40. O'Halpin explains that the under secretary's position "was the pivotal post in Irish government. An assertive incumbent, consistently backed by his minister, could dominate administration as no one else could" (*The Decline of the Union*, 9). See also McDowell, *The Irish Administration*, 63.
41. The great exception to this was London's Metropolitan Police Force, which reported directly to the Home Secretary. For more on this see David Philips and Robert D. Storch, *Policing Provincial England, 1829–1856: The Politics of Reform* (London: Leicester University Press, 1999); and Phillip Thurmond Smith, *Policing Victorian London: Political Policing, Public Order, and the London Metropolitan Police* (Westport, C.T.: Greenwood Press, 1985).
42. Even in the case of the London Metropolitan Police, the Home Secretary made most policing decisions independent of parliamentary debate.
43. See Jim Herlihy, *The Dublin Metropolitan Police: A Short History and Genealogical Guide* (Dublin: Four Courts Press, 2001), chapter 2.
44. See Donal J. O'Sullivan, *The Irish Constabularies, 1822–1922* (Dingle, County Kerry: Brandon Book Publishers, 1999), chapter 1.
45. See Stanley H. Palmer, *Police and Protest in England and Ireland, 1780–1850* (Cambridge: Cambridge University Press, 1988), chapters 4, 7, and 9.
46. See Townshend, *Political Violence in Ireland*, 67–84.
47. Moran, *Patrick Pearse and the Politics of Redemption*, 175.
48. Dangerfield, *The Damnable Question*, 4.
49. See also Ruth Dudley Edwards, *Patrick Pearse: The Triumph of Failure* (New York: Taplinger Publishing, 1978).
50. Charles Townshend, *The British Campaign in Ireland, 1919–1921: The Development of Political and Military Policies* (Oxford: Oxford University Press, 1975), 204.
51. Ibid., 205.
52. See also Joost Augusteijn, *From Public Defiance to Guerrilla Warfare: The Experience of Ordinary Volunteers in the Irish War of Independence, 1916–1921* (Dublin: Irish Academic Press, 1996); William H. Kautt, *The Anglo-Irish War, 1916–1921: A People's War* (Westport, C.T.: Praeger Publishers, 1999); David Fitzpatrick, *Politics and Irish Life, 1913–21: Provincial Experience of War and*

Revolution (Dublin: Gill & Macmillan, 1977); Arthur Mitchell, *Revolutionary Government in Ireland: Dáil Éireann, 1919–22* (Dublin: Gill & Macmillan, 1995); and Peter Hart, *The I.R.A. and Its Enemies: Violence and Community in Cork, 1916–1923* (New York: Clarendon Press, 1998).

53. Elizabeth A. Muenger, *The British Military Dilemma in Ireland: Occupation Politics, 1886–1914* (Dublin: Gill & Macmillan, 1991), 81–82.
54. O'Sullivan, *The Irish Constabularies*, 175.
55. Ibid., 175.
56. Herlihy, *The Dublin Metropolitan Police*, 122–127.
57. Ibid., 131–137.

Part I   The Period of Overt Militancy, 1912–1914

1. The Lords agreed to pass the bill only because the Prime Minister extracted from King George V a pledge to create a new contingent of Liberal peers that could outnumber the Conservatives in the Lords if they did not carry the bill. The Conservative peers, faced with this threat, decided that they would rather be a less powerful Conservative majority than a powerless minority under a powerful Liberal majority.
2. Jeremy Smith, *The Tories and Ireland: Conservative Party Politics and the Home Rule Crisis, 1910–1914* (Dublin: Irish Academic Press, 2000), 21–22.
3. The Irish Nationalist Party had 82 Members of Parliament, the Liberals 275, and the Conservatives 273.
4. See James Loughlin, *Gladstone, Home Rule and the Ulster Question, 1882–93* (Atlantic Highlands, N.J.: Humanities Press International Inc., 1987).
5. Stewart, *The Ulster Crisis*, 39. For more on the Ulster Party, see Alvin Jackson, *The Ulster Party: Irish Unionists in the House of Commons, 1884–1911* (Oxford: Clarendon Press, 1989). For more on Walter Long's leadership of the party, see Charles Petrie, *Walter Long and His Times* (London: Hutchinson & Co. Ltd., 1936).
6. H. Montgomery Hyde, *Carson: The Life of Sir Edward Carson, Lord Carson of Duncairn* (London: William Heinemann Ltd., 1953), 5–7, 12.
7. A.T.Q. Stewart, *Edward Carson* (Dublin: Gill & Macmillan, 1981), 6.
8. Hyde, *Carson*, 18.
9. William Gladstone was British Prime Minister during the 1886 and 1893 Home Rule debates. Charles Stewart Parnell was leader of the Irish Home Rule Party during the same time.
10. Buckland, *Irish Unionism: Two*, 48.
11. St. John Ervine, *Craigavon: Ulsterman* (London: George Allen & Unwin Ltd., 1949), 63.
12. Ibid., 125–131.
13. Ibid., 181–191.
14. Stewart, *The Ulster Crisis*, 21–22.
15. Ibid., 47.
16. Ibid., 48.

17. Prior to 1707, there was no such thing as Great Britain. Wales had become officially united with England in 1536, and since the death of Elizabeth I in 1603, England and Scotland had shared a common monarchy. Not until 1707, however, did the Parliament at Westminster pass an Act of Union that officially linked Scotland with England and Wales, dissolved the Scottish Parliament, and created the entity of Great Britain. Even then, nothing remotely similar to a unified nation had been created. It was a union on paper only. Those living in England looked with suspicion at their northern neighbors, and in Wales (even more so than in Scotland) the people spoke an entirely different language. In the years that followed, however, Linda Colley argues that two elements came together to create a common sense of Britishness, which transcended these earlier regional identities. These elements were Protestantism and Francophobia. Beginning in the early eighteenth century, troops from the British Isles began to fight the Catholic French throughout Britain's emerging empire, most notably in North America, but also in India. As these troops from England, Scotland, and Wales fought side by side, they realized that they had a common identity that forged them together as British, setting them apart from the French. That identity was Protestant. Ireland, being a Catholic nation, was distanced from this sense of shared Britishness. See Linda Colley, *Britons: Forging the Nation, 1707–1837* (New Haven: Yale University Press, 1992).

18. See A.G. Dickens, *The English Reformation*, second edition (University Park, P.A.: Pennsylvania State University Press, 1991).

19. See Felicity Heal, *Reformation in Britain and Ireland* (Oxford: Oxford University Press, 2003); Alan Ford, *The Protestant Reformation in Ireland, 1590–1641*, second edition (Dublin: Four Courts Press, 1997); and Samantha A. Meigs, *The Reformations in Ireland: Tradition and Confessionalism, 1400–1690* (New York: St. Martin's Press, 1997).

20. See Diarmaid MacCulloch, *The Boy King: Edward VI and the Protestant Reformation* (New York: Palgrave, 2001).

21. See D.M. Loades, *The Reign of Mary Tudor: Politics, Government, and Religion in England, 1553–1558*, second edition (London: Longman, 1991); and Jasper Godwin Ridley, *Bloody Mary's Martyrs: The Story of England's Terror* (New York: Carroll and Graf Publishers, 2001).

22. See Diarmaid MacCulloch, *The Later Reformation in England, 1547–1603*, second edition (New York: Palgrave, 2001).

23. A.T.Q. Stewart states, correctly, that it was the failure of the English Reformation in Ireland that lies at the root of all Anglo-Irish troubles (*The Ulster Crisis*, 27).

24. For more on the theory and practice of these plantations, see Nicholas Canny, *Making Ireland British, 1580–1650* (Oxford: Oxford University Press, 2001).

25. See John McGurk, *The Elizabethan Conquest of Ireland: The 1590s Crisis* (Manchester: Manchester University Press, 1997); and ibid., chapter 3.

26. See Canny, *Making Ireland British*, chapter 4; and Raymond Gillespie, *Colonial Ulster: The Settlement of East Ulster, 1600–1641* (Cork: Cork University Press, 1985).

27. For more on this, see John McCavitt, *The Flight of the Earls* (Dublin: Gill & Macmillan, 2002).

28. For an excellent account of these distracting events within England, see Christopher Hill, *The Century of Revolution, 1603–1714* (New York: W.W. Norton, 1982).

29. See Hilary Sims, "Violence in County Armagh, 1641," in Brian Mac Cuarta, ed., *Ulster 1641: Aspects of the Rising* (Belfast: Institute of Irish Studies, Queen's University of Belfast, 1997).

30. At the time of the rising, in 1641, the total Irish population was between 1.5 and 2 million people. In the 10 years that followed, this number fell to 850,000 (in 1652). Not all of these losses occurred during Cromwell's subjugation, however. During the years 1642 and 1649, many battles of the English Civil War took place in Ireland, with English Catholic Royalists taking sanctuary amongst the Catholic population there. For more on this, see James Scott Wheeler, *Cromwell in Ireland* (Dublin: Gill & Macmillan, 1999).

31. For a thoroughly delightful account of these years, see G.M. Trevelyan, *The English Revolution, 1688–1689* (London: T. Butterworth Ltd., 1938; reprinted Oxford: Oxford University Press, 1981). See also John Miller, "The Glorious Revolution" and James McGuire, "James II and Ireland, 1685–90," both in W.A. Maguire, ed., *Kings in Conflict: The Revolutionary War in Ireland and Its Aftermath, 1689–1750* (Belfast: Blackstaff Press, 1990).

32. William Brown, *An Army with Banners: The Real Face of Orangeism* (Belfast: Beyond the Pale Publications, 2003), 10.

33. Ibid., 11. See also S.J. Connolly, "The Penal Laws," in Maguire, ed., *Kings in Conflict*.

34. Brown, *An Army with Banners*, 11. See also W.A. Maguire, "The Land Settlement," in Maguire, ed., *Kings in Conflict*.

35. Brown, *An Army with Banners*, vii.

36. The Peep O'Day Boys, along with other Protestant groups such as the Orange Boys and the Bleary Boys, had been formed in the years after 1778, when the Parliament at Westminster passed an act overturning some of the earlier penal acts. Most significantly, this act allowed Catholics to lease land for 999 years, essentially paving the way for Catholic property ownership. These Protestant groups formed in an attempt to intimidate Catholics from leasing this land. The Defenders had come into existence to protect Catholic homes from vigilante attacks by these Protestants. For more on this, see Kevin Haddick-Flynn, *Orangeism: The Making of a Tradition* (Dublin: Wolfhound Press, 1999), 120–121, 127–131.

37. For a detailed account of this battle, see ibid., 132–138.

38. For more on the 1798 reforms of the Orange Order, see Brown, *An Army with Banners*, 25–27.

39. See Haddick-Flynn, *Orangeism*, 257–271.

40. See Frank Wright, *Two Lands on One Soil: Ulster Politics before Home Rule* (Dublin: Gill & Macmillan, 1996), 476–509.

41. Stewart, *The Ulster Crisis*, 32.

42. Ibid., 32.
43. The other members of the Commission of Five were Colonel Sharman Crawford, Colonel R.H. Wallace, Thomas Sinclair, and Edward Sclater.
44. By far the best single-volume biography on Churchill is Roy Jenkins, *Churchill: A Biography* (New York: Farrar, Straus and Giroux, 2001).
45. Stewart, *The Ulster Crisis*, 48. Carson, when addressing the willingness of the Ulster Unionists to face the army and the navy, referenced a challenge by Secretary of State for Agriculture, Thomas Wallace Russell, saying, "Mr. Russell asks, Are we going to fight the army and the navy? No, we are not going to fight the army and the navy, but if the army and the navy under a British Government come up to displace us, they will displace us at their peril. It is not that we mean to fight them. God forbid that any loyal Irishman should ever shoot or think of shooting the British soldier or sailor. But, believe you me, any Government will ponder long before it dares to shoot a loyal Ulster Protestant, devoted to his country and loyal to his King. And I ask Mr. Russell and those who foolishly think that this is mere bravado and brag, I ask them what do you think would be the condition of affairs throughout the length and breadth of England and Scotland and Wales if, because you were loyal to your King and want to remain as citizens of a United Kingdom, British troops were turned out to shoot you? I venture to think that a fire would burn throughout England that would not only displace the Government, but would within a few days lead to the repeal of the iniquitous measure that could produce such disastrous results" (Ervine, *Craigavon*, 193).
46. Winston S. Churchill, "Speech on Foreign and Domestic Policy," Constituency Meeting, Kinnaird Hall, Dundee, October 3, 1911, in Robert Rhodes James, ed., *Winston S. Churchill: His Complete Speeches, 1897–1963: Volume II, 1908–1913* (New York: Chelsea House Publishers, 1974), 1882.
47. Ibid., 1883.
48. Major General Edward Gleichen was at this time commander of the 15th Infantry Division, stationed in Belfast. He wrote that Churchill was originally scheduled to speak at the Ulster Hall, one of Ulster's "holy of holies," but the night before his speech members of the Orange Order seized the hall and threatened to kidnap Churchill if he proceeded. The Liberal Association, therefore, hurriedly found an alternate site, the Celtic Park Football Ground. Gleichen sought guarantees from the prominent unionist leaders that there would be no trouble, but they "would not promise anything." Gleichen, therefore, arranged for four battalions and a squadron of extra troops to be brought to Victoria Barracks and three battalions to Holywood Barracks. Three of these battalions, as well as the squadron, were ordered to be present at the football ground on the day of the speech; the remaining three were held in reserve at various places across the city. When Churchill finally arrived, the reception from unionist crowds was so hostile that his car was lifted from the ground several times and was only prevented from being tipped over because his wife accompanied him and propriety forbade it. See Major General Lord Edward Gleichen, *A Guardsman's Memories: A Book of Recollections* (Edinburgh and London: William Blackwood & Sons Ltd., 1932), 360–362.

49. Winston S. Churchill, "Speech on Irish Home Rule," Celtic Park Football Ground, City of Belfast, February 8, 1912, in James, ed., *Winston S. Churchill: His Complete Speeches, 1897–1963: Volume II, 1908–1913*, 1909.

50. Catherine B. Shannon, *Arthur J. Balfour and Ireland, 1874–1922* (Washington, D.C.: Catholic University of America Press, 1988), 174; and Stewart, *The Ulster Crisis*, 55.

51. Fitzpatrick, *The Two Irelands*, 44.

52. Jeremy Smith, *The Tories and Ireland*, 67–68.

53. Stewart, *The Ulster Crisis*, 57. See also D.G. Boyce, "British Conservative Opinion, the Ulster Question, and the Partition of Ireland, 1912–1921," *Irish Historical Studies*, volume 17, number 65 (March 1970).

54. Stewart, *The Ulster Crisis*, 61. The Scottish Covenant was drafted in 1581 by John Craig, a Dominican monk who became a Protestant during Mary I's Counter-Reformation and for doing so was nearly burnt at the stake.

55. The exact wording of the Covenant was as follows: "Being convinced in our consciences that Home Rule would be disastrous to the material well-being of Ulster as well as the whole of Ireland, subversive to our civil and religious freedom, destructive of our citizenship, and perilous to the unity of the Empire, we, whose names are underwritten, men of Ulster, loyal subjects of His Gracious Majesty King George V, humbly relying on the God whom our fathers in days of stress and trial confidently trusted, do hereby pledge ourselves in solemn Covenant throughout this our time of threatened calamity to stand by one another in defending for ourselves and our children our cherished position of equal citizenship in the United Kingdom, and in using all means which may be found necessary to defeat the present conspiracy to set up a Home Rule Parliament in Ireland. And in the event of such a Parliament being forced upon us we further solemnly and mutually pledge ourselves to refuse to recognize its authority. In sure confidence that God will defend the right we hereto subscribe our names. And further, we individually declare that we have not already signed this Covenant. God save the King."

56. Stewart, *The Ulster Crisis*, 61–62.

57. Ibid., 63.

58. Ibid., 66.

59. Jeremy Smith, *The Tories and Ireland*, 69.

60. *Hansard's Parliamentary Debates*, House of Commons, fifth series, volume XLII, October 28–November 14, 1912 (London: His Majesty's Stationary Office, 1912), 1765–1774.

61. Ibid., 2039.

62. Ibid., 2041.

63. Ibid., 2042.

64. Stewart, *The Ulster Crisis*, 67.

65. *Hansard's Parliamentary Debates*, House of Commons, fifth series, volume XLII, October 28–November 14, 1912, 2054. The Speaker said, "It is quite obvious to the House that it is useless to continue. . . . [I]n the circumstances, it is quite obvious that the Opposition having determined not to allow further business,

I am compelled to say that a state of grave disorder has arisen, and, under the Standing Order, I must adjourn the House until tomorrow."

66. Stewart, *The Ulster Crisis*, 67–68.
67. Ervine, *Craigavon*, 233.
68. Stewart, *The Ulster Crisis*, 69.
69. Townshend, *Political Violence in Ireland*, 249.
70. Stewart, *The Ulster Crisis*, 69.
71. *Hansard's Parliamentary Debates*, House of Commons, fifth series, volume XLII, October 7–October 25, 1912, 787.
72. Ibid., 787–788.
73. CO 904 / 27 / 1: 107, Letter from the War Office to Under Secretary J.B. Dougherty, Dublin Castle, February 5, 1913.
74. CO 904 / 27 / 1: 196, Confidential Report submitted by Sergeant Henry Conway to the Crimes Special Branch, September 9, 1912.
75. CO 904 / 27 / 1: 205–206, Report submitted by Sergeant Patrick Hughes to District Inspector J.W. Mahon, Linaskea, September 4, 1912.
76. CO 904 / 27 / 1: 196, Copies of two circulars published by Trimble, submitted by Sergeant Henry Conway to Crimes Special Branch, September 6, 1912.
77. CO 904 / 27 / 1: 198, Circular written by W. Copeland Trimble, August 30, 1912.
78. CO 904 / 27 / 1: 196, Report submitted by Sergeant Henry Conway to Crimes Special Branch, September 6, 1912.
79. CO 904 / 27 / 1: 197, Circular written by W. Copeland Trimble, September 3, 1912.
80. CO 904 / 27 / 1: 194, Report submitted by Sergeant Joseph Ruddock to District Inspector C.E. Armstrong, Enniskillen, September 7, 1912.
81. CO 904 / 27 / 1: 193, Report submitted by Sergeant Patrick Hughes to the Crimes Special Branch, September 8, 1912.
82. CO 904 / 27 / 1: 191, List of men from the Lisbellow subdistrict involved in the Carrowkeel drill of September 7, 1912, submitted by Sergeant William Agnew, September 8, 1912.
83. CO 904 / 27 / 1: 180, Report submitted by County Inspector, County Fermanagh, to Inspector General Neville Chamberlain, September 17, 1912.
84. Hyde, *Carson*, 319.
85. Ibid., 321–322.
86. CO 904 / 27 / 1: 176, Report submitted by Sergeant William McDowell to District Inspector J. Cahill, Kesh, October 27, 1912.
87. CO 904 / 27 / 1: 177, Query from District Inspector J. Cahill, Kesh, October 28, 1912.
88. CO 904 / 27 / 1: 174–175, Report submitted by Sergeant William McDowell to District Inspector J. Cahill, Kesh, November 1, 1912.
89. CO 904 / 27 / 1: 172–173, Report submitted by the County Inspector, County Fermanagh, to Inspector General Neville Chamberlain, November 2, 1912.
90. CO 904 / 27 / 1: 169, Report submitted by Acting Sergeant William Pyne to District Inspector J.W. Mahon, Linaskea, November 9, 1912.

91. CO 904 / 27 /1: 167, Report submitted by Acting Sergeant William Pyne to the Crimes Special Branch, November 21, 1912.
92. CO 904 / 27 / 1: 152–153, Report submitted by Acting Sergeant Jacob Martin to District Inspector C.E. Armstrong, Enniskillen, November 22, 1912.
93. CO 904 / 27 / 1: 150, Report submitted by Acting Sergeant Jacob Martin to District Inspector C.E. Armstrong, Enniskillen, December 1, 1912.
94. CO 904 / 27 / 1: 148–149, Report submitted by Sergeant Michael Headon to District Inspector C.E. Armstrong, Enniskillen, December 2, 1912. Included amongst their number were Thomas Johnston, who was "an ex-soldier and pensioner and acts as drill instructor," and J.R. Carson, who was "a pensioner from the Cape Mounted Police and also gives instruction."
95. CO 904 / 27 / 1: 157–158, Report submitted by Sergeant Patrick Hughes to District Inspector J.W. Mahon, Linaskea, December 5, 1912.
96. CO 904 / 27 / 1: 155, Report submitted by Acting Sergeant William Pyne to District Inspector J.W. Mahon, Linaskea, December 6, 1912.
97. CO 904 / 27 / 1: 156, Report submitted by Sergeant John Taggart to District Inspector J.W. Mahon, Linaskea, December 6, 1912.
98. CO 904 / 27 / 1: 163, Printed Memo from the Chief Secretary's Office, Ireland, to the Royal Irish Constabulary, December 9, 1912.
99. CO 904 / 27 / 1: 138, Newspaper Clipping from the *Evening Mail*, December 30, 1912.
100. CO 904 / 27 / 1: 135–136, Report submitted by Acting Sergeant David Reilly to District Inspector C.E. Armstrong, Enniskillen, January 2, 1913.
101. CO 904 / 27 / 1: 133–134, Letter from the County Inspector, County Fermanagh, to Inspector General Neville Chamberlain, January 6, 1913.
102. CO 904 / 27 / 2A: 442–446, Memorandum from Acting Sergeant Joseph Edwards to the Detective Department, City of Belfast, December 15, 1912.
103. CO 904 / 27 / 2A: 440, Note from Deputy Inspector General W. O'Connell to Commissioner, City of Belfast, December 17, 1912. O'Connell wrote to the Belfast Commissioner asking on what basis Edwards had received the information (CO 904 / 27 / 2A: 437). The Commissioner replied, stating, "Acting Sergeant Edwards assures me that his informant is quite reliable and was present both at the meeting and dinner" (CO 904 / 27 / 2A: 437).
104. CO 904 / 27 / 2A: 440, Note from Under Secretary J.B. Dougherty to Chief Secretary Augustine Birrell, December 17, 1912.
105. CO 904 / 27 / 2A: 440, Note from Chief Secretary Augustine Birrell to Under Secretary J.B. Dougherty, December 18, 1912.
106. CO 904 / 27 / 2A: 439, Letter from Under Secretary J.B. Dougherty to Inspector General Neville Chamberlain [written date illegible; stamped by the Crimes Special Branch, having received it from Chamberlain, on December 24, 1912]. Dougherty wrote personally to the Inspector General, Colonel Neville Chamberlain, telling him that Edwards deserved credit for the "zeal and intelligence displayed by him in having succeeded in obtaining the information contained in his report."
107. O'Halpin, *The Decline of the Union*, 81.

108. Leon Ó Broin, *The Chief Secretary: Augustine Birrell in Ireland* (Edinburgh: Archon Books, 1970), 7.
109. O'Halpin, *The Decline of the Union*, 81.
110. Ó Broin, *The Chief Secretary*, 139.
111. Jalland, *The Liberals and Ireland*, 32.
112. Andrew Philip Magill, *From Dublin Castle to Stormont: The Memoirs of Andrew Philip Magill, 1913–1925*, ed. Charles W. Magill (Cork: Cork University Press, 2003), 17–18.
113. Ibid., 18–19.
114. Ibid., 22.
115. CO 904 / 27 / 2A: 432–435, Report submitted by Sergeant James English to Acting District Inspector P. Masterson, Dungannon, December 23, 1912.
116. CO 904 / 27 / 2A: 420–421, Report submitted by Sergeant William James Blair to District Inspector S.R. Livingstone, Cookstown, December 28, 1912.
117. CO 904 / 27 / 2A: 424–426, Report submitted by District Inspector S.R. Livingstone, Cookstown, to County Inspector, County Tyrone, December 28, 1912.
118. CO 904 / 27 / 2A: 418, Clipping from the *Northern Whig*, December 23, 1912.
119. CO 904 / 27 / 2A: 415, Report submitted by District Inspector Robert Dunlop, City of Belfast, to Inspector General Neville Chamberlain, January 3, 1913.
120. CO 904 / 27 / 2A: 409–413, Report submitted by County Inspector N.I. Marrion, County Antrim, to Inspector General Neville Chamberlain, January 3, 1913.
121. CO 904 / 27 / 2A: 408, Report submitted by Under Secretary J.B. Dougherty to Chief Secretary Augustine Birrell, January 4, 1913.
122. CO 904 / 27 / 2A: 414, Report submitted by Under Secretary J.B. Dougherty to Chief Secretary Augustine Birrell, January 4, 1913.
123. CO 904 / 27 / 2A: 414, Note from Chief Secretary Augustine Birrell to Under Secretary J.B. Dougherty, January 4, 1913.
124. CO 904 / 27 / 2A: 406, Report submitted by District Inspector S.R. Livingstone, Cookstown, to County Inspector, County Tyrone, January 3, 1913. This report was forwarded by the County Inspector, County Tyrone, to Chief Inspector Augustine Birrell, on January 6, 1913 (CO 904 / 27 / 2A: 405).
125. CO 904 / 27 / 2A: 358–359, Report submitted by Constable Henry Fyfe to Commissioner, City of Belfast, January 4, 1913.
126. CO 904 / 27 / 2A: 324–327, Report submitted by County Inspector N.I. Marrion, County Antrim, to Inspector General Neville Chamberlain, January 8, 1913.
127. CO 904 / 27 / 2A: 396, Report submitted by Sergeant William Hall to Crimes Special Branch, January 17, 1913; CO 904 / 27 / 2A: 397, Report submitted by District Inspector Patrick Culhane, County Armagh, to County Inspector C.C. Oulton, County Armagh, January 18, 1913; CO 904 / 27 / 2A: 375–381, Report submitted by District Inspector Vere Richard Gregory, Lisburn, to County Inspector N.I. Marrion, County Antrim, January 22, 1913; CO 904 / 27 / 2A: 349–350, Report submitted by Constable Samuel Ferguson to Sergeant Thomas Cusack, January 17, 1913; CO 904 / 27 / 2A: 347, Report

submitted by Sergeant Thomas Cusack to Commissioner, City of Belfast, January 17, 1913; CO 904 / 27 / 2A: 345–346, Report submitted by Sergeant Thomas Cusack to Commissioner, City of Belfast, January 23, 1913; Report submitted by CO 904 / 27 / 2A: 354–355, Constable Henry Fyfe to Sergeant Thomas Cusack, January 20, 1913; CO 904 / 27 / 2A: 344, Report submitted by Constable Samuel Ferguson to Sergeant Thomas Cusack, January 24, 1913; CO 904 / 27 / 2A: 342–343, Report submitted by Sergeant Thomas Cusack to Commissioner, City of Belfast, January 24, 1913; CO 904 / 27 / 2A: 331–335, Report submitted by District Inspector Vere Richard Gregory, Lisburn, to County Inspector N.I. Marrion, County Antrim, January 26, 1913; and CO 904 / 27 / 2A: 337–338, Report submitted by District Inspector J. Ross, Ballymeena, to County Inspector N.I. Marrion, County Antrim, January 26, 1913.

128. CO 904 / 27 / 2A: 316–319, Report submitted by County Inspector N.I. Marrion, County Antrim, to Inspector General Neville Chamberlain, January 17, 1913; CO 904 / 27 / 2A: 397, County Inspector C.C. Oulton, County Armagh, to Inspector General Neville Chamberlain, January 19, 1913; CO 904 / 27 / 2A: 389–393, Report submitted by County Inspector N.I. Marrion, County Antrim, to Inspector General Neville Chamberlain, January 17, 1913; CO 904 / 27 / 2A: 384–385, Report submitted by County Inspector N.I. Marrion, County Antrim, to Inspector General Neville Chamberlain, January 22, 1913; CO 904 / 27 / 2A: 341, Report submitted by Commissioner, City of Belfast, to Inspector General Neville Chamberlain, January 24, 1913; and CO 904 / 27 / 2A: 329–330, Reports submitted by County Inspector N.I. Marrion, County Antrim, to Inspector General Neville Chamberlain, January 27, 1913.

129. CO 904 / 27 / 2A: 396, Report submitted by Sergeant William Hall to Crimes Special Branch, January 17, 1913.

130. CO 904 / 27 / 2A: 398–404, The Ulster Volunteer Force Little Book, as copied by Sergeant William Hall.

131. CO 904 / 27 / 2A: 375–381, Report submitted by District Inspector Vere Richard Gregory, Lisburn, to County Inspector N.I. Marrion, County Antrim, January 22, 1913.

132. CO 904 / 27 / 2A: 331–335, Report submitted by District Inspector Vere Richard Gregory, Lisburn, to County Inspector N.I. Marrion, County Antrim, January 26, 1913.

133. CO 904 / 27 / 2A: 314–315, Report submitted by Inspector General Neville Chamberlain to Chief Secretary Augustine Birrell, January 30, 1913.

134. CO 904 / 89: 2, Note from Under Secretary J.B. Dougherty to Chief Secretary Augustine Birrell, February 20, 1913.

135. CO 904 / 14 / 1: 3, Note from Under Secretary J.B. Dougherty to Chief Secretary Augustine Birrell, February 20, 1913.

136. For a summary of police reports in February and March, see CO 904 / 89: 217–219, Confidential County Report for February 1913, County Armagh; CO 904 / 89: 209–210, Confidential Monthly Report for February 1913, County Antrim; CO 904 / 89: 260–262, Confidential Monthly Report for February 1913, County Fermanagh; CO 904 / 89: 350–351, Confidential

Monthly Report for February 1913, County Tyrone; CO 904 / 89: 221–223, Confidential Monthly Report for February 1913, City of Belfast; CO 904 / 89: 254–255, Confidential County Report for February 1913, County Down; CO 904 / 89: 198–201, Inspector General's Monthly Report for February 1913; CO 904 / 89: 393–402, Confidential County Report for March 1913, County Antrim; CO 904 / 89: 404–406, Confidential County Report for March 1913, County Armagh; CO 904 / 89: 449–450, Confidential County Report for March 1913, County Down; CO 904 / 89: 455–457, Confidential County Report for March 1913, County Fermanagh; CO 904 / 89: 380–382, Inspector General's Monthly Report for March 1913.

137. CO 904 / 27 / 3: 694–696, Summary of the weekly reports submitted for February and March regarding the situation in Ulster, submitted by Under Secretary J.B. Dougherty to Chief Secretary Augustine Birrell, March 10, 1913.

138. Magill, *From Dublin Castle to Stormont*, 19.

139. Ó Broin, *The Chief Secretary*, 17.

140. O'Halpin, *The Decline of the Union*, 91.

141. Ó Broin, *The Chief Secretary*, 17.

142. O'Halpin, *The Decline of the Union*, 249.

143. CO 904 / 89: 579–583, Inspector General's Monthly Report for April 1913.

144. CAB 37 / 115 / 1913: 25, "Memorandum A: Memorandum Re Condition of Things in Ulster in View of the Home Rule Bill," March 23, 1913, distributed to the cabinet by Chief Secretary Augustine Birrell, April 22, 1913.

145. CAB 37 / 115 / 1913: 25, "Memorandum B: Response by Augustine Birrell to Memorandum A," April 15, 1913, distributed to the cabinet by Chief Secretary Augustine Birrell, April 22, 1913.

146. CO 904 / 90: 17, Inspector General's Monthly Report for May 1913; CO 904 / 27 / 2A: 307–310, Report submitted by Acting Sergeant Joseph Edwards to the Crimes Special Branch, May 20, 1913.

147. CO 904 / 14 / 1: 35, Précis of Information obtained by the Crimes Special Branch as to Secret Societies, etc., during the month of June 1913.

148. CO 904 / 14 / 1: 62, Précis of Information obtained by the Crimes Special Branch as to Secret Societies, etc., during the month of July 1913.

149. See CO 904 / 90: 211–213, Inspector General's Monthly Report for June 1913; CO 904 / 90: 221–226, Confidential City Report for June 1913, City of Belfast; CO 904 / 90: 227–232, Confidential County Report for June 1913, County Antrim; CO 904 / 90: 234–236, Confidential County Report for June 1913, County Armagh; CO 904 / 90: 269–271, Confidential County Report for June 1913, County Down; Co 904 / 90: 397–405, Report on the activities of Secret Societies in Ireland during July 1913, submitted by the Crimes Special Branch to Colonel Neville Chamberlain, Inspector General, August 14, 1913; CO 904 / 27 / 2A: 297–301, report submitted by Acting Sergeant Joseph Edwards to Crimes Special Branch, July 24, 1913; CO 904 / 90: 420, Inspector General's Monthly Report for July 1913; CO 904 / 90: 430–449, Confidential County Report for July 1914, County Antrim; CO 904 / 90: 511–515, Confidential County Report for July 1913, County Down; CO 904 / 90: 521–525,

Confidential County Report for July 1913, County Fermanagh; CO 904 / 90: 457–465, Confidential City Report for July 1913, City of Belfast.

150. CO 904 / 14 / 1: 88, Précis of Information obtained by the Crimes Special Branch as to Secret Societies, etc., during the month of August 1913.

151. CO 904 / 14 / 1: 85, Note from Under Secretary J.B. Dougherty to Chief Secretary Augustine Birrell, attached to the Précis of Information obtained by the Crimes Special Branch as to Secret Societies, etc., during the month of August 1913.

152. CO 904 / 27 / 3: 628–635, Report on the condition of Ulster, submitted by Colonel Neville Chamberlain, Inspector General, to Chief Secretary Augustine Birrell, August 26, 1913.

153. CO 904 / 27 / 3: 625–627, Note from Under Secretary J.B. Dougherty to Chief Secretary Augustine Birrell, attached to Colonel Neville Chamberlain's Report of August 26, 1913.

154. CO 904 / 27 / 2B: 533, Note from Deputy Inspector General W. O'Connell, to Under Secretary J.B. Dougherty, September 19, 1913. This information was initially reported by Acting Sergeant Joseph Edwards in two separate reports: CO 904 / 27 / 2B: 540–541, Report from Acting Sergeant Joseph Edwards to the Crimes Special Branch, September 14, 1913; CO 904 / 27 / 2B: 534–535, Report from Acting Sergeant Joseph Edwards to the Detective Department, City of Belfast, September 16, 1913.

155. Stewart, *The Ulster Crisis*, 76–77.

156. CO 904 / 27 / 2B: 545, Cutting from the *News Letter* newspaper, September 12, 1913; CO 904 / 27 / 2B: 546, Cutting from the *Northern Whig* newspaper, September 12, 1913.

157. CO 904 / 27 / 2B: 503, Letter from a Belfast civilian to Justice of the Peace Mr. T.J. Smith, September 18, 1913, given to the Crimes Special Branch that same day.

158. CO 904 / 27 / 2B: 504–505, "Ulster Volunteer Force: Extract from Summary of Orders Which Will Be Issued by the G.O.C. for the Parade of the Belfast Division for Inspection by Sir Edward Carson." Submitted to the Crimes Special Branch on September 18, 1913.

159. CO 904 / 27 / 2B: 498, "Ulster Volunteer Force (Belfast Division)," Inspection Orders. The names and ranks given were as follows: Lt. General Sir George Richardson (General Officer Commanding), Col. Hacket Pain (Chief Staff Officer), W.B. Spender (Assistant Quartermaster General), Lt. Col. T.V.P. McCammon (Officer in Command of Administration and Officer Commanding the First Battalion, North Belfast Regiment), Captain F. Hall (Military Secretary), A. Sayers (Overall Commander, Signaling and Dispatch Riding Corps, Belfast Section), J. Windrim (Commander of Signalers), J. Windrim (Commander of Dispatch Riders), Fred May (Conductor, Divisional Musical Band), Colonel R.H. Wallace (Officer Commanding the North Belfast Regiment), Captain A.C.S. Chichester (Officer Commanding the West Belfast Regiment), Major F.H. Crawford (Officer Commanding the South Belfast Regiment), Major R.C. McCalmont (Officer Commanding the

East Belfast Regiment), C.O. Slacks (Officer Commanding, Second Battalion, North Belfast Regiment), George Clark (Officer Commanding, Third Battalion, North Belfast Regiment), B.W.D. Montgomery (Officer Commanding, Fourth Battalion, North Belfast Regiment), Stewart Blacker Quin (Officer Commanding, First Battalion, West Belfast Regiment), John Graham (Officer Commanding, Second Battalion, West Belfast Regiment), W.A. Lenox-Conyngham (Officer Commanding, First Battalion, South Belfast Regiment), Captain Holt Waring (Officer Commanding, Second Battalion, South Belfast Regiment), Captain Frank Dixon (Officer Commanding, Third Battalion, South Belfast Regiment), Captain H.N.B. Cunningham (Fourth Battalion, South Belfast Regiment), Arthur Gregg (Officer Commanding, First Battalion, East Belfast Regiment), H.V. Coates (Officer Commanding, Second Battalion, East Belfast Regiment), Dr. William Gibson (Officer Commanding, Third Battalion, East Belfast Regiment), and C.W. Henderson (Officer Commanding, Fourth Battalion, East Belfast Regiment).

160. CO 904 / 27 / 2B: 490–491, Report submitted by Acting Sergeant Joseph Edwards to the Detective Department, City of Belfast, October 4, 1913; CO 904 / 91 / 235–240, Confidential Report as to the State of the City, City of Belfast, 1913, submitted by Colonel Neville Chamberlain, Inspector General, to Chief Secretary Augustine Birrell.

161. CO 904 / 14 / 1: 128, Précis of Information obtained by the Crimes Special Branch as to Secret Societies, etc., during the month of September 1913.

162. CO 904 / 27 / 1: 199–202, Inspector General's Monthly Report to Under Secretary J.B. Dougherty, October 1913.

163. Birrell sent to the cabinet a report on the U.V.F. and attached the following note: "Some members of the Cabinet having expressed a wish to be kept informed as to the reports I receive as to the 'goings-on' in Ulster. I am circulating some extracts from recent reports, and will continue to do so from time to time" (CAB 37 / 116 / 1913: 69, Note from Chief Secretary Augustine Birrell to the cabinet, October 21, 1913).

164. F.X. Martin, "Introduction," in F.X. Martin, ed., *The Irish Volunteers, 1913–1915: Recollections and Documents* (Dublin: James Duffy & Co. Ltd., 1963), viii.

165. Eoin MacNeill, "The North Began," *An Claidheamh Soluis*, November 1, 1913, reprinted in Martin, ed., *Irish Volunteers*, 59.

166. Bulmer Hobson, "Foundation and Growth of the Irish Volunteers, 1913–14," in Martin, ed., *The Irish Volunteers*, 23–24.

167. Hobson later noted, "MacNeill's value lay in the fact that he was a great intellectual figure, able, clear-headed, sincere and well liked, that he quarreled with nobody and could pour oil on the most troubled waters. These qualities made him an ideal chairman in the early stages of the movement, and enabled him to keep the Volunteer Committee and the Volunteers together in circumstances of great difficulty in the year that followed the start of the movement" (ibid., 24–25).

168. Eoin MacNeill, "Memoirs of Eoin MacNeill," unpublished, October 1932, reprinted in Martin, ed., *The Irish Volunteers*, 71.
169. Ibid., 72.
170. Michael O'Rahilly, *The Secret History of the Irish Volunteers*, Dublin, 1915, reprinted in Martin, ed., *The Irish Volunteers*, 76. Those invited were Bulmer Hobson, Patrick Pearse, Sean McDermott, W.J. Ryan, Eamonn Ceannt, Sean Fitzgibbon, James A. Deakin, Piaras Beaslai, Joseph Campbell, and, of course, Eoin MacNeill and Michael O'Rahilly.
171. Hobson, "Foundation and Growth of the Irish Volunteers," 25. He writes, "I was generally regarded as an extreme nationalist, and thought it better at this initial stage to absent myself from Dublin on business that evening."
172. See Seán T. Ó Ceallaigh, "The Founding of the Irish Volunteers," *The Capuchin Annual*, 1963, reprinted in Martin, ed., *The Irish Volunteers*, 88–90.
173. Piaras Beaslai, "The National Army Is Founded," *Irish Independent*, January 5, 1953, reprinted in Martin, ed., *The Irish Volunteers*, 80–81.
174. Of these, twelve were members of the I.R.B., four were from the Irish Parliamentary Party, four were from the Ancient Order of Hibernians (a Catholic equivalent of the Protestant Orange Order), and ten were unaffiliated with any party. Of this latter ten, four would later join the I.R.B., in addition to being members of the Irish Volunteers (Hobson, "Foundation and Growth of the Irish Volunteers," 30–31).
175. Joseph P. Finnan, *John Redmond and Irish Unity, 1912–1918* (Syracuse: Syracuse University Press, 2004), 12.
176. Ibid., 13.
177. For a concise account of the rise of Parnell, see Lee, *The Modernisation of Irish Society*, 74–114.
178. Finnan, *John Redmond and Irish Unity*, 16.
179. Throughout the 1880s, Parnell was involved in an extramarital affair with Katherine O'Shea, the wife of Captain William O'Shea, a fellow Irish Nationalist Member of Parliament. Captain O'Shea was fully aware of the affair and held no personal grudge against Parnell; the captain's was a marriage of convenience only. As Parnell and Katherine became ever close, however, the captain became concerned that he might be excluded from his wife's recent inheritance. He sued for divorce, therefore, believing that doing so would give him just the leverage he needed to contest for a share in the will. As grounds for the divorce, he cited his wife's affair with Parnell.
180. Finnan, *John Redmond and Irish Unity*, 18.
181. Ibid., 19.
182. The four were John Gore, Laurence Kettle, T.M. Kettle, and Colonel Maurice Moore.
183. O'Rahilly, *Secret History of the Irish Volunteers*, 77.
184. Ibid., 77.
185. Bulmer Hobson writes, "The arrangements for the meeting in the Rotunda were made by me. I went to the then Lord Mayor, Lorcan Sherlock, and asked him for the use of the Mansion House. He refused. I then engaged the large concert hall in the Rotunda. This hall held only about five hundred people, as

at first we were too dubious of the amount of popular support we would get to risk taking the bigger room. As the day approached for the holding of the meeting I took the Rotunda Rink, a large temporary building in the grounds of the Rotunda Gardens. The Rink was then the biggest hall in Dublin and held about four thousand people" ("Foundation and Growth of the Irish Volunteers," 27).

186. Eamonn Ceannt, "The Founding of the Irish Volunteers," *The Irish Volunteer*, June 20, 1914, reprinted in Martin, ed., *The Irish Volunteers*, 78.
187. Beaslai, "The National Army Is Founded," 82.
188. Hobson, "Foundation and Growth of the Irish Volunteers," 28.
189. Eoin MacNeill, *Manifesto of Irish Volunteers*, November 25, 1913, reprinted in Martin, ed., *The Irish Volunteers*, 98–101.
190. CO 904 / 14 / 1: 237, Précis of Information obtained by the Crimes Special Branch as to Secret Societies, etc., during the month of December 1913.
191. Stewart, *The Ulster Crisis*, 79.
192. Ibid., 80.
193. CAB 37 / 116 / 1913: 59, "The Constitutional Position of the Sovereign," distributed to the cabinet by Prime Minister Herbert Asquith, September 1913.
194. Dangerfield, *The Damnable Question*, 101.
195. Ibid., 99–100. See also John Newsinger, *Rebel City: Larkin, Connolly and the Dublin Labour Movement* (London: Merkin Press, 2004), particularly part 1.
196. For background on James Connolly, see W.K. Anderson, *James Connolly and the Irish Left* (Dublin: Irish Academic Press, 1994).
197. Dangerfield, *The Damnable Question*, 104.
198. Ibid., 106.
199. General Sir Nevil Macready, *Annals of an Active Life*, 2 volumes (London: Hutchinson & Co. Ltd., 1924), 171.
200. Ibid., 166.
201. Ibid., 171.
202. Stewart, *The Ulster Crisis*, 107.
203. CAB 37 / 117 / 1913: 81, "Power to Prevent Importation of Arms into Ulster," Memorandum distributed to the cabinet by Attorney General John Allsebrook Simon, November 26, 1913.
204. Stewart, *The Ulster Crisis*, 107.
205. Ibid., 91.
206. Fred H. Crawford, *Guns for Ulster* (Belfast: Graham & Heslip Ltd., 1947), 16.
207. Crawford writes, "I obtained some specimens and prices of arms. I shall never forget the look of horror that came over the faces of these good and peaceful citizens who had been talking so glibly about rifles and armed resistance when, one day after they had concluded their deliberations, I asked them to step into a room where I had laid out some rifles and bayonets which I had recently obtained. When some of my friends saw the cold steel of bayonets, the rows of cartridges, and the very businesslike look of the rifles, they told me that they had no idea I really meant that sort of thing. After that their attendance at Committee meetings became very rare and some resigned" (ibid., 17).
208. Ibid., 18–19.

209. The government was aware of such activities on several occasions. In October 1912, for example, Birrell circulated to the cabinet a report that detailed some of the smuggling activities. It spoke of revolvers already stored in Belfast, contacts that had been made with the Birmingham Small Arms Factory, and "a quantity of modern magazine rifles" that were stored in the district of Warrenpoint. These rifles were "to be issued when the necessity arises," and were "not intended for use against the army, but against the forces directly under the control of the Irish Government, should that Government be created." There were also 450 rifles stored in Dungannon and 100 rifles promised to the Unionist Club in Derry (including two that had already been provided by Major Ross Smyth for drill practice). Furthermore, the report stated, the Earl of Roden in Newcastle, County Down, had obtained a supply of Lee-Metford and Martini-Henry rifles and was constructing a closed rifle range near his residence. His son Lord Jocelyn had a similar arrangement at his residence at Bryansford. In County Armagh, there were 200 snider rifles stored at Lord Caledon's residence, and 50 Martini-Henry rifles at Lord Annesley's seat at Castlewellan (CAB 37 / 112 / 1912: 112, Report circulated for the cabinet by Chief Secretary Augustine Birrell, October 11, 1912).

210. Henry Maxwell, *Ulster Was Right* (London: Hutchinson & Co. Ltd., 1934), 28.

211. O'Halpin, *The Decline of the Union*, 88.

212. Crawford, *Guns for Ulster*, 25–26.

213. Ibid., 27.

214. Ibid., 27–28.

215. CO 904 / 28 / 1: 175–188, Reports compiled by Acting Sergeant Joseph Edwards, sent to the Chief Secretary's Office, October 31–November 14, 1913.

216. CAB 37 / 117 / 1913: 82, "Memorandum on Illegalities in Ulster," drafted by Attorney General John Allsebrook Simon, November 26, 1913, distributed to the cabinet in December 1913.

217. CAB 37 / 117 / 1913: 87, "Memorandum: Position of the Army with Regard to the Situation in Ulster," distributed to the cabinet by Colonel John Seely, Secretary of State for War, December 9, 1913.

218. CAB 37 / 119 / 1914: 20, "Memorandum: Suggestions in Regard to Irish Government Bill," distributed by Chief Secretary Augustine Birrell, January 1914.

219. Stewart, *The Ulster Crisis*, 76.

220. Ibid., 76.

221. Charles Hobhouse, *Diaries*, printed in Edward David, ed., *Inside Asquith's Cabinet: From the Diaries of Charles Hobhouse* (New York: St. Martin's Press, 1977), 147. Charles Hobhouse had first entered the Westminster Parliament in 1892 as the Liberal Member for Wiltshire East but was defeated and lost his seat in 1895. He returned to parliament in 1900 as the Member for East Bristol. He was a backbencher until 1907, when he gained office as under secretary at the India Office. From 1907 to 1908, he was Chairman of the Royal Commission on Decentralization of Government in India, and then became Financial Secretary to the Treasury in 1908. He remained at the Treasury until

October 1911, when he entered the cabinet as Chancellor of the Duchy of Lancaster, a post he remained at until February 1914 when he became Postmaster General. As a cabinet member from October 1911 until May 1915 (when the Liberal government fell), he was in an excellent position to report on the inner happenings of the cabinet during the Ulster Crisis, which he did in detail in his diaries.

222. Stewart, *The Ulster Crisis*, 80–81.
223. Ibid., 81–82.
224. Hobhouse, *Diaries*, 149–150.
225. Ibid., 156–157.
226. Ibid., 157.
227. CO 903 / 17: 115–117, Intelligence Notes for 1912–1913 (Confidential Print: Ireland, Chief Secretary's Office, Judicial Division).
228. CO 903 / 17: 124–125, Intelligence Notes for 1912–1913 (Confidential Print: Ireland, Chief Secretary's Office, Judicial Division).
229. CO 903 / 17: 126–129, Intelligence Notes for 1912–1913 (Confidential Print: Ireland, Chief Secretary's Office, Judicial Division).
230. Hobhouse, *Diaries*, 163.
231. John Hostettler, *Sir Edward Carson: A Dream Too Far* (Chichester: Barry Rose Law Publishers, 1997), 196.
232. At the beginning of March, the R.I.C. forwarded a report to the Chief Secretary, which in part read as follows: "It is stated that one of the first offensive moves of the Ulster Volunteer Force will be the seizure of all arms in the R.I.C. It is understood that such an occasion might arise even before the Home Rule Bill becomes law, should the police have to use their arms against the U.V. Force, or should they attempt to seize any large store of Ulster Volunteer arms" (CO 904 / 14 / 2: 20, Précis of Information relating to Secret Societies and the Ulster Volunteer Movement against Home Rule, March 1914).
233. Hobhouse, *Diaries*, 164; CAB 41 / 35 / 1914: 7, Letter from Prime Minister Herbert Asquith to King George V, March 12, 1914.
234. Churchill said, "Bloodshed, gentlemen, no doubt is lamentable. . . . But there are worse things than bloodshed, even on an extreme scale. An eclipse of the central Government of the British Empire would be worse. The abandonment by our public men of the righteous aims to which they are pledged in honor would be worse. The trampling down of law and order which, under the conditions of a civilized state, assure life, liberty, and the pursuit of happiness—all this would be worse than bloodshed. . . . If Ulster seeks peace and fair-play, she can find it. . . . If Ulstermen extend the hand of friendship it will be clasped by Liberals and by their Nationalist countrymen in all good faith and in all goodwill. But if there is no wish for peace, if every concession that is made is spurned and exploited, if every effort to meet their views is only to be used as a means of breaking down Home Rule and of barring the way to the rest of Ireland, if Ulster is to become a tool in party calculations, if the civil and Parliamentary systems under which we have dwelt and our fathers before us for so many years are to be brought to the crude challenge of force, if the Government and the

Parliament of this great country and greater Empire is to be exposed to menace and brutality, if all the loose, wanton, and reckless chatter we have been forced to listen to all these many months is in the end to disclose a sinister and revolutionary purpose—then, gentlemen, I can only say to you let us go forward together and put these grave matters to the proof" (Winston S. Churchill, "Speech on the Ulster Situation," St. George's Hall, Bradford, March 14, 1914, in Robert Rhodes James, ed., *Winston S. Churchill: His Complete Speeches, 1897–1963: Volume III, 1914–1922* [New York: Chelsea House Publishers, 1974], 2230–2233).

235. Hobhouse, *Diaries*, 164; CAB 41 / 35 / 1914: 9, Letter from Prime Minister Herbert Asquith to King George V, March 18, 1914.

236. Gleichen, *A Guardsman's Memories*, 375.

237. Ibid., 376.

238. General Sir Hubert Gough, *Soldiering On* (London: Arthur Barker Ltd., 1954), 99.

239. Ibid., 101–102.

240. Ibid., 102.

241. Ibid., 103.

242. Ibid., 103–104.

243. For a more detailed account of this, see A.P. Ryan, *Mutiny at the Curragh* (London: Macmillan & Co. Ltd., 1956); and Sir James Ferguson, *The Curragh Incident* (London: Faber and Faber Limited, 1964).

244. Gleichen, *A Guardsman's Memories*, 381. For an insider's account of these negotiations, see Gough, *Soldiering On*, 105–109.

245. Gough, *Soldiering On*, 109.

246. Hobhouse, *Diaries*, 165.

247. Birrell's private secretary, commenting on this matter, wrote, "It was not our [the Irish Office's] business and I am afraid I took a certain satisfaction in seeing another department in hot water, especially as I thought the whole affair had been clumsily handled. To ask an Irish officer whether he would prefer to resign, or act against his own countrymen with whom he was probably in sympathy politically, was merely asking for trouble. Anyhow, Col. Seely resigned over the incident and Mr. Asquith took over the War Office temporarily" (Magill, *From Dublin Castle to Stormont*, 28).

248. Gleichen, *A Guardsman's Memories*, 381.

249. Macready, *Annals of an Active Life*, 178–179.

250. CO 904 / 29 / 1: 58, Telegram from Sir Henry Lowther to Sir Edward Grey, March 31, 1914.

251. CO 904 / 29 / 1: 48–51, Letter from Sir Henry Lowther to Sir Edward Grey, April 1, 1914; CO 904 / 29 / 1: 46–47, Letter from Walter R. Hearn, British Consulate General, Hamburg, to Sir Edward Grey, April 3, 1914. Lowther informed Grey that the *Fanny* had taken on cargo from a German lighter, the *Carl Kiehn*, off Langeland in the neighborhood of Rudkjobing. Hearn's letter specified that the cargo contained 15,770 cases of new Winchester rifles, which had been loaded onto a British steamer, the *Brinkburn*, at New York, originally destined for Mexico. The *Brinkburn* had instead taken them to Odessa, where

it transferred the rifles onto a German steamer, the *Pernau*. This then traveled to Hamburg, where it transferred them to the *Carl Kiehn*.

252. Crawford, *Guns for Ulster*, 38–53.
253. For an account of the *Balmarino* decoy, see CO 904 / 29 / 1: 67–70, Report from Surveyor of Customs and Excise Methuselah Jones, May 2, 1914; CO 904 / 29 / 1: 71, Report from Officer of Customs and Excise George Victor Acheson, May 2, 1914; CO 904 / 29 / 1: 72–74, Report from Preventive Officer of Customs Patrick Wallace, May 2, 1914; CO 904 / 29 / 1: 75–76, Report from Customs Preventive Man Matthew MacDonald, May 2, 1914; CO 904 / 29 / 1: 77, Report from Officer of Customs and Excise Andrew McMullan, May 2, 1914; CO 904 / 29 / 1: 78–80, Report from Officer of Customs and Excise James Francis MacWilliams, May 2, 1914.
254. CO 904 / 29 / 1: 98–99, Report from Surveyor of Customs and Excise George Goodman, May 2, 1914.
255. CO 904 / 29 / 1: 95–96, Report from Head Constable James McHugh, May 2, 1914.
256. CO 904 / 29 / 1: 92–94, Report from District Inspector William Sneyd Moore, May 2, 1914.
257. CO 904 / 29 / 1: 97, Report from Acting Sergeant Robert Gordon, May 2, 1914.
258. CO 904 / 29 / 1: 95–96, Report from Head Constable James McHugh, May 2, 1914.
259. CO 904 / 29 / 1: 92–94, Report from District Inspector William Sneyd Moore, May 2, 1914.
260. CO 904 / 29 / 1: 95–96, Report from Head Constable James McHugh, May 2, 1914.
261. CO 904 / 29 / 1: 92–94, Report from District Inspector William Sneyd Moore, May 2, 1914.
262. CO 904 / 29 / 1: 108–109, Report from Sergeant George Phillips, May 2, 1914.
263. CO 904 / 29 / 1: 117–118, Report from District Inspector John Shankey, May 2, 1914.
264. The following reports were submitted to the Chief Secretary: CO 904 / 29 / 1: 81–84, Report from Preventive Officer of Customs Adam Henry Fitzsimmons, May 2, 1914; CO 904 / 29 / 1: 85–86, Report from Customs Preventive Man John Clarke, May 2, 1914; CO 904 / 29 / 1: 87–88, Report from Officer of Customs and Excise James Francis MacWilliams, May 2, 1914; CO 904 / 29 / 1: 89–91, Report from Acting Sergeant Joseph Edwards, May 4, 1914; CO 904 / 29 / 1: 98–99, Report from Surveyor of Customs and Excise George Goodman, May 2, 1914; CO 904 / 29 / 1: 95–96, Report from Head Constable James McHugh, May 2, 1914; CO 904 / 29 / 1: 92–94, Report from District Inspector William Sneyd Moore, May 2, 1914; CO 904 / 29 / 1: 97, Report from Acting Sergeant Robert Gordon, May 2, 1914; CO 904 / 29 / 1: 103–107, "List of Cars Used in Connection with the Landing at Larne," May 2, 1914; CO 904 / 29 / 1: 108–109, Report from Sergeant George Phillips, May 2, 1914;

CO 904 / 29 / 1: 110–111, Report from Chief Officer of the Coastguard Richard Fowler, May 2, 1914; CO 904 / 29 / 1: 116, Report from Chief Officer of the Coastguard William Hitt, May 2, 1914; CO 904 / 29 / 1: 117–118, Report from District Inspector John Shankey, May 2, 1914; CO 904 / 29 / 1: 112–113, Report from Lieutenant Commander Gerald Ducat, Royal Navy Divisional Officer of the Coastguard, May 2, 1914; CO 904 / 29 / 1: 114–115, Report from Officer of Customs and Excise Robert Smith, May 2, 1914; CO 904 / 29 / 1: 120–123, Return of motor cars used in the removal of arms from the Donaghadee Pier, April 25, 1914.

265. CO 904 / 29 / 1: 190, Crimes Special Branch Memorandum, December 1914.

266. Magill, *From Dublin Castle to Stormont*, 24.

267. Letter from Chief Secretary Augustine Birrell to Prime Minister Herbert Asquith, April 26, 1914, quoted in Jalland, "A Liberal Chief Secretary and the Irish Question," 444.

268. Magill, *From Dublin Castle to Stormont*, 24.

269. Immediately following the gunrunning, General Macready once again traveled to Ireland to see for himself the situation on the ground. He found Birrell's under secretary, Dougherty, in a near hysterical state, alternating between anger at the humiliation suffered by the government and incredulity that Birrell and Asquith had not ordered the military to dig up half of the country estates in Ulster to look for arms, regardless of the police intelligence. Commenting on this meeting, Macready wrote in his memoirs, "Sir James Dougherty, who had been a minister of religion before entering the Civil Service, struck me as being far too old to hold any position in which steady nerves and calm judgment were required; but Dublin Castle has, I believe, always been famous for the human curiosities within its walls, of whom it has been my fortune to see not a few" (*Annals of an Active Life*, 185–186).

270. CO 904 / 14 / 2: 28–30, Précis of Information relating to Secret Societies and the Ulster Volunteer Movement against Home Rule, March 1914.

271. CO 904 / 14 / 2: 67, Précis of the Principal Reports relative to Secret Societies, &c., in the Dublin Metropolitan Police District, May 1914; CO 903 / 18: 39, Intelligence Notes for 1914 (Confidential Print: Ireland, Chief Secretary's Office, Judicial Division).

272. CO 903 / 18: 51, Intelligence Notes for 1914 (Confidential Print: Ireland, Chief Secretary's Office, Judicial Division).

273. Macready, *Annals of an Active Life*, 191.

274. Hobson, "Foundation and Growth of the Irish Volunteers," 43–47.

275. Hobson, "The Provisional Committee Submits but Protests," June 16, 1914, printed in Martin, ed., *The Irish Volunteers*, 141–143.

276. CAB 37 / 120 / 1914: 81, "A Memorandum by the Military Members of the Army Council on the Military Situation in Ireland," July 4, 1914.

277. See George H. Cassar, *Asquith as War Leader* (London: Hambledon Press, 1994), chapter 1.

278. Macready, *Annals of an Active Life*, 193–194.

279. On this policy, Macready commented scathingly, "So far as the political government of Ireland was concerned I was entirely indifferent, having no interest of any kind in the island. The policy I did advocate, whether applicable to the North or to the South, was 'Govern or get out,' and that is exactly what in 1914 Mr. Asquith would not do" (ibid., 198).

280. In a remarkable instance of prescience, General Gleichen noted the following in his diary on July 25: "Another item of news is that Serbia has refused to give in to the outrageous demands of Austria, and that Germany and Russia are mobilizing! It will be really comic if the assassination of Franz Ferdinand is going to settle the Irish Question!" (*A Guardsman's Memories*, 394).

281. Michael MacDonagh, *The Irish on the Somme* (London: Hodder and Stoughton, 1917), 32–33.

282. Stewart, *The Ulster Crisis*, 236.

283. Keith Jeffery, *Ireland and the Great War* (Cambridge, U.K.: Cambridge University Press, 2000), 56.

284. Tom Johnstone, *Orange, Green and Khaki: The Story of the Irish Regiments in the Great War, 1914–18* (Dublin: Gill & Macmillan, 1992), 229.

285. Brian Gardner, *The Big Push: A Portrait of the Battle of the Somme* (New York: William Morrow and Company, 1963), 84.

286. MacDonagh, *The Irish on the Somme*, 37.

287. Gardner, *The Big Push*, 84.

288. Ibid., 85.

289. Jeffery, *Ireland and the Great War*, 56.

290. Gardner, *The Big Push*, 92.

291. Stewart, *The Ulster Crisis*, 234.

292. Fitzpatrick, *The Two Irelands*, 51–52.

293. Hobhouse, *Diaries*, 190.

294. Ibid., 189–190.

295. Ibid., 192.

296. Stewart, *The Ulster Crisis*, 234–235.

297. See the introduction for an overview of this historiography.

298. Jalland, *The Liberals and Ireland*, 245.

299. Ó Broin, *The Chief Secretary*, 94.

300. Stewart, *The Ulster Crisis*, 207.

Part II   The Period of Clandestine Organization, 1914–1916

1. CO 904 / 14 / 2: 95, Summary of County Inspectors' Confidential Reports, and Précis of Information Received in the Crimes Special Branch During the Month of July 1914.

2. CO 904 / 14 / 2: 97, Summary of County Inspectors' Confidential Reports, and Précis of Information Received in the Crimes Special Branch During the Month of July 1914.

3. CO 904 / 14 / 2: 99, Summary of County Inspectors' Confidential Reports, and Précis of Information Received in the Crimes Special Branch During the Month of July 1914.

4. Hobson, "Foundation and Growth of the Irish Volunteers," 33.

5. The information in the following three paragraphs is taken from Roger Sawyer, *Casement: The Flawed Hero* (London: Routledge & Kegan Paul, 1984), 18–108.

6. Jeffrey Dudgeon, *Roger Casement: The Black Diaries, with a Study of His Background, Sexuality, and Irish Political Life* (Belfast: Belfast Press, 2002), 91–92.

7. Sawyer, *Casement*, 42–52.

8. For more on the Gaelic League and Irish cultural nationalism, see John Hutchinson, *The Dynamics of Cultural Nationalism: The Gaelic Revival and the Creation of the Irish Nation State* (London: Allen & Unwin, in association with the London School of Economics and Political Science, 1987).

9. Dudgeon, *Roger Casement*, 167–175.

10. Jim Ring, *Erskine Childers* (London: John Murray, 1996), 138–139.

11. These books were *In the Ranks of the C.I.V.: A Narrative and Diary of Personal Experiences with the C.I.V. Battery (Honorary Battery Company) in South Africa* (London: Smith, Elder and Company, 1901) and *The H.A.C. in South Africa: A Record of the Services Rendered in the South African War by Members of the Honourable Artillery Company* (London: Smith, Elder and Company, 1903), coauthored with Basil Williams.

12. See Ring, *Erskine Childers*, 105–139.

13. Leonard Piper, *Dangerous Waters: The Life and Death of Erskine Childers* (London: Hambledon, 2003), 123.

14. Ibid., 124.

15. Dudgeon, *Roger Casement*, 418–419.

16. Townshend, *Political Violence in Ireland*, 238–242.

17. Hobson, "Foundation and Growth of the Irish Volunteers," 19–20.

18. Ibid., 21.

19. Ibid., 33.

20. Ibid., 34.

21. CO 904 / 14 / 2: 104–105, Summary of County Inspectors' Confidential Reports, and Précis of Information received in the Crimes Special Branch during the month of July 1914.

22. CO 904 / 14 / 2: 105–113, Summary of County Inspectors' Confidential Reports, and Précis of Information received in the Crimes Special Branch during the month of July 1914.

23. Hobson, "Foundation and Growth of the Irish Volunteers," 35.

24. Ibid., 36.

25. Macready, *Annals of an Active Life*, 194–195.

26. Hobson, "Foundation and Growth of the Irish Volunteers," 37–38.

27. Ibid., 38–39.

28. Dangerfield, *The Damnable Question*, 121.

29. CO 904 / 94: 407, Inspector General's Monthly Report for September 1914.

30. Birrell's private secretary, Andrew Magill, writes the following in his memoirs: "There was a great outcry and a commission was appointed to enquire into the whole proceedings in connection with the landing of the arms. The late Lord Shaw of Dunfermline was the chairman and how he managed it I cannot say, but he secured the assent of the other two commissioners to a report which censured Mr. Harrel, who had to retire" (*From Dublin Castle to Stormont*, 25).

31. Macready, *Annals of an Active Life*, 195–196.

32. Magill, *From Dublin Castle to Stormont*, 25–26.

33. Ibid., 26.

34. Magill relates a further incident in which Birrell acted inappropriately towards Harrell during this investigation: "When Mr. Birrell spoke to me about the affair I told him that the only thing for which I blamed Mr. Harrel was that he let the military return through the city unaccompanied by any police. The military are of no use in a street row; the only thing they can do is to fire on the people, whereas the police are accustomed to handling crowds, and a few police armed with batons are usually more than a match for any average crowd. I was very sorry I said this, for Mr. Birrell seized upon it as usual, and made it one of the charges against Mr. Harrel that he had not sent back the police with the military" (*From Dublin Castle to Stormont*, 26).

35. Hobhouse, *Diaries*, 177.

36. CO 904 / 94: 11, Inspector General's Monthly Report for July 1914.

37. CO 904 / 94: 70–71, County Inspector's Confidential Monthly Report for July 1914, County Dublin.

38. Ibid.

39. Date of revocation given in CO 903 / 18, Intelligence Notes, 1914 (Confidential Print: Ireland, Chief Secretary's Office, Judicial Division).

40. See Ben Novick, "The Arming of Ireland: Gun-Running and the Great War, 1914–16," in Adrian Gregory and Senia Pašeta, eds., *Ireland and the Great War: "A War to Unite Us All"?* (Manchester: Manchester University Press, 2002), 97–99.

41. CO 903 / 18: 61, Intelligence Notes, 1914 (Confidential Print: Ireland, Chief Secretary's Office, Judicial Division).

42. CO 904 / 94: 11–12, Inspector General's Monthly Report for July 1914.

43. CO 904 / 94: 203–211, Précis of County Inspector's Reports for the month of August 1914.

44. Terence Denman, *Ireland's Unknown Soldiers: The 16th (Irish Division) in the Great War, 1914–1918* (Dublin: Irish Academic Press, 1992), 20.

45. *Hansard's Parliamentary Debates*, House of Commons, fifth series, volume LXV, July 20–August 10, 1914 (London: His Majesty's Stationary Office, 1914).

46. Denman, *Ireland's Unknown Soldiers*, 21.

47. Johnstone, *Orange, Green and Khaki*, 1. Parliament consented on August 6 to increase the regular army by 500,000 men. On August 11, a general proclamation was issued calling for 100,000 men to volunteer for three years or the duration of the war, whichever was longer. This force became the First New Army, known

as K1. On September 13, a further 100,000 men were called for, creating the Second New Army, or K2. An Irish Division was planned for each of these armies.

48. Denman, *Ireland's Unknown Soldiers*, 22–23.
49. Ibid., 23.
50. Stewart, *The Ulster Crisis*, 234; Fitzpatrick, *The Two Irelands*, 51–52.
51. Hobhouse, *Diaries*, 181.
52. Ibid., 190.
53. Ibid., 191.
54. Ibid., 192.
55. John Redmond, "Speech at Woodenbridge," September 20, 1914, reprinted in Martin, ed., *The Irish Volunteers*, 148.
56. See Cyril Falls, *The History of the 36th Ulster Division* (Belfast: M'Caw, Stephenson, and Orr, 1922); Denman, *Ireland's Unknown Soldiers*; and Timothy Bowman, "The Ulster Volunteer Force and the Formation of the 36th (Ulster) Division," *Irish Historical Studies*, volume 37, number 128 (November 2001).
57. CO 904 / 94: 203–211, Précis of County Inspector's Reports for the month of August 1914.
58. Hobson, "The Provisional Committee Submits but Protests," 141–143.
59. CO 904 / 94: 213–214, Inspector General's Monthly Report for August 1914.
60. "Open Letter to the Irish Volunteers," signed by Eoin MacNeill, Chairman Provisional Committee; Ua Rathghaille, Treasurer Provisional Committee; Thomas MacDonagh; Joseph Plunkett; Piaras Beaslai; Michael J. Judge; Peter Paul Macken; Sean Mac Giobuin; P.H. Pearse; Padraic Ó Riain; Bulmer Hobson; Eamonn Martin; Conchubhair Ó Colbaird; Eamonn Ceannt; Sean Mac Diarmada; Seamus Ó Conchubhair; Liam Mellows; L. Colm Ó Lochlainn; Liam Ua Gogan; and Peter Waite, September 24, 1914, in Martin, ed., *The Irish Volunteers*, 152–155.
61. Hobson, "Foundation and Growth of the Irish Volunteers," 53.
62. "Proposed Constitution of the Irish Volunteers," Passed at a Special Meeting of the Provisional Committee, October 10, 1914, reprinted in Martin, ed., *The Irish Volunteers*, 159–162; "First Convention," *The Irish Volunteer*, October 31, 1914, reprinted in Martin, ed., *The Irish Volunteers*, 162–169; and "The Volunteers Declare Their Policy," *The Irish Volunteer*, October 31, 1914, reprinted in Martin, ed., *The Irish Volunteers*, 169–170.
63. Hobson wrote that the provisional committee "knew that the number of men that would adhere to us would be relative small," but maintained that it was important for "the men throughout the country who were in earnest about maintaining an Irish Volunteer Force" on its original ideology to be given that chance. ("Foundation and Growth of the Irish Volunteers," 53).
64. CO 904 / 95: 216, Inspector General's Monthly Report for November 1914.
65. See CO 904 / 94: 416, Précis of Information received in the Crimes Special Branch during September 1914; CO 904 / 95: 3, Inspector General's Monthly Report for October 1914; CO 904 / 95: 216, Inspector General's Monthly Report for November 1914; CO 904 / 95: 435, Inspector General's Monthly Report for December 1914; CO 904 / 96: 3, Inspector General's Monthly

Report for January 1915; CO 904 / 96: 14, Précis of Information received in the Crimes Special Branch during January 1915; CO 904 / 96: 208, Inspector General's Monthly Report for February 1915; CO 904 / 96 / 216, Précis of Information received in the Crimes Special Branch during February 1915; CO 904 / 96: 397, Inspector General's Monthly Report for March 1915; CO 904 / 96: 407, Précis of Information Received in the Crimes Special Branch during March 1915; CO 904 / 96: 598, Inspector General's Monthly Report for April 1915; and CO 903 / 19 / Part 1, Intelligence Notes, 1915 (Confidential Print: Ireland, Chief Secretary's Office, Judicial Division).

66. CO 904 / 97: 3, Inspector General's Monthly Report for May 1915.
67. CO 904 / 94: 406, Inspector General's Monthly Report for September 1914.
68. CO 904 / 94: 431–433, References in the Inspector General's Confidential Report for September 1914, to the State of Public Feeling in Ireland in Connection with the War.
69. CO 904 / 94: 433–435, References in the Inspector General's Confidential Report for September 1914, to the State of Public Feeling in Ireland in Connection with the War.
70. CO 904 / 94: 434, References in the Inspector General's Confidential Report for September 1914, to the State of Public Feeling in Ireland in Connection with the War.
71. CO 904 / 95: 3–14, Inspector General's Monthly Report for October 1914.
72. CO 904 / 95: 15–18, References in the Inspector General's Confidential Report for October 1914, to the State of Public Feeling in Ireland in Connection with the War.
73. CO 904 / 95: 216, Inspector General's Monthly Report for November 1914.
74. CO 904 / 95: 436, Inspector General's Monthly Report for December 1914.
75. CO 904 / 95: 444, Inspector General's Monthly Report for December 1914.
76. CO 904 / 96: 3–11, Inspector General's Monthly Report for January 1915.
77. CO 904 / 96: 20–27, Précis of Information Received in the Crimes Special Branch during January 1915.
78. CO 904 / 96: 213–214, Inspector General's Monthly Report for February 1915.
79. CO 904 / 96: 208, Inspector General's Monthly Report for February 1915.
80. CO 904 / 96: 397, Inspector General's Monthly Report for March 1915.
81. CO 904 / 96: 415, Précis of Information Received in the Crimes Special Branch during March 1915.
82. CO 904 / 96: 220–221, Précis of Information Received in the Crimes Special Branch during February 1915.
83. CO 904 / 96: 597–599, Inspector General's Monthly Report for April 1915.
84. CO 904 / 96: 596, Note from Under Secretary Matthew Nathan to Chief Secretary Augustine Birrell, May 15, 1915.
85. CO 904 / 96: 596, Note from Chief Secretary Augustine Birrell to Under Secretary Matthew Nathan, May 17, 1915.
86. Edwards, *Patrick Pearse*, 14–152.
87. See Brian P. Murphy, *Patrick Pearse and the Lost Republican Ideal* (Dublin: James Duffy & Co. Ltd., 1991), chapter 1.

88. Moran, *Patrick Pearse and the Politics of Redemption*, 127–128.
89. Edwards, *Patrick Pearse*, 154–173.
90. Moran, *Patrick Pearse and the Politics of Redemption*, 129.
91. Edwards, *Patrick Pearse*, 173.
92. Moran, *Patrick Pearse and the Politics of Redemption*, 140–145.
93. CO 904 / 97: 4, Inspector General's Monthly Report for May 1915.
94. CO 904 / 97: 4–5, Inspector General's Monthly Report for May 1915.
95. CO 904 / 97: 183–184, Précis of Information Received in the Crimes Special Branch during May 1915.
96. CO 904 / 97: 203–204, Inspector General's Monthly Report for June 1915.
97. CO 904 / 97: 413–416, Précis of Information Received in the Crimes Special Branch during July 1915.
98. CO 904 / 97: 406, Inspector General's Monthly Report for July 1915.
99. CO 904 / 97: 624–625, Précis of Information Received in the Crimes Special Branch during August 1915.
100. CO 904 / 97: 636, Note from Under Secretary Matthew Nathan to Chief Secretary Augustine Birrell, September 15, 1915.
101. CO 904 / 97: 611–619, Inspector General's Monthly Report for August 1915.
102. CO 904 / 98: 3–5, Inspector General's Monthly Report for September 1915.
103. CO 904 / 98: 183–189, Inspector General's Monthly Report for October 1916.
104. CO 904 / 98: 182, Note from Under Secretary Matthew Nathan to Chief Secretary Augustine Birrell, November 11, 1915.
105. CO 904 / 98: 362–368, Inspector General's Monthly Report for November 1915.
106. CO 904 / 98: 532–535, Inspector General's Monthly Report for December 1915.
107. CO 904 / 99: 7–8, Inspector General's Monthly Report for January 1916.
108. CO 904 / 99: 10–11, Inspector General's Monthly Report for January 1916.
109. CO 904 / 99: 11, Inspector General's Monthly Report for January 1916.
110. CO 904 / 99: 224, Inspector General's Monthly Report for February 1916.
111. CO 904 / 23 / 3A: 57, Secret, Report from Granite, February 24, 1916, Detective Department, Dublin Metropolitan Police.
112. CO 904 / 23 / 3A: 48–49, Secret, Report from Chalk, March 16, 1916, Detective Department, Dublin Metropolitan Police.
113. CO 904 / 23 / 3A: 54–55, Secret, Report from Chalk, March 27, 1916, Detective Department, Dublin Metropolitan Police.
114. CO 904 / 23 / 3A: 56, Secret, Report from Granite, March 27, Detective Department, Dublin Metropolitan Police.
115. CO 904 / 99: 429–431, Inspector General's Monthly Report for March 1916.
116. CO 904 / 99: 432, Inspector General's Monthly Report for March 1916.
117. CO 904 / 99: 641, Inspector General's Confidential Report, April 1–May 31, 1916: Secret Report on the Easter Rising.
118. Reinhard R. Doerries, *Prelude to the Easter Rising: Sir Roger Casement in Imperial Germany* (London: Frank Cass, 2000), 1–4.
119. Ibid., 3.

120. John Devoy, *Recollections of an Irish Rebel* (New York: Chas. P. Young, 1929), 403, quoted in ibid., 3.

121. Declaration from Clan na Gael to His Imperial Majesty, The German Emperor, August 25, 1914, printed in Doerries, *Prelude to the Easter Rising*, 4.

122. Casement's logic here did indeed have some grounds. Following the establishment of the Irish Free State in 1921, Great Britain retained control of three strategic ports along the Irish sea coast, which gave them greater access to the Atlantic Ocean. In 1937, however, the British Prime Minister, Neville Chamberlain, relinquished these ports to the Irish government. As a result, during the Second World War the radius of the Royal Navy's operations in the Atlantic was reduced by between 200 and 400 miles. See Benjamin Grob-Fitzgibbon, *The Irish Experience During the Second World War: An Oral History* (Dublin: Irish Academic Press, 2004), 7–9.

123. Quoted in Doerries, *Prelude to the Easter Rising*, 5.

124. Ibid., 6–7.

125. In his November 1914 Monthly Report, the Inspector General of the R.I.C., Neville Chamberlain, noted that "from information with regard to the mission to Berlin of Sir Roger Casement, who has undoubtedly been in association with revolutionary extremists both in this Country and in America, it is also probable that an attempt may be made to send an expedition from America and perhaps arms and officers from Germany for the purpose of stirring up insurrection in Ireland" (CO 904 / 95: 216, Inspector General's Monthly Report for November 1914).

126. Doerries, *Prelude to the Easter Rising*, 8–9.

127. Ibid., 9–17.

128. Ibid.

129. CO 904 / 99: 641, Inspector General's Confidential Report, April 1–May 31, 1916: Secret Report on the Easter Rising.

130. CO 904 / 23 / 3A: 63, Secret, Report from Chalk, April 22, 1916, Detective Department, Dublin Metropolitan Police.

131. CO 904 / 99: 641–642, Inspector General's Confidential Report, April 1–May 31, 1916: Secret Report on the Easter Rising.

132. CO 904 / 99: 642, Inspector General's Confidential Report, April 1–May 31, 1916: Secret Report on the Easter Rising.

133. Foy and Barton, *The Easter Rising*, 46.

134. Ibid., 48–50.

135. CO 903 / 19 / 2: 31, Special Report: The Sinn Fein or Irish Volunteers and the Rebellion, Intelligence Notes, 1916 (Confidential Print: Ireland, Chief Secretary's Office, Judicial Division).

136. Foy and Barton, *The Easter Rising*, 54, 56, 71, and 124.

137. The following account is taken from *Sinn Fein Rebellion Handbook, Easter 1916*, compiled by the *Weekly Irish Times* (Dublin, 1916).

138. Inspector General Chamberlain later reported that "the 'underworld' of the City quickly realized their opportunity," and looting became widespread, beginning on Lower Sackville Street where "the windows were smashed and hordes of people

crowded into the shops, returning with bundles of wearing apparel of all descriptions." The "younger section of the roughs," Chamberlain said, also became active and "made merry with boxes of chocolates, sweets, etc., all the afternoon". CO 903 / 19 / 2: 32–33, Special Report: The Sinn Fein or Irish Volunteers and the Rebellion. Intelligence Notes, 1916 (Confidential Print: Ireland, Chief Secretary's Office, Judicial Division).

139. CO 903 / 19 / 2: 33, Special Report: The Sinn Fein or Irish Volunteers and the Rebellion. Intelligence Notes, 1916 (Confidential Print: Ireland, Chief Secretary's Office, Judicial Division).

140. CO 904 / 23 / 2B: 17. The full proclamation read, "Whereas an attempt, instigated and designed by the foreign enemies of our King and Country to incite rebellion in Ireland, and thus endanger the safety of the United Kingdom, has been made by a reckless though small body of men, who have been guilty of insurrectionary acts: Now We, Ivor Churchill, Baron Wimborne, Lord Lieutenant General and General Governor of Ireland, DO HEREBY WARN all His Majesty's Subjects that the sternest measures are being, and will be, taken for the prompt suppression of the existing disturbances and the restoration of order: And we do hereby enjoin all loyal and law-abiding citizens to abstain from any acts or conduct which might interfere with the action of the executive Government, and, in particular, WE WARN ALL CITIZENS of the danger of unnecessarily frequenting the streets or public places, or of assembling in crowds: Given under Our Seal on the 24th day of April, 1916. WIMBOURNE."

141. CO 904 / 23 / 2B / 13 and 21. The Martial Law Proclamation of April 25, on which the April 29 Proclamation was based, read as follows: "Whereas, in the City of Dublin and County of Dublin certain evilly disposed persons and association, with the intent to subvert the supremacy of the Crown in Ireland, have committed divers acts of violence, and have with deadly weapons attacked the Forces of the Crown, and have resisted by armed force the lawful Authority of His Majesty's Police and Military Forces. And whereas by reason thereof several of His Majesty's liege Subjects have been killed and many others severely injured, and much damage to property has been caused. And, whereas, such armed resistance to His Majesty's authority still continues. Now, I, Ivor Churchill, Baron Wimborne, Lord Lieutenant-General and General-Governor of Ireland, by virtue of all the powers me thereunto enabling DO HEREBY PROCLAIM that from and after the date of this Proclamation, and for the period of One Month thereafter (unless otherwise ordered) the City of Dublin and County of Dublin are under and subject to MARTIAL LAW And I do hereby call on all loyal and well affected Subjects of the Crown to aid in upholding and maintaining the peace of this Realm and the supremacy and authority of the Crown. And I warn all peaceable and law-abiding Subjects within such area of the danger of frequenting, or being in any place in or in the vicinity of which His Majesty's Forces are engaged in the suppression of disorder. And I do hereby enjoin upon such Subjects the duty and necessity, so far as practicable, of remaining within their own homes so long as these dangerous conditions prevail. And I do hereby declare that all persons found carrying Arms without

lawful authority are liable to be dealt with by virtue of this Proclamation. Given at Dublin this 25th day of April, 1916. Wimborne."

142. CO 904 / 23 / 2B: 14, Proclamation of Martial Law.
143. CAB 41 / 37: 17, Letter from Prime Minister Herbert Asquith to King George V, April 27, 1916.
144. Quoted in Foy and Barton, *The Easter Rising*, 220.
145. Ibid., 221.
146. CO 904 / 99: 643, Inspector General's Confidential Report, April 1–May 31, 1916: Secret Report on the Easter Rising.
147. *Sinn Fein Rebellion Handbook*, 9–10.
148. Ibid., 10. As the flames spread, civilians began to appear from their homes, and whilst some men, women, and children "emerged from their houses and fled to the sanctuary of the Custom House," others were too scared or injured to move. Eventually, "a soldier crept from Butt Bridge to the burning block and managed to encourage some of the occupants to leave. They included young women who fell on their knees and kissed his hand" (Foy and Barton, *The Easter Rising*, 210).
149. His declaration read, "In order to prevent further slaughter of unarmed people and in the hope of saving the lives of our followers, now surrounded and hopelessly outnumbered, members of the Provisional Government at present at headquarters have agreed to unconditional surrender, and the commanders of all units of the republican forces will order their followers to lay down their arms. P.H. Pearse, 29th day of April, 1916."
150. Connolly's declaration read, "I agree to these conditions for the men only under my command in the Moore street district, and for the men in the Stephen's Green Command. James Connolly." McDonagh's declaration read, "April 29th, 1916. On consultation with Commandant Ceannt and other officers, I have decided to agree to unconditional surrender also. Thomas MacDonagh."
151. *Sinn Fein Rebellion Handbook*, 11.
152. The following account is taken from CO 904 / 99: 644–648, Inspector General's Confidential Report, April 1–May 31, 1916: Secret Report on the Easter Rising.
153. CO 903 / 19 / 2: 39, Special Report: The Sinn Fein or Irish Volunteers and the Rebellion. Intelligence Notes, 1916 (Confidential Print: Ireland, Chief Secretary's Office, Judicial Division).
154. *Sinn Fein Rebellion Handbook*, 28.
155. Ibid., 11.
156. Tim Pat Coogan writes, "The initial outrage that greeted all this was hardly surprising. Dubliners, some with husbands and relatives at the Front, had hooted and jeered at the prisoners as they were marched through the city they had shattered. Vegetables were thrown at them, even the contents of chamberpots, as they passed by, dirty, weary, [and] hungry" (Tim Pat Coogan, *1916: The Easter Rising* [Dublin: Cassell & Co., 2001], 135).
157. Foy and Barton, *The Easter Rising*, 203–204.
158. CO 904 / 99: 651, Inspector General's Confidential Report, April 1–May 31, 1916: Secret Report on the Easter Rising.

159. CO 903 / 19 / 2: 38, Special Report: The Sinn Fein or Irish Volunteers and the Rebellion. Intelligence Notes, 1916 (Confidential Print: Ireland, Chief Secretary's Office, Judicial Division).

160. CO 904 / 99: 651, Inspector General's Confidential Report, April 1–May 31, 1916: Secret Report on the Easter Rising. The R.I.C. estimated that there were approximately 1,100 rifles, 730 shot guns, and 1,200 revolvers that had not been recovered. These weapons were retained by the Irish Volunteers.

161. CO 903 / 19 / 2: 38–40, Special Report: The Sinn Fein or Irish Volunteers and the Rebellion. Intelligence Notes, 1916 (Confidential Print: Ireland, Chief Secretary's Office, Judicial Division).

162. Ibid.

163. Quoted in Coogan, *1916: The Easter Rising*, 136.

164. Ibid.

165. CAB 41 / 37 / 19, Letter from Prime Minister Herbert Asquith to King George V, May 6, 1916. Asquith informed George V in a letter that General Maxwell had "commuted the sentence of death passed by Court Martial on the Countess Markievitch [*sic*] to one of penal servitude for life. He was instructed [by the cabinet] not to allow the capital sentence to be carried out in the case of any woman."

166. Coogan, *1916: The Easter Rising*, 136.

167. Foy and Barton, *The Easter Rising*, 239–242.

168. CO 903 / 19 / 2: 38–40, Special Report: The Sinn Fein or Irish Volunteers and the Rebellion. Intelligence Notes, 1916 (Confidential Print: Ireland, Chief Secretary's Office, Judicial Division). Of those who were not executed, 10 were sentenced to penal servitude for life, 1 was sentenced to 20 years' penal servitude, 33 were sentenced to 10 years' penal servitude, 3 were sentenced to 8 years' penal servitude, 1 was sentenced to 7 years' penal servitude, 18 were sentenced to 5 years' penal servitude, 56 were sentenced to 3 years' penal servitude, 2 were sentenced to 2 years' imprisonment with hard labor, 17 were sentenced to 1 years' imprisonment with hard labor, and 4 were sentenced to 6 months' imprisonment with hard labor.

169. CO 904 / 99: 649–651, Inspector General's Confidential Report, April 1–May 31, 1916: Secret Report on the Easter Rising.

170. Ibid.

171. CO 904 / 100: 197–203, Inspector General's Confidential Report for June 1916.

172. CO 904 / 100: 196, Note from Assistant Under Secretary Edward O'Farrell, to the Under Secretary Robert Chalmers, July 18, 1916.

173. CO 904 / 100: 392, Inspector General's Confidential Report for July 1916.

174. O'Halpin, *The Decline of the Union*, 124.

175. Magill, *From Dublin Castle to Stormont*, 39.

176. Foy and Barton, *The Easter Rising*, 224.

177. Magill, *From Dublin Castle to Stormont*, 39.

178. Foy and Barton, *The Easter Rising*, 223.

Part III The Period of Guerrilla War, 1916–1921

1. Eunan O'Halpin writes, "[Maxwell] came to Ireland to put an end to rebellion; he soon realized that he had, in the eyes of the civil authorities and of most Irishmen, a broader mandate to govern the country as he wished." To his credit, Maxwell believed that such a position was not in the interests of the Irish people or government, and in June he offered his resignation "lest his presence jeopardize the prospects of a home rule settlement." Asquith, however, refused to accept this resignation, and he was kept in place until Duke's appointment as Chief Secretary. See O'Halpin, *The Decline of the Union*, 122–123.

2. Ibid., 121–122.

3. On May 31, 1915, a year before his appointment, Duke had confessed to Conservative leader Bonar Law that he was "destitute . . . of what is usually called ambition." See D.G. Boyce and Cameron Hazlehurst, "The Unknown Chief Secretary: H.E. Duke and Ireland, 1916–1918," *Irish Historical Studies*, volume 20, number 79 (March 1977).

4. O'Halpin, *The Decline of the Union*, 124.

5. The position had initially gone to Sir Robert Chalmers, who had been appointed on an interim basis immediately following Sir Matthew Nathan's resignation. He served from May to September 1916, at which time Byrne was brought in as his permanent replacement.

6. Unionists had hoped for Sir Henry Robinson; Nationalists had asked that T.P. Gill be given the job.

7. O'Halpin, *The Decline of the Union*, 125.

8. Ibid., 125–126.

9. CO 904 / 101: 2–9, Deputy Inspector General's Confidential Report for September 1916.

10. CO 904 / 101: 217, Deputy Inspector General's Confidential Report for October 1916.

11. CO 904 / 101: 603–607, Inspector General's Confidential Report December 1916.

12. O'Halpin, *The Decline of the Union*, 126–127.

13. See Bentley B. Gilbert, *David Lloyd George: A Political Life* (London: Batsford Publishers, 1992).

14. O'Halpin, *The Decline of the Union*, 126; and Dangerfield, *The Damnable Question*, 251–252.

15. Dangerfield, *The Damnable Question*, 258.

16. O'Halpin, *The Decline of the Union*, 103–104, 129.

17. CO 904 / 157: 222, Report from Intelligence Officer Captain G. Whitfield, Northern District, to Brigadier General G.W. Hacket Pain, Commanding Northern District, October 30, 1916, copied to Major Ivor Price, October 31, 1916, forwarded to the Chief Secretary H.E. Duke, November 4, 1916.

18. CO 904 / 157: 224, Monthly Confidential Report for Midlands and Connaught District, Prepared by Major F.C. Burke, Intelligence Officer, Midland District

and Connaught, for Major Ivor Price, October 31, 1916, forwarded to the Chief Secretary H.E. Duke, November 4, 1916.

19. CO 904 / 157: 228–229, Report from Captain T.W. Dickie, Intelligence Officer, Southern District, to Major General B. Doran, General Officer Commanding Southern District, October 30, 1916, copied to Major Ivor Price, October 31, 1916, forwarded to the Chief Secretary H.E. Duke, November 4, 1916.

20. CO 904 / 157: 206, Memorandum from Under Secretary William Byrne to Assistant Under Secretary Edward O'Farrell, December 7, 1916.

21. CO 904 / 157: 206, Unsigned Note from Assistant Under Secretary Edward O'Farrell to Under Secretary William Byrne, December 11, 1916.

22. CO 904 / 157: 192, Report from Captain T.W. Dickie, Intelligence Officer, Southern District, December 30, 1916.

23. CO 904 / 157: 194, Report from Captain G. Whitfield, Intelligence Officer, Northern District, December 30, 1916.

24. CO 904 / 157: 195, Report from Major F.C. Burke, Intelligence Officer, Midland District and Connaught, December 30, 1916.

25. Cassar, *Asquith as War Leader*, 185, 191.

26. Ibid., 196.

27. Fitzpatrick, *The Two Irelands*, 64.

28. Ibid., 64.

29. For a detailed account of this election, see Michael Laffan, "The Unification of Sinn Fein in 1917," *Irish Historical Studies*, volume 17, number 67 (March 1971), 358–361.

30. The candidate who, by his death, vacated this seat was J.J. O'Kelly, one of Charles Stewart Parnell's original colleagues, a veteran of the Land Wars of the 1870s and the Home Rule debates of the 1880s and 1890s, and a close friend of John Redmond. He had held the County Roscommon seat for the Home Rule/Nationalist Party for over 30 years.

31. CO 904 / 102: 7, Inspector General's Monthly Report for January 1917.

32. CO 904 / 102: 7–8, Inspector General's Monthly Report for January 1917.

33. O'Halpin, *The Decline of the Union*, 136.

34. Dangerfield, *The Damnable Question*, 253.

35. Townshend, *The British Campaign in Ireland*, 3.

36. CO 904 / 102: 10–12, Inspector General's Monthly Report for January 1917.

37. CO 904 / 157: 175–176, Report from Captain T.W. Dickie, Intelligence Officer, Southern District, February 27, 1917.

38. CO 904 / 157: 178–179, Report for Captain George Whitfield, Intelligence Officer, Northern District, February 28, 1917.

39. CO 904 / 157: 180–181, Report from Major F.C. Burke, Intelligence Officer, Midland District and Connaught, February 28, 1917.

40. CO 904 / 102: 217–218, Inspector General's Monthly Report for February, 1917.

41. CO 904 / 102: 416, Inspector General's Monthly Report for March 1917; CO 904 / 102: 599, Inspector General's Monthly Report for April 1917.

42. CO 904 / 157: 160, Report from Captain T.W. Dickie, Intelligence Officer, Southern District, April 30, 1917.

43. CO 903 / 19 / 3A: 9, "County Longford," Intelligence Notes, 1917 (Confidential Print: Ireland, Chief Secretary's Office, Judicial Division).
44. Dangerfield, *The Damnable Question*, 254.
45. CO 904 / 103: 9, Inspector General's Monthly Report for May 1917.
46. Dangerfield, *The Damnable Question*, 254.
47. Patrick Maume, *The Long Gestation: Irish Nationalist Life, 1891–1918* (Dublin: Gill & Macmillan, 1999), 194–195.
48. Dangerfield, *The Damnable Question*, 253–254.
49. CO 904 / 23 / 3B: 21, Police Notes on the South Longford Election.
50. CO 904 / 23 / 3B: 26–27, Police Notes on the South Longford Election.
51. CO 904 / 103: 10, Inspector General's Monthly Report for May 1917. For more on the South Longford byelection, see Marie Coleman, *County Longford and the Irish Revolution, 1910–1923* (Dublin: Irish Academic Press, 2003), chapter 2, 45–67.
52. CO 904 / 23 / 3B: 31–32, Police Notes on the South Longford Election.
53. CO 904 / 103: 10–11, Inspector General's Monthly Report for May 1917.
54. See Terence Denman, *A Lonely Grave: The Life and Death of William Redmond* (Dublin: Irish Academic Press, 1995), 118–122.
55. CO 904 / 103: 201, Inspector General's Monthly Report for June 1917.
56. Dangerfield, *The Damnable Question*, 258.
57. Finnan, *John Redmond and Irish Unity*, 213.
58. Denman, *A Lonely Grave*, 119–120.
59. Ibid., 119–121.
60. Finnan, *John Redmond and Irish Unity*, 213.
61. For the most comprehensive biography of de Valera's life, see Tim Pat Coogan, *Eamon de Valera: The Man Who Was Ireland* (New York: Dorset Press, 1993).
62. Ibid., 94.
63. CO 903 / 19 / 3A: 11, "County Clare," Intelligence Notes, 1917 (Confidential Print: Ireland, Chief Secretary's Office, Judicial Division).
64. Captain Maunsell, writing for Captain Dickie (on leave) of the military southern district, stated, "Drilling is practiced, chiefly in the Co. Clare since the beginning of the Parliamentary Contest there, is no longer clandestine, but on the contrary, perfectly open. The Irish Volunteers are being reconstituted" (CO 904 / 157: 148, Report from Captain R.J.C. Maunsell, Intelligence Officer, Southern District, July 31, 1917, to Captain T.W. Dickie, absent on sick leave).
65. CO 903 / 19 / 3A: 11, "County Clare," Intelligence Notes, 1917 (Confidential Print: Ireland, Chief Secretary's Office, Judicial Division).
66. CO 904 / 23 / 3B: 41–43, Police Notes on the East Clare Election.
67. Coogan, *Eamon de Valera*, 94.
68. Finnan, *John Redmond and Irish Unity*, 216.
69. Ibid., 217.
70. CO 903 / 19 / 3A: 11, "County Clare," Intelligence Notes, 1917 (Confidential Print: Ireland, Chief Secretary's Office, Judicial Division).
71. CO 903 / 19 / 3A: 8, "County Kilkenny," Intelligence Notes, 1917 (Confidential Print: Ireland, Chief Secretary's Office, Judicial Division).
72. Ibid.

73. CO 904 / 23 / 3B: 44–49, Police Notes on the Kilkenny City Election.
74. Dangerfield, *The Damnable Question*, 259.
75. Ibid., 260–263.
76. In the monthly intelligence reports, there is no indication of such unification until November 1918.
77. CO 903 / 19 / 3A: 7, "County Carlow" and "County Dublin," Intelligence Notes, 1917 (Confidential Print: Ireland, Chief Secretary's Office, Judicial Division).
78. CO 903 / 19 / 3A: 8, "King's County" and "County Kilkenny," Intelligence Notes, 1917 (Confidential Print: Ireland, Chief Secretary's Office, Judicial Division).
79. CO 903 / 19 / 3A: 9–10, "County Louth" and "County Westmeath," Intelligence Notes, 1917 (Confidential Print: Ireland, Chief Secretary's Office, Judicial Division).
80. CO 903 / 19 / Part 3: 7–11, "Leinster Province," Intelligence Notes, 1917 (Confidential Print: Ireland, Chief Secretary's Office, Judicial Division).
81. CO 903 / 19 / Part 3: 11, "County Clare," Intelligence Notes, 1917 (Confidential Print: Ireland, Chief Secretary's Office, Judicial Division).
82. CO 903 / 19 / 3A: 11, "County Clare," Intelligence Notes, 1917 (Confidential Print: Ireland, Chief Secretary's Office, Judicial Division).
83. CO 903 / 19 / 3A: 12, "County Cork, East Riding," Intelligence Notes, 1917 (Confidential Print: Ireland, Chief Secretary's Office, Judicial Division).
84. Ibid.
85. CO 903 / 19 / 3A: 13–14, "County and City of Limerick," Intelligence Notes, 1917 (Confidential Print: Ireland, Chief Secretary's Office, Judicial Division).
86. CO 903 / 19 / 3A: 15–18, "County Tipperary, North Riding," "County Tipperary, South Riding," "County Waterford," "County Galway, West Riding," and "County Sligo," Intelligence Notes, 1917 (Confidential Print: Ireland, Chief Secretary's Office, Judicial Division).
87. CO 903 / 19 / 3A: 11–18, "Munster Province" and "Connaught Province," Intelligence Notes, 1917 (Confidential Print: Ireland, Chief Secretary's Office, Judicial Division).
88. CO 903 / 19 / 3A: 5–6, "County Antrim" and "County Down," Intelligence Notes, 1917 (Confidential Print: Ireland, Chief Secretary's Office, Judicial Division).
89. CO 903 / 19 / 3A: 6, "County Armagh" and "County Donegal," Intelligence Notes, 1917 (Confidential Print: Ireland, Chief Secretary's Office, Judicial Division).
90. CO 903 / 19 / 3A: 6–7, "County Tyrone" and "County Cavan," Intelligence Notes, 1917 (Confidential Print: Ireland, Chief Secretary's Office, Judicial Division).
91. CO 903 / 19 / 3A: 6, "County Fermanagh," Intelligence Notes, 1917 (Confidential Print: Ireland, Chief Secretary's Office, Judicial Division).
92. CO 903 / 19 / 3A: 7, "County Monaghan," Intelligence Notes, 1917 (Confidential Print: Ireland, Chief Secretary's Office, Judicial Division).
93. This national figure is given in the following document: CO 904 / 104: 737, Inspector General's Monthly Report for December 1917.

94. CO 904 / 157: 82, Report from Captain George Whitfield, Intelligence Officer, Northern District, December 31, 1917.
95. CO 904 / 157: 83–84, Report from Captain R.J.C. Maunsell, Intelligence Officer, Southern District, December 31, 197.
96. CO 904 / 157: 87–90, Report from Major R.C. Holmes, Intelligence Officer, Midland and Connaught District, December 31, 1917.
97. CO 904 / 122 / 1, Memorandum by Under Secretary William Byrne, December 11, 1917.
98. CO 904 / 157: 72, Report from Captain R.J.C. Maunsell, Intelligence Officer, Southern District, January 31, 1918.
99. CO 904 / 157: 75, Report from Major R.C. Holmes, Intelligence Officer, Midland and Connaught District, January 31, 1918.
100. CO 904 / 105: 15–19, Inspector General's Monthly Report for January 1918.
101. Dangerfield, *The Damnable Question*, 152.
102. Fitzpatrick, *The Two Irelands*, 54–56.
103. For a discussion of Duke's use of D.O.R.A, see O'Halpin, *The Decline of the Union*, 143–146.
104. For more on the hunger strike, see ibid., 145–146. The Irish penal system was, at this time, badly in need of reform, and had not been updated since the 1870s. For more on the origins of this problem, see Patrick Carroll-Burke, *Colonial Discipline: The Making of the Irish Convict System* (Dublin: Four Courts Press, 2000).
105. Coogan, *Eamon de Valera*, 100.
106. O'Halpin, *Decline of the Union*, 146.
107. Coogan, *Eamon de Valera*, 100.
108. Ibid., 101.
109. O'Halpin, *The Decline of the Union*, 146.
110. Ibid., 147.
111. Coogan, *Eamon de Valera*, 101.
112. CO 904 / 105: 19, Inspector General's Monthly Report for January 1918.
113. For details of these battles, see Johnstone, *Orange, Green and Khaki*, 282–317.
114. Ibid., 318–337.
115. CO 904 / 105: 296–298, Inspector General's Monthly Report for February 1918.
116. CO 904 / 105: 298–311, Inspector General's Monthly Report for February 1918.
117. CO 904 / 157: 62–63, Report from Captain R.J.C. Maunsell, Intelligence Officer, Southern District, February 28, 1918.
118. CO 904 / 157: 66–67, Report from Major R.C. Holmes, Intelligence Officer, Midland and Connaught District, February 28, 1918.
119. CO 904 / 157: 58, Note from Chief Secretary H.E. Duke to Under Secretary William Byrne, March 3, 1918.
120. CO 904 / 157: 58, Note from Under Secretary William Byrne, to Chief Secretary H.E. Duke, March 6, 1918.

121. CO 904 / 187: 40, Note from Chief Secretary's Office (unsigned) to Under Secretary William Byrne, March 2, 1918.
122. CO 904 / 187: 40, Note from Under Secretary William Byrne to the Chief Secretary, the Military Commander, and the Inspector General, March 3, 1918.
123. CO 904 / 187: 42–65, Memorandum on the Military Aid of the Civil Power in Ireland, 1882–1882, General Sir John Ross of Bladensburg, December 11, 1882.
124. The Chief Secretary initialed the date that he had read these intelligence documents, as he did with each report that crossed his desk.
125. Duke did not commit such a policy to paper. However, upon reading the memorandum (as evidenced by his initials), he did not make additional comment, and was content to let the under secretary's remarks stand unchallenged: "The arrangements which are now in force for the cooperation of soldiers and police have been made very quickly, [but] promise to work well" (CO 904 / 187: 40, Note from Under Secretary William Byrne to the Chief Secretary, the Military Commander, and the Inspector General, March 3, 1918).
126. Quoted (without authorship) in O'Halpin, *The Decline of the Union*, 151.
127. Quoted in ibid., 151.
128. Ibid., 154–155.
129. Ibid., 157.
130. For the development of this system of Irish governance, see McDowell, *The Irish Administration*, 52–77.
131. Dangerfield, *The Damnable Question*, 284.
132. Richard Holmes, *The Little Field Marshal: Sir John French* (London: Jonathan Cape, 1981), 15–34.
133. For an account of this action, see George H. Cassar, *The Tragedy of Sir John French* (Newark, N.J.: University of Delaware Press, 1985), 22–28; and Holmes, *The Little Field Marshal*, 34–42.
134. Holmes, *The Little Field Marshal*, 44–47.
135. Cassar, *The Tragedy of Sir John French*, 29.
136. Holmes, *The Little Field Marshal*, 50–52.
137. For more detail on French's South Africa service, see Cassar, *The Tragedy of Sir John French*, 32–60; ibid., 53–117; and Brian L. Kieran, *Success of a General: General French and the Relief of Kimberley* (Honiton: Token, 2001).
138. Cassar, *The Tragedy of Sir John French*, 67–70.
139. For more on the Curragh incident, see 1, "The Period of Overt Militancy." For detail on French's role in such, see Cassar, *The Tragedy of Sir John French*, 74–80; and Holmes, *The Little Field Marshal*, 166–194.
140. Holmes, *The Little Field Marshal*, 196–205.
141. For the most comprehensive account of French's wartime leadership, see Cassar, *The Tragedy of Sir John French*.
142. Holmes, *The Little Field Marshal*, 323–327.
143. Ibid., 335.
144. O'Halpin, *The Decline of the Union*, 158–159.
145. CO 904 / 105: 856–864, Inspector General's Monthly Report for April 1918.

146. O'Halpin, *The Decline of the Union*, 159–160.
147. Ibid., 160–162.
148. CO 904 / 106: 2–14, Inspector General's Monthly Report for May 1918.
149. Dangerfield, *The Damnable Question*, 295.
150. The information in this paragraph is taken from Sheila Lawlor, *Britain and Ireland, 1914 to 1923* (Dublin: Gill & Macmillan, 1983), 279. For a more in-depth biography of Michael Collins, see T. Ryle Dwyer, *Big Fellow, Long Fellow: A Joint Biography of Collins and De Valera* (Dublin: Gill & Macmillan, 1998).
151. For more on this reorganization, see Peter Hart, *The I.R.A. at War, 1916 to 1923* (Oxford: Oxford University Press, 2003).
152. CO 904 / 157: 2–43, Military Intelligence Reports for May, June, July, and August 1918.
153. CO 904 / 106: 261–271, Inspector General's Monthly Report for June 1918; CO 904 / 106: 504–517, Inspector General's Monthly Report for July 1918.
154. CO 904 / 106: 762, Inspector General's Monthly Report for August 1918.
155. The final military intelligence report was submitted to the Chief Secretary's Office and copied to the Lord Lieutenant in August 1918.
156. CO 904 / 107, 254, Inspector General's Monthly Report for October 1918.
157. CO 904 / 107: 476, Inspector General's Monthly Report for November 1918.
158. Michael Laffan, *The Resurrection of Ireland: The Sinn Fein Party, 1916–1923* (Cambridge, U.K.: Cambridge University Press, 1999), 155.
159. See ibid., chapter 6, "Policy: Beliefs and Attitudes," 214–265.
160. CO 904 / 107: 703–704, Inspector General's Monthly Report for December 1918.
161. CO 904 / 107: 476, Inspector General's Monthly Report for November 1918.
162. CO 903 / 19 / 4: 19, Intelligence Notes, 1918 (Confidential Print: Ireland, Chief Secretary's Office, Judicial Division).
163. CO 903 / 19 / 4: 23–24, Intelligence Notes, 1918 (Confidential Print: Ireland, Chief Secretary's Office, Judicial Division). Italics are in the original document.
164. CO 903 / 19 / 4: 27, Intelligence Notes, 1918 (Confidential Print: Ireland, Chief Secretary's Office, Judicial Division).
165. See CO 903 / 19 / 4: 18–49, Intelligence Notes, 1918 (Confidential Print: Ireland, Chief Secretary's Office, Judicial Division).
166. Laffan, *The Resurrection of Ireland*, 164–165.
167. Ibid.
168. CO 904 / 107: 703, Inspector General's Monthly Report for December 1918.
169. CO 904 / 107: 704, Inspector General's Monthly Report for December 1918.
170. Dangerfield, *The Damnable Question*, 301.
171. For complete copies of the declaration of independence and the Message to the Free Nations of the World, see Michael Hopkinson, *The Irish War of Independence* (Dublin: Gill & Macmillan, 2002), appendixes C and D, 207–209. For a detailed analysis of the content of the constitution, see Dangerfield, *The Damnable Question*, 302–304.
172. CO 904 / 108: 13–15, Inspector General's Monthly Report for January 1919.

173. CO 904 / 108: 15–18, Inspector General's Monthly Report for January 1919.
174. Quoted in O'Halpin, *The Decline of the Union*, 185.
175. Coogan, *Eamon de Valera*, 130.
176. In part, the declaration read, "We solemnly declare foreign government in Ireland to be an invasion of our national right which we will never tolerate, and we demand the evacuation of our country by the English Garrison."
177. There is no mention whatsoever in any intelligence documents of the contents of the Dáil's declaration of independence, nor is there any acknowledgment that the Dáil intended to act on its newly declared independence.
178. Dan Breen, *My Fight for Irish Freedom* (Dublin: Talbot Press, 1924; repr., Tralee, County Kerry: Anvil Books, 1964), 39. Reference is to the Anvil Books edition.
179. For a full first hand account of this ambush, see ibid., 38–58. Dan Breen, in command of the I.R.A. contingent, described the killings in this way: "In answer to our challenge they raised their rifles, and with military precision held them at the ready. They were Irishmen, too, and would rather die than surrender. We renewed our demand for surrender. We would have preferred to avoid bloodshed; but they were inflexible. Further appeal was useless. It was a matter of our lives or theirs. We took aim. The two policemen fell, mortally wounded" (ibid., 40).
180. Ibid., 41.
181. CO 904 / 108: 8, Inspector General's Monthly Report for January 1919.
182. In his intelligence reports, the Inspector General was always meticulous about listing Irish Volunteer actions under political crime and about identifying those involved as belonging to the Irish Volunteers or Sinn Fein if he believed that to be the case. He only listed actions as ordinary crime if he believed that they had no relation to the Irish Volunteers or Sinn Fein.
183. O'Halpin, *The Decline of the Union*, 185–186.
184. For details of these crimes, see CO 904 / 105–107, Inspector General's Monthly Reports for January 1918–December 1918.
185. In no secondary sources written by historians nor primary sources written by Irish Volunteers or I.R.A. men is there any mention of such actions being carried out by the separatist movement before January 1919.
186. CO 903 / 19 / 5: 22, "County Longford," Intelligence Notes, 1919 (Confidential Print: Ireland, Chief Secretary's Office, Judicial Division).
187. CO 903 / 19 / 5: 15, "County Tyrone," Intelligence Notes, 1919 (Confidential Print: Ireland, Chief Secretary's Office, Judicial Division).
188. CO 903 / 19 / 5: 30, "County Galway, West Riding," Intelligence Notes, 1919 (Confidential Print: Ireland, Chief Secretary's Office, Judicial Division).
189. CO 903 / 19 / 5: 14, "County Monaghan," Intelligence Notes, 1919 (Confidential Print: Ireland, Chief Secretary's Office, Judicial Division).
190. CO 903 / 19 / 5: 31, "County Galway, West Riding," Intelligence Notes, 1919 (Confidential Print: Ireland, Chief Secretary's Office, Judicial Division).
191. CO 903 / 19 / 5: 29, "County Galway, East Riding," Intelligence Notes, 1919 (Confidential Print: Ireland, Chief Secretary's Office, Judicial Division).

192. CO 903 / 19 / 5: 37–38, "County Cork, East Riding," Intelligence Notes, 1919 (Confidential Print: Ireland, Chief Secretary's Office, Judicial Division).
193. CO 904 / 19 / 5: 39–40, "County Cork, West Riding," Intelligence Notes, 1919 (Confidential Print: Ireland, Chief Secretary's Office, Judicial Division).
194. CO 903 / 19 / 5: 43, "County Limerick," Intelligence Notes, 1919 (Confidential Print: Ireland, Chief Secretary's Office, Judicial Division).
195. CO 904 / 19 / 5: 44, "County Tipperary, North Riding," Intelligence Notes, 1919 (Confidential Print: Ireland, Chief Secretary's Office, Judicial Division).
196. CO 903 / 19 / 5: 36–37, "County Clare," Intelligence Notes, 1919 (Confidential Print: Ireland, Chief Secretary's Office, Judicial Division).
197. Dangerfield, *The Damnable Question*, 312.
198. For a full first hand account of this ambush, see Breen, *My Fight for Irish Freedom*, 63–70.
199. Ibid., 83–96.
200. CO 904 / 108: 243–258, Inspector General's Monthly Report for February 1919.
201. CO 904 / 108: 492–508, Inspector General's Monthly Report for March 1919.
202. Ibid.
203. CO 904 / 108: 734–747, Inspector General's Monthly Report for April 1919.
204. CO 904 / 109: 253, Inspector General's Monthly Report for June 1919.
205. CO 904 / 109: 261, Inspector General's Monthly Report for June 1919.
206. CO 904 / 109: 738–756, Inspector General's Monthly Report for August 1919.
207. Ibid.
208. CO 904 / 110: 6, Inspector General's Monthly Report for September 1919.
209. CO 904 / 110: 6–9, Inspector General's Monthly Report for September 1919; CO 904 / 110: 244–246, Inspector General's Monthly Report for October 1919; and CO 904 / 110: 477–480, Inspector General's Monthly Report for November 1919.
210. CO 904 / 110: 3–19, Inspector General's Monthly Report for September 1919.
211. O'Halpin, *The Decline of the Union*, 180–181.
212. Townshend, *The British Campaign in Ireland*, 20. Shortt had been appointed Home Secretary following the resignation of Duke in April 1918.
213. Ibid., 21.
214. Quoted in O'Halpin, *The Decline of the Union*, 186–187.
215. Townshend, *The British Campaign in Ireland*, 23–24.
216. O'Halpin, *The Decline of the Union*, 187–188.
217. WO 35 / 214, War Office: Army of Ireland: Administrative and Easter Rising Record, a Report of the Intelligence Branch of the Chief of Police, Dublin Castle, from May 1920 to July 1921, 19–21.
218. See O'Halpin, *The Decline of the Union*, 186–189.
219. Townshend, *The British Campaign in Ireland*, 22.
220. O'Halpin, *The Decline of the Union*, 190.
221. Quoted in O'Halpin, *The Decline of the Union*, 191.
222. Townshend, *The British Campaign in Ireland*, 31.
223. O'Halpin, *The Decline of the Union*, 194–195.

224. Quoted in Townshend, *The British Campaign in Ireland*, 45.
225. Quoted in O'Halpin, *The Decline of the Union*, 194.
226. Townshend, *The British Campaign in Ireland*, 45.
227. O'Halpin, *The Decline of the Union*, 248.
228. Macready, *Annals of an Active Life*, 438.
229. CO 904 / 110: 702–714, Inspector General's Monthly Report for December 1919.
230. Dangerfield, *The Damnable Question*, 314. The man killed was Martin Savage. The ten who escaped were Dan Breen, Mick McDonnell, Tom Kehoe, Sean Treacy, Seamus Robinson, Sean Hogan, Paddy Daly, Vincent Byrne, Tom Kilkoyne, and Joe Leonard. For a detailed first hand account of this ambush from the point of view of the I.R.A. men involved, see Breen, *My Fight for Irish Freedom*, 83–96. See also various police records and witness statements of this event in CO 904 / 198, Sir John Anderson's Private Papers, 1919–1921.
231. O'Halpin, *The Decline of the Union*, 198–199.
232. Townshend, *The British Campaign in Ireland*, 42.
233. CO 904 / 111: 3–17, Inspector General's Monthly Report for January 1920.
234. Quoted in O'Halpin, *The Decline of the Union*, 200.
235. Mitchell, *Revolutionary Government in Ireland*, 128–129.
236. See Laffan, *The Resurrection of Ireland*, 310–318.
237. See O'Halpin, *The Decline of the Union*, 192–207.
238. Townshend, *The British Campaign in Ireland*, 42.
239. Hopkinson, *The Irish War of Independence*, 49.
240. O'Sullivan, *The Irish Constabularies*, 308–309. Charles Townshend suggests that such recruitment actually began some months earlier than this, with a special recruiting officer beginning to travel in England in late 1919 and the first English recruit joining on January 2, another 110 following that month. It seems, however, that recruitment did not start in earnest until March 1920. See Townshend, *The British Campaign in Ireland*, 43–46.
241. O'Sullivan, *The Irish Constabularies*, 308–309.
242. Ibid., 309–310. For a detailed account of the Black and Tans, see Richard Bennett, *The Black and Tans* (London: Edward Hulton and Co. Ltd., 1959).
243. O'Sullivan, *The Irish Constabularies*, 322–324. For a first hand account of the Auxiliaries, see Brigadier-General F.P. Crozier, *Impressions and Recollections* (London: T. Werner Laurie Ltd., 1930), chapter 12, 250–309.
244. He accepted the position against his better judgment, and later wrote, "On 23rd March, 1920, while lunching at Garrick, a telephone message was brought in from the Prime Minister asking me to go round to 10, Downing Street at once. I had an uneasy foreboding that it had something to do with the island I hoped never to set foot in again. . . . The deciding factor, indeed the only one that weighed with me, was the evident desire of my old Chief, Lord French, that I should take the appointment. But for that nothing would have induced me to return to a country to which I was never attracted, or to take up a task which

I instinctively felt would be affected by every variation of the political weathercock, and in which it was doubtful if any satisfactory result could be attained" (Macready, *Annals of an Active Life*, 425).

245. Quoted in Townshend, *The British Campaign in Ireland*, 74.
246. Quoted in Michael Hopkinson, "Introduction," in Mark Sturgis, *The Last Days of Dublin Castle: The Diaries of Mark Sturgis*, ed. Michael Hopkinson (Dublin: Irish Academic Press, 1999), 4.
247. Macready, *Annals of an Active Life*, 425.
248. O'Sullivan, *The Irish Constabularies*, 307. See also Townshend, *The British Campaign in Ireland*, 81–83.
249. Townshend, *The British Campaign in Ireland*, 78.
250. O'Halpin, *The Decline of the Union*, 200–201.
251. Hopkinson, "Introduction," 2–3.
252. Ibid., 5–6.
253. Quoted in O'Halpin, *The Decline of the Union*, 210.
254. Sturgis, *Last Days of Dublin Castle*, 11.
255. Macready, *Annals of an Active Life*, 426.
256. Sturgis, *Last Days of Dublin Castle*, 13. The italics are Sturgis'.
257. Ibid., 16.
258. Ibid., 17.
259. Prior to this appointment, Winter was serving as Boundary Commissioner to Schleswig-Holstein, having taken leave prematurely finding there to be "a surfeit of Brigadier-Generals wandering about the country" after the armistice. He described his selection as intelligence chief in the following manner: "I arrived in Dublin and met Tudor, who took me to interview General Sir Nevil Macready, the recently appointed Commander in Chief of the forces in Ireland. At lunch we discussed the situation, and afterwards I asked Tudor what exactly my position would be. He told me I would be nominated Deputy Chief of Police, an appointment which would enable me to replace him at any time during his absence, and would also cover my actual position which was to be the Chief of the Combined Intelligence Services. He would in no way interfere with my work. . . . On these terms I accepted the post" (Brigadier General Sir Ormonde de L'Épée Winter, *Winter's Tale: An Autobiography* [London: Richards Press, 1955], 288–289).
260. Sturgis, *Last Days of Dublin Castle*, 32.
261. WO 35 / 214, War Office: Army of Ireland: Administrative and Easter Rising Record, a Report of the Intelligence Branch of the Chief of Police, Dublin Castle, from May 1920 to July 1921, 11–14.
262. Ibid., 14.
263. In his autobiography, Winter explained this process: "Immediately after any raid, all documents were at once submitted by its personnel to a close scrutiny, epitomes completed, and copies made for distribution. . . . The result was that practically all documents came into the Central Bureau and an efficient card index system was organized. . . . A list of all persons arrested was forwarded to me, and the

duty devolved on me of deciding who should be liberated, interned, or prosecuted from the evidence available in the Raid Bureau" (Winter, *Winter's Tale*, 304–305).

264. WO 35 / 214, War Office: Army of Ireland: Administrative and Easter Rising Record, a Report of the Intelligence Branch of the Chief of Police, Dublin Castle, from May 1920 to July 1921, 15.

265. Ibid., 26–29.

266. Ibid., 23–29.

267. See CO 904 / 193–216, Files on Sinn Fein and Republican Suspects.

268. Townshend, *The British Campaign in Ireland*, 214. For details of most of these actions, see CO 906 / 19, Ireland, 1920–21, Disorders and Telegrams, etc.

269. CO 904 / 188, Letter from General Nevil Macready, Commander-in-Chief, Ireland, to Sir Hamar Greenwood, Chief Secretary, July 17, 1920.

270. CO 904 / 188, Letter from Joint Under secretary Sir John Anderson to Sir Chief Secretary Hamar Greenwood, July 20, 1920.

271. CO 904 / 188, Memorandum for the cabinet by Sir John Anderson, joint under secretary, July 25, 1920.

272. CO 904 / 188, Memorandum by General Nevil Macready, Commander-in-Chief, Ireland, July 26, 1920, distributed to the cabinet by Winston Churchill, Secretary of State for War, August 6, 1920.

273. Hopkinson, *Irish War of Independence*, 80.

274. CO 904 / 188, Memorandum by General Nevil Macready, Commander-in-Chief Ireland, no date. References contained within the memo suggest it was written in late October 1920.

275. Francis Costello, *The Irish Revolution and Its Aftermath, 1916–1923: Years of Revolt* (Dublin: Irish Academic Press, 2003), 70–71.

276. Hart, *I.R.A. at War*, 77–78.

277. Costello, *Irish Revolution and Its Aftermath*, 52.

278. Winter, *Winter's Tale*, 309.

279. Costello, *Irish Revolution and Its Aftermath*, 92–96. Some of the witness statements of these killings, particularly from the officers' wives, are quite chilling. For example, Mrs. Keenlyside, wife of Captain B.C.H. Keenlyside, wrote, "About ten past nine on Sunday Morning Nov 21st my husband and myself were asleep, when we were awakened by a loud knocking and 20 to 22 men dressed in overcoats and rain coats and wearing cloth caps and felt hats filed methodically into the bedroom. They shouted roughly to my husband 'Get up you and put up your hands' which he did. They then hustled him downstairs clad only in pajamas. I protested and begged them not to hurt him holding the arm of one of the raiders. He assured me that I should not be hurt and pushed me roughly back into the room. I followed them immediately out and saw another officer being taken downstairs with his hands up. They then placed him and my husband side by side in the hall, demanded their names, and fired at them, wounding the officer in the back, and my husband in the jaw, both arms, and upper part of the forearm." For this and other reports see CO 904 / 168: 170–195, Dublin Metropolitan Police Records.

280. O'Sullivan, *The Irish Constabularies*, 335.
281. Costello, *Irish Revolution and Its Aftermath*, 98–99.
282. Winter, *Winter's Tale*, 341.
283. See Hopkinson, *The Irish War of Independence*, 92–96.

Conclusion

1. Dangerfield, *The Damnable Question*, 328–331. For a detailed account of these negotiations, see S.M. Lawlor, "Ireland from Truce to Treaty: War or Peace? July to October 1921," *Irish Historical Studies*, volume 22, number 85 (March 1980).
2. Dangerfield, *The Damnable Question*, 331–342.
3. For a discussion of the unionist acceptance of this treaty, see John D. Fair, "The Anglo-Irish Treaty of 1921: Unionist Aspects of the Peace," *Journal of British Studies*, volume 12, number 1 (November 1972). For a discussion of the nationalist acceptance, see F.M.A. Hawkings, "Defense and the Role of Erskine Childers in the Treaty Negotiations of 1921," *Irish Historical Studies*, volume 22, number 87 (March 1981).
4. For a detailed analysis of the terms of the treaty, see Nicholas Mansergh, *The Unresolved Question: The Anglo-Irish Settlement and Its Undoing, 1912–72* (New Haven: Yale University Press, 1991), especially chapter 8, 190–198.
5. Ibid., 207.
6. Coogan, *Eamon de Valera*, 301.
7. See Michael Hopkinson, *Green against Green: The Irish Civil War* (New York: St. Martin's Press, 1988).
8. This republic came about in a somewhat unusual fashion. Following the Civil War, which the pro-treaty forces won, de Valera was ostracized from Irish political life. In 1926, however, he broke from the abstention policies of Sinn Fein and formed his own party, Fianna Fail. He entered the Dáil, and in 1932, his party won a majority of seats in the General Election and de Valera became Prime Minister. He immediately set about dismantling the provisions of the Anglo-Irish Treaty, and in 1937, he wrote a new constitution, renaming the Irish Free State Eire, claiming sovereignty over the whole island (including the six-county Northern Ireland), and declaring independence from the British Empire. The British government did not recognize this new constitution, and continued to deal with Eire as a British dominion. Following the Second World War, however, during which Eire remained neutral and continued to maintain diplomatic relations with both Germany and Japan, Great Britain accepted the constitution, and when the government of Eire officially declared itself the Irish Republic in 1949, the British government did not object and allowed the republic to remove itself from the British Commonwealth. Ironically, de Valera, as Prime Minister from 1932 to 1948, used many of the same tactics against the I.R.A. as had the British in the years 1916 to 1921. Unlike the British, however, and perhaps having a greater understanding of the militant's mind, he allowed

the hunger strikers to starve themselves to death if they so chose. By unrelentingly using such tactics, de Valera had eliminated the I.R.A. as a serious threat in southern Irish life by the close of the Second World War. See Uinseann MacEoin, *The IRA in the Twilight Years, 1923–1948* (Dublin: Argenta Publications, 1997).

9. See Tim Pat Coogan, *The IRA* (London: HarperCollins, 2000).
10. David McKittrick, Seamus Kelters, Brian Feeney, and Chris Thornton, *Lost Lives: The Stories of the Men, Women, and Children Who Died as a Result of the Northern Ireland Troubles* (Edinburgh: Mainstream Publishing Company, 1999, 2001), 1494–1496. Reference is to the 2001 edition.
11. Marc Mulholland, *The Longest War: Northern Ireland's Troubled History* (Oxford: Oxford University Press, 2002), 184.

Bibliography

Unpublished Primary Sources

National Archives, Kew, Richmond-Upon-Thames, United Kingdom

Cabinet Office 37 (Cabinet Papers, 1880–1916)
Box 112, 1912
Box 115, 1913
Box 116, 1913
Box 117, 1913
Box 119, 1914
Box 120, 1914

Cabinet Office 41 (Cabinet Letters in the Royal Archives, 1868–1916)
Box 34, 1913
Box 35, 1914
Box 37, 1916

Colonial Office 903 (Confidential Print: Ireland)
Box 17, "Chief Secretary's Office, Judicial Division: Intelligence Notes for 1912–1913"
Box 18, "Chief Secretary's Office, Judicial Division: Intelligence Notes for 1914"
Box 19, Part 1, "Chief Secretary's Office, Judicial Division: Intelligence Notes for 1915";
    Part 2, "Chief Secretary's Office, Judicial Division: Intelligence Notes for 1916";
    Part 3, "Chief Secretary's Office, Judicial Division: Intelligence Notes for 1917";
    Part 4, "Chief Secretary's Office, Judicial Division: Intelligence Notes for 1918";
    Part 5, "Chief Secretary's Office, Judicial Division: Intelligence Notes for 1919"

Colonial Office 904 (Dublin Castle Records)
Box 14, Part 1, "Secret Societies. Précis of Information and Reports Relating to the
    D.M.P. District, 1913"; Part 2, "Secret Societies. Précis of Information and Reports
    Relating to the D.M.P. District, 1914"
Box 23, Part 2, "Sinn Fein Movement. Easter Rising—Proclamations, 1916";
    Part 3A, "Sinn Fein Movement. Meetings and Other Activities, 1916"; Part 3B,
    "Sinn Fein Movement. Meetings and Other Activities, 1917"

Box 27, Part 1, "Ulster Unionists. Drilling of Volunteers—Enniskillen Horse, 1911–1914"; Part 2, "Ulster Unionists. Formation and Organization of Ulster Volunteers, 1913"; Part 3, "Ulster Unionists. Unionist Movement in Ulster Opposing Home Rule, 1913–1914"

Box 28, Part 1, "Arms and Ammunition. Illegal Importation and Distribution of Arms and Reports of Seizures of Arms, 1886–1913"

Box 29, Part 1, "Arms and Ammunition. Gun-Running—reports, returns, statements, etc., 1914"

Box 89, "Inspector General's and County Inspector's Monthly Confidential Reports: January to April, 1913"

Box 94, "Inspector General's and County Inspector's Monthly Confidential Reports: July to September, 1914"

Box 95, "Inspector General's and County Inspector's Monthly Confidential Reports: October to December, 1914"

Box 96, "Inspector General's and County Inspector's Monthly Confidential Reports: January to April, 1915"

Box 97, "Inspector General's and County Inspector's Monthly Confidential Reports: May to August, 1915"

Box 98, "Inspector General's and County Inspector's Monthly Confidential Reports: September to December, 1915"

Box 99, "Inspector General's and County Inspector's Monthly Confidential Reports: January to April, 1916"

Box 100, "Inspector General's and County Inspector's Monthly Confidential Reports: May to August, 1916"

Box 101, "Inspector General's and County Inspector's Monthly Confidential Reports: September to December, 1916"

Box 102, "Inspector General's and County Inspector's Monthly Confidential Reports: January to April, 1917"

Box 103, "Inspector General's and County Inspector's Monthly Confidential Reports: May to July, 1917"

Box 104, "Inspector General's and County Inspector's Monthly Confidential Reports: September to December, 1917"

Box 105, "Inspector General's and County Inspector's Monthly Confidential Reports: January to April, 1918"

Box 106, "Inspector General's and County Inspector's Monthly Confidential Reports: May to August, 1918"

Box 107, "Inspector General's and County Inspector's Monthly Confidential Reports: September to December, 1918"

Box 108, "Inspector General's and County Inspector's Monthly Confidential Reports: January to April, 1919"

Box 109, "Inspector General's and County Inspector's Monthly Confidential Reports: May to August, 1919"

Box 110, "Inspector General's and County Inspector's Monthly Confidential Reports: September to December, 1919"

Box 111, "Inspector General's and County Inspector's Monthly Confidential Reports: January to February, 1920"

Box 112, "Inspector General's and County Inspector's Monthly Confidential Reports: June to August, 1920"

Box 113, "Inspector General's and County Inspector's Monthly Confidential Reports: October to December, 1920"

Box 114, "Inspector General's and County Inspector's Monthly Confidential Reports: January to March, 1921"

Box 115, "Inspector General's and County Inspector's Monthly Confidential Reports: April to June, 1921"

Box 116, "Inspector General's and County Inspector's Monthly Confidential Reports: July to September, 1921"

Box 120, Part 2, "Précis of Information Received by the Special Branch, R.I.C., April to December, 1915"; Part 3, "Report on the State of the Counties, 1916"

Box 122, Part 1, "Illegal Drilling: Dublin, November to December, 1916"; Part 2, "Illegal Drilling: Clarecastle, Cork, Kiltimagh, Kinvarra, Midlands and Connaught Districts, October to December, 1917; Southern District, November to December, 1917; Various Countries, November to December, 1917"; Part 3, "Illegal Drilling: Northern District, December 1917 to January 1918"

Box 148, "Weekly Summaries of Outrages against the Police, April to July, 1920"

Box 149, "Weekly Summaries of Outrages against the Police, August to December, 1920"

Box 150, "Weekly Summaries of Outrages Against the Police, January to December, 1921"; "Summary of Outrages Against the Police, etc."

Box 157, Part 1, "Military Reports. Intelligence Officers, 1916–1918"

Box 168, Part 1, "Statements to the Press, 1920"; Part 2, "Statements to the Press, 1921" and "Intelligence Summaries, etc., and Establishment of Organization for Counter-Propaganda"

Box 188, "Sir John Anderson's Private Papers, 1919–1921"

Boxes 193–216, "Files on Sinn Fein and Republican Suspects"

Colonial Office 906 (Irish Office Records)
Box 19, "Ireland, 1920–21, Disorders and Telegrams, etc."

War Office 35 (Army of Ireland: Administrative and Easter Rising Records)
Box 214, "A Report of the Intelligence Branch of the Chief of Police, Dublin Castle, from May 1920 to July 1921"

Published Primary Sources

Anonymous, "First Convention," *The Irish Volunteer*, October 31, 1914, reprinted in F.X. Martin, ed., *The Irish Volunteers, 1913–1915: Recollections and Documents* (Dublin: James Duffy & Co. Ltd., 1963).

Anonymous, "The Volunteers Declare Their Policy," *The Irish Volunteer*, October 31, 1914, reprinted in F.X. Martin, ed., *The Irish Volunteers, 1913–1915: Recollections and Documents* (Dublin: James Duffy & Co. Ltd., 1963).

Beaslai, Piaras, "The National Army Is Founded," *Irish Independent*, January 5, 1953, reprinted in F.X. Martin, ed., *The Irish Volunteers, 1913–1915: Recollections and Documents* (Dublin: James Duffy & Co. Ltd., 1963).

Breen, Dan, *My Fight for Irish Freedom* (Dublin: Talbot Press, 1924; Tralee, County Kerry: Anvil Books, 1964).

Callwell, Major-General Sir C.E., *Field-Marshall Sir Henry Wilson: His Life and Diaries*, 2 volumes (London: Cassell & Company Ltd., 1927).

Ceannt, Eamonn, "The Founding of the Irish Volunteers," *The Irish Volunteer*, June 20, 1914, reprinted in F.X. Martin, ed., *The Irish Volunteers, 1913–1915: Recollections and Documents* (Dublin: James Duffy & Co. Ltd, 1963).

Childers, Erskine, *In the Ranks of the C.I.V.: A Narrative and Dairy of Personal Experiences with the C.I.V. Battery (Honorary Battery Company) in South Africa* (London: Smith, Elder and Company, 1901).

Childers, Erskine, and Williams, Basil, *The H.A.C. in South Africa: A Record of the Services Rendered in the South African War by Members of the Honourable Artillery Company* (Smith, Elder and Company, 1903).

Churchill, Winston S., "Speech on Foreign and Domestic Policy," Constituency Meeting, Kinnaird Hall, Dundee, October 3, 1911, in Robert Rhodes James, ed., *Winston S. Churchill: His Complete Speeches, 1897–1963: Volume II, 1908–1913* (New York: Chelsea House Publishers, 1974).

———— "Speech on Irish Home Rule," Celtic Park Football Ground, Belfast, February 8, 1912, in Robert Rhodes James, ed., *Winston S. Churchill: His Complete Speeches, 1897–1963: Volume II, 1908–1913* (New York: Chelsea House Publishers, 1974).

———— "Speech on the Ulster Situation," St. George's Hall, Bradford, March 14, 1914, in Robert Rhodes James, ed., *Winston S. Churchill: His Complete Speeches, 1897–1963: Volume III, 1914–1922* (New York: Chelsea House Publishers, 1974).

Crawford, Fred H., *Guns for Ulster* (Belfast: Graham & Heslip Ltd., 1947).

Crozier, Brigadier-General F.P., *Impressions and Recollections* (London: T. Werner Laurie Ltd., 1930).

Devoy, John, *Recollections of an Irish Rebel* (New York: Chas. P. Young, 1929).

Gleichen, Major-General Lord Edward, *A Guardsman's Memories: A Book of Recollections* (Edinburgh and London: William Blackwood & Sons Ltd., 1932).

Gough, General Sir Hubert, *Soldiering On* (London: Arthur Barker Ltd., 1954).

Hansard's Parliamentary Debates, House of Commons, fifth series, volume XLII, October 7–25, 1912 (London: His Majesty's Stationary Office, 1912).

———— House of Commons, fifth series, volume XLIII, October 28–November 14, 1912 (London: His Majesty's Stationary Office, 1912).

———— House of Commons, fifth series, volume LXV, July 20–August 10, 1914 (London: His Majesty's Stationary Office, 1914).

Hobhouse, Charles, *Diaries*, printed in Edward David, ed., *Inside Asquith's Cabinet: From the Diaries of Charles Hobhouse* (New York: St. Martin's Press, 1977).

Hobson, Bulmer, "The Provisional Committee Submits but Protests," June 16, 1914, reprinted in F.X. Martin, ed., *The Irish Volunteers, 1913–1915: Recollections and Documents* (Dublin: James Duffy & Co. Ltd., 1963).

———— "Foundation and Growth of the Irish Volunteers, 1913–14," in F.X. Martin, ed., *The Irish Volunteers, 1913–1915: Recollections and Documents* (Dublin: James Duffy & Co. Ltd., 1963).

MacNeill, Eoin, *Manifesto of Irish Volunteers*, November 25, 1913, reprinted in F.X. Martin, ed., *The Irish Volunteers, 1913–1915: Recollections and Documents* (Dublin: James Duffy & Co. Ltd., 1963).

———— "Memoirs of Eoin MacNeill," unpublished, October 1932, reprinted in F.X. Martin, ed., *The Irish Volunteers, 1913–1915: Recollections and Documents* (Dublin: James Duffy & Co. Ltd., 1963).

———— "The North Began," *An Claidheamh Soluis*, November 1, 1913, reprinted in F.X. Martin, ed., *The Irish Volunteers, 1913–1915: Recollections and Documents* (Dublin: James Duffy & Co. Ltd., 1963).

MacNeill, Eoin, and Nineteen Others, "Open Letter to the Irish Volunteers," September 24, 1914, reprinted in F.X. Martin, ed., *The Irish Volunteers, 1913–1915: Recollections and Documents* (Dublin: James Duffy & Co. Ltd., 1963).

Macready, General Sir Nevil, *Annals of an Active Life*, 2 volumes (London: Hutchinson & Co. Ltd., 1924).

Magill, Andrew Philip, *From Dublin Castle to Stormont: The Memoirs of Andrew Philip Magill, 1913–1925*, Charles W. Magill, ed. (Cork: Cork University Press, 2003).

Ó Ceallaigh, Seán T., "The Founding of the Irish Volunteers," *The Capuchin Annual*, 1963, reprinted in F.X. Martin, ed., *The Irish Volunteers, 1913–1915: Recollections and Documents* (Dublin: James Duffy & Co. Ltd, 1963).

O'Rahilly, Michael, *The Secret History of the Irish Volunteers*, Dublin, 1915, reprinted in F.X. Martin, ed., *The Irish Volunteers, 1913–1915: Recollections and Documents* (Dublin: James Duffy & Co. Ltd, 1963).

Sinn Fein Rebellion Handbook, Easter 1916, compiled by the *Weekly Irish Times*, Dublin, 1916.

Sturgis, Mark, *The Last Days of Dublin Castle: The Diaries of Mark Sturgis*, introduction by Michael Hopkinson, ed. (Dublin: Irish Academic Press, 1999).

Winter, Brigadier-General Sir Ormonde de L'Épée, *Winter's Tale: An Autobiography* (London: Richards Press, 1955).

Secondary Sources

Books

Anderson, W.K., *James Connolly and the Irish Left* (Dublin: Irish Academic Press, 1994).

Augusteijn, Joost, *From Public Defiance to Guerrilla Warfare: The Experience of Ordinary Volunteers in the Irish War of Independence, 1916–1921* (Dublin: Irish Academic Press, 1996).

————, ed., *The Irish Revolution, 1913–1923* (New York: Palgrave, 2002).

Barton, Brian, *From Behind a Closed Door: Secret Court Martial Records of the 1916 Easter Rising* (Belfast: Blackstaff Press, 2002).

Bennett, Richard, *The Black and Tans* (London: Edward Hulton & Company Ltd., 1959).

Boyce, D. George, and Alan O'Day, eds., *Defenders of the Union: A Survey of British and Irish Unionism since 1801* (London: Routledge, 2001).

Brown, William, *An Army with Banners: The Real Face of Orangeism* (Belfast: Beyond the Pale Publications, 2003).

Buckland, Patrick, *Irish Unionism: Two: Ulster Unionism and the Origins of Northern Ireland, 1886–1922* (Dublin: Gill & Macmillan, 1973).

Cannadine, David, *Ornamentalism: How the British Saw Their Empire* (Oxford: Oxford University Press, 2001).

Canny, Nicholas, *Making Ireland British, 1580–1650* (Oxford: Oxford University Press, 2001).

Carroll-Burke, Patrick, *Colonial Discipline: The Making of the Irish Convict System* (Dublin: Four Courts Press, 2000).

Cassar, George H., *Asquith as War Leader* (London: Hambledon Press, 1994).

———, *The Tragedy of Sir John French* (Newark, N.J.: University of Delaware Press, 1985).

Coleman, Marie, *County Longford and the Irish Revolution, 1910–1923* (Dublin: Irish Academic Press, 2003).

Colley, Linda, *Britons: Forging the Nation, 1707–1837* (New Haven: Yale University Press, 1992).

Collier, Basil, *Brasshat: A Biography of Sir Henry Wilson* (London: Secker & Warburg, 1961).

Colvin, Ian, *The Life of Lord Carson*, 2 volumes (London: Victor Gollancz Ltd., 1934).

Coogan, Tim Pat, *Eamon de Valera: The Man Who Was Ireland* (New York: Dorset Press, 1993).

——— *The IRA* (London: HarperCollins, 2000).

——— *1916: The Easter Rising* (Dublin: Cassell & Company Ltd., 2001).

Costello, Francis, *The Irish Revolution and Its Aftermath, 1916–1923: Years of Revolt* (Dublin: Irish Academic Press, 2003).

Cronin, S., *Protest in Arms: The Young Ireland Rebellion of July–August 1848* (Dublin: Gill & Macmillan, 1984).

Curtin, Nancy J., *The United Irishmen: Popular Politics in Ulster and Dublin, 1791–1798* (Oxford: Oxford University Press, 1994).

Dangerfield, George, *The Damnable Question: A Study in Anglo-Irish Relations* (Boston: Little, Brown & Company, 1976).

Denman, Terence, *Ireland's Unknown Soldiers: The 16th (Irish) Division in the Great War, 1914–1918* (Dublin: Irish Academic Press, 1992).

——— *A Lonely Grave: The Life and Death of William Redmond* (Dublin: Irish Academic Press, 1995).

Dickens, A.G., *The English Reformation*, second edition (University Park, P.A.: Pennsylvania State University Press, 1991).

Doerries, Reinhard R., *Prelude to the Easter Rising: Sir Roger Casement in Imperial Germany* (London: Frank Cass, 2000).

Dungeon, Jeffrey, *Roger Casement: The Black Diaries, with a Study of His Background, Sexuality, and Irish Political Life* (Belfast: Belfast Press, 2002).

Dwyer, T. Ryle, *Big Fellow, Long Fellow: A Joint Biography of Collins and De Valera* (Dublin: Gill & Macmillan, 1998).

Edwards, Ruth Dudley, *Patrick Pearse: The Triumph of Failure* (London: Victor Gollancz Ltd., 1977).

Elliot, Marianne, *Partners in Revolution: The United Irishmen and France* (New Haven: Yale University Press, 1982).

Ervine, St. John, *Craigavon: Ulsterman* (London: George Allen & Unwin Ltd., 1949).

Falls, Cyril, *The History of the 36th Ulster Division* (Belfast: M'Caw, Stephenson, and Orr, 1922).

Ferguson, Sir James, *The Curragh Incident* (London: Faber and Faber Ltd., 1964).

Finnan, Joseph P., *John Redmond and Irish Unity, 1912–1918* (Syracuse: Syracuse University Press, 2004).

Fitzpatrick, David, *Politics and Irish Life, 1913–21: Provincial Experience of War and Revolution* (Dublin: Gill & Macmillan, 1977).

——— *The Two Irelands, 1912–1939* (Oxford: Oxford University Press, 1998).

Ford, Alan, *The Protestant Reformation in Ireland, 1590–1641*, second edition (Dublin: Four Courts Press, 1997).

Foy, Michael, and Brian Barton, *The Easter Rising* (Stroud, U.K.: Sutton Publishing, 1999).

Gardner, Brian, *The Big Push: A Portrait of the Battle of the Somme* (New York: William Morrow & Company, 1963), 92.

Gilbert, Bentley B., *David Lloyd George: A Political Life* (London: Batsford Publishers, 1992).

Gillespie, Raymond, *Colonial Ulster: The Settlement of East Ulster, 1600–1641* (Cork: Cork University Press, 1985).

Gregory, Adrian, and Senia Pašeta, eds., *Ireland and the Great War: "A War to Unite Us All"?* (Manchester: Manchester University Press, 2002).

Grob-Fitzgibbon, Benjamin, *The Irish Experience During the Second World War: An Oral History* (Dublin: Irish Academic Press, 2004).

Haddick-Flynn, Kevin, *Orangeism: The Making of a Tradition* (Dublin: Wolfhound Press, 1999).

Hart, Peter, *The I.R.A. and Its Enemies: Violence and Community in Cork, 1916–1923* (New York: Clarendon Press, 1998).

——— *The I.R.A. at War, 1916–1923* (Oxford: Oxford University Press, 2003).

Heal, Felicity, *Reformation in Britain and Ireland* (Oxford: Oxford University Press, 2003).

Herlihy, Jim, *The Dublin Metropolitan Police: A Short History and Genealogical Guide* (Dublin: Four Courts Press, 2001).

Hill, Christopher, *The Century of Revolution, 1603–1714* (New York: W.W. Norton, 1982).

Holmes, Richard, *The Little Field-Marshall: Sir John French* (London: Jonathan Cape, 1981).

Hopkinson, Michael, *Green against Green: The Irish Civil War* (New York: St. Martin's Press, 1988).

———— *The Irish War of Independence* (Dublin: Gill & Macmillan, 2002).

Hostettler, John, *Sir Edward Carson: A Dream Too Far* (Chichester: Barry Rose Law Publishers, 1997).

Hutchinson, John, *The Dynamics of Cultural Nationalism: The Gaelic Revival and the Creation of the Irish Nation State* (London: George Allen & Unwin Ltd., in association with the London School of Economics and Political Science, 1987).

Hyde, H. Montgomery, *Carson: The Life of Sir Edward Carson, Lord Carson of Duncairn* (London: William Heinemann Ltd., 1953).

Jackson, Alvin, *The Ulster Party: Irish Unionists in the House of Commons, 1885–1911* (Oxford: Clarendon Press, 1989).

Jalland, Patricia, *The Liberals and Ireland: The Ulster Question in British Politics to 1914* (New York: St. Martin's Press, 1980).

James, Robert Rhodes, ed., *Winston S. Churchill: His Complete Speeches, 1897–1963: Volume II, 1908–1913; Volume III, 1914–1922* (New York: Chelsea House Publishers, 1974).

Jeffery, Keith, *Ireland and the Great War* (Cambridge: Cambridge University Press, 2000), 56.

Jenkins, Roy, *Churchill: A Biography* (New York: Farrar, Straus and Giroux, 2001).

Johnstone, Tom, *Orange, Green and Khaki: The Story of the Irish Regiments in the Great War, 1914–18* (Dublin: Gill & Macmillan, 1992).

Kautt, William H., *The Anglo-Irish War, 1916–1921: A People's War* (Westport, C.T.: Praeger Publishers, 1999).

Kieran, Brian L., *Success of a General: General French and the Relief of Kimberley* (Honiton: Token Publishing, 2001).

Laffan, Michael, *The Resurrection of Ireland: The Sinn Fein Party, 1916–1923* (Cambridge: Cambridge University Press, 1999).

Lawlor, Sheila, *Britain and Ireland, 1914 to 1923* (Dublin: Gill & Macmillan, 1983).

Lee, Joseph, *The Modernisation of Irish Society, 1848–1918* (Dublin: Gill & Macmillan, 1989).

Loades, D.M., *The Reign of Mary Tudor: Politics, Government, and Religion in England, 1553–1558*, second edition (London: Longman, 1991).

Loughlin, James, *Gladstone, Home Rule and the Ulster Question, 1882–93* (Atlantic Highlands, N.J.: Humanities Press International Inc., 1987).

Lower, A.R.M., *Colony to Nation: A History of Canada* (Toronto: Longmans, Green & Company, 1946).

Mac Cuarta, Brian, ed., *Ulster 1641: Aspects of the Rising* (Belfast: Institute of Irish Studies, Queen's University of Belfast, 1997).

MacCulloch, Diarmaid, *The Boy King: Edward VI and the Protestant Reformation* (New York: Palgrave, 2001).

———— *The Later Reformation in England, 1547–1603*, second edition (New York: Palgrave, 2001).

MacDonagh, Michael, *The Irish on the Somme* (London: Hodder & Stoughton, 1917).

MacEoin, Uinseann, *The IRA in the Twilight Years, 1923–1948* (Dublin: Argenta Publications, 1997).

Maguire, W.A., ed., *Kings in Conflict: The Revolutionary War in Ireland and Its Aftermath, 1689–1750* (Belfast: Blackstaff Press, 1990).

Mansergh, Nicholas, *The Unresolved Question: The Anglo-Irish Settlement and Its Undoing, 1912–72* (New Haven: Yale University Press, 1991).

Martin, F.X., ed., *The Irish Volunteers, 1913–1915: Recollections and Documents* (Dublin: James Duffy & Co. Ltd., 1963).

———, ed., *Leaders and Men of the Easter Rising: Dublin 1916* (Ithaca, N.Y.: Cornell University Press, 1967).

Matthews, Kevin, *Fatal Influence: The Impact of Ireland on British Politics, 1920–1925* (Dublin: University College Dublin Press, 2004).

Maume, Patrick, *The Long Gestation: Irish Nationalist Life, 1891–1918* (Dublin: Gill & Macmillan, 1999).

Maxwell, Henry, *Ulster Was Right* (London: Hutchinson & Co. Ltd., 1934).

McCavitt, John, *The Flight of the Earls* (Dublin: Gill & Macmillan, 2002).

McDowell, R.B., *The Irish Administration: 1801–1914* (London: Routledge & Kegan Paul, 1964).

McGurk, John, *The Elizabethan Conquest of Ireland: The 1590s Crisis* (Manchester: Manchester University Press, 1997).

McKittrick, David, Seamus Kelters, Brian Feeney, and Chris Thornton, *Lost Lives: The Stories of the Men, Women, and Children Who Died As a Result of the Northern Ireland Troubles* (Edinburgh: Mainstream Publishing Company, 1999, 2001). Reference is to the 2001 edition.

Meigs, Samantha A., *The Reformations in Ireland: Tradition and Confessionalism, 1400–1690* (New York: St. Martin's Press, 1997).

Mitchell, Arthur, *Revolutionary Government in Ireland: Dáil Éireann, 1919–22* (Dublin: Gill & Macmillan, 1995).

Moran, Sean Farrell, *Patrick Pearse and the Politics of Redemption: The Mind of the Easter Rising, 1916* (Washington, D.C.: The Catholic University Press, 1994).

Muenger, Elizabeth A., *The British Military Dilemma in Ireland: Occupation Politics, 1886–1914* (Dublin: Gill & Macmillan, 1991).

Mulholland, Marc, *The Longest War: Northern Ireland's Troubled History* (Oxford: Oxford University Press, 2002).

Murphy, Brian P., *Patrick Pearse and the Lost Republican Ideal* (Dublin: James Duffy & Co. Ltd., 1991).

Newsinger, John, *Rebel City: Larkin, Connolly and the Dublin Labour Movement* (London: Merlin Press, 2004).

Ó Broin, Leon, *The Chief Secretary: Augustine Birrell in Ireland* (Edinburgh: Archon Books, 1970), 7.

——— *Dublin Castle and the 1916 Rising* (New York: New York University Press, 1971).

Ó Broin, Leon, *Revolutionary Underground: The Story of the Irish Republican Brotherhood, 1858–1924* (Totowa, N.J.: Rowman & Littlefield Publishers, 1976).

O'Halpin, Eunan, *The Decline of the Union: British Government in Ireland, 1892–1920* (Dublin: Gill & Macmillan, 1987).

O'Sullivan, Donal J., *The Irish Constabularies, 1822–1922* (Dingle, County Kerry: Brandon Books, 1999).

Palmer, Stanley H., *Police and Protest in England and Ireland, 1780–1850* (Cambridge: Cambridge University Press, 1988).

Petrie, Charles, *Walter Long and His Times* (London: Hutchinson & Co. Ltd., 1936).

Philips, David, and Robert D. Storch, *Policing Provincial England, 1829–1856: The Politics of Reform* (London: Leicester University Press, 1999).

Piper, Leonard, *Dangerous Waters: The Life and Death of Erskine Childers* (London: Hambledon Press, 2003).

Ridley, Jasper Goodwin, *Bloody Mary's Martyrs: The Story of England's Terror* (New York: Carroll and Graf Publishers, 2001).

Ring, Jim, *Erskine Childers* (London: John Murray, 1996).

Ryan, A.P., *Mutiny at the Curragh* (London: Macmillan & Co. Ltd., 1956).

Sawyer, Roger, *Casement: The Flawed Hero* (London: Routledge & Kegan Paul, 1984).

Shannon, Catherine B., *Arthur J. Balfour and Ireland, 1874–1922* (Washington, D.C.: Catholic University of America Press, 1988).

Smith, Jeremy, *The Tories and Ireland: Conservative Party Politics and the Home Rule Crisis, 1910–1914* (Dublin: Irish Academic Press, 2000).

Smith, Phillip Thurmond, *Policing Victorian London: Political Policing, Public Order, and the London Metropolitan Police* (Westport, C.T.: Greenwood Press, 1985).

Stewart, A.T.Q., *Edward Carson* (Dublin: Gill & Macmillan, 1981).

———— *The Ulster Crisis: Resistance to Home Rule, 1912–1914* (Belfast: Blackstaff Press, 1967).

Townshend, Charles, *The British Campaign in Ireland, 1919–1921: The Development of Political and Military Polices* (Oxford: Oxford University Press, 1975).

———— *Political Violence in Ireland: Government and Resistance since 1848* (Oxford: Clarendon Press, 1983).

Trevelyan, G.M., *The English Revolution, 1688–1689* (London: T. Butterworth Ltd., 1938; reprinted Oxford: Oxford University Press, 1981).

Wheeler, James Scott, *Cromwell in Ireland* (Dublin: Gill & Macmillan, 1999).

Williams, Desmond, ed., *The Irish Struggle, 1916–1926* (Toronto: University of Toronto Press, 1966).

Wright, Frank, *Two Lands on One Soil: Ulster Politics before Home Rule* (Dublin: Gill & Macmillan, 1996).

Articles, Essays, and Chapters

Bowman, Timothy, "The Ulster Volunteer Force and the Formation of the 36th (Ulster) Division," *Irish Historical Studies*, volume 32, number 128 (November 2001).

Boyce, D.G., "British Conservative Opinion, the Ulster Question, and the Partition of Ireland, 1912–1921," *Irish Historical Studies*, volume 17, number 65 (March 1970).

Boyce, D.G., and Cameron Hazlehurst, "The Unknown Chief Secretary: H.E. Duke and Ireland, 1916–1918," *Irish Historical Studies*, volume 20, number 79 (March 1977).

Connolly, S.J., "The Penal Laws," in W.A. Maguire, ed., *Kings in Conflict: The Revolutionary War in Ireland and Its Aftermath, 1689–1750* (Belfast: Blackstaff Press, 1990).

Fair, John D., "The Anglo-Irish Treaty of 1921: Unionist Aspects of the Peace," *Journal of British Studies*, volume 12, number 1 (November 1972).

Hawkings, F.M.A., "Defense and the Role of Erskine Childers in the Treaty Negotiations of 1921," *Irish Historical Studies*, volume 22, number 87 (March 1981).

Hopkinson, Michael, "Introduction," in Mark Sturgis, *The Last Days of Dublin Castle: The Diaries of Mark Sturgis*, introduction by Michael Hopkinson, ed. (Dublin: Irish Academic Press, 1999).

Jalland, Patricia, "A Liberal Chief Secretary and the Irish Question: Augustine Birrell, 1907–1914," *The Historical Journal*, volume 19, number 2 (June 1976).

Laffan, Michael, "The Unification of Sinn Fein in 1917," *Irish Historical Studies*, volume 17, number 67 (March 1971).

Lawlor, S.M., "Ireland from Truce to Treaty: War or Peace? July to October 1921," *Irish Historical Studies*, volume 22, number 85 (March 1980).

Maguire, W.A., "The Land Settlement," in W.A. Maguire, ed., *Kings in Conflict: The Revolutionary War in Ireland and Its Aftermath, 1689–1750* (Belfast: Blackstaff Press, 1990).

McGuire, James, "James II and Ireland, 1685–90," in W.A. Maguire, ed., *Kings in Conflict: The Revolutionary War in Ireland and Its Aftermath, 1689–1750* (Belfast: Blackstaff Press, 1990).

Miller, John, "The Glorious Revolution," in W.A. Maguire, ed., *Kings in Conflict: The Revolutionary War in Ireland and Its Aftermath, 1689–1750* (Belfast: Blackstaff Press, 1990).

Novick, Ben, "The Arming of Ireland: Gun-Running and the Great War, 1914–16," in Adrian Gregory and Senia Paseta, eds., *Ireland and the Great War: "A War to Unite Us All"?* (Manchester: Manchester University Press, 2002).

Sims, Hillary, "Violence in County Armagh, 1641," in Brian Mac Cuarta, ed., *Ulster 1641: Aspects of the Rising* (Belfast: Institute of Irish Studies, Queen's University of Belfast, 1997).

Index